THE METAPHYSICS OF POWER

THE METAPHYSICS OF POWER

Understanding the Deep Structure of Ripening Being

Anthony E. Mansueto

◆PICKWICK *Publications* · Eugene, Oregon

THE METAPHYSICS OF POWER
Understanding the Deep Structure of Ripening Being

Copyright © 2025 Anthony E. Mansueto. All rights reserved. Except for brief quotations in critical publications or reviews, no part of this book may be reproduced in any manner without prior written permission from the publisher. Write: Permissions, Wipf and Stock Publishers, 199 W. 8th Ave., Suite 3, Eugene, OR 97401.

Pickwick Publications
An Imprint of Wipf and Stock Publishers
199 W. 8th Ave., Suite 3
Eugene, OR 97401

www.wipfandstock.com

PAPERBACK ISBN: 979-8-3852-1786-1
HARDCOVER ISBN: 979-8-3852-1787-8
EBOOK ISBN: 979-8-3852-1788-5

Cataloguing-in-Publication data:

Names: Mansueto, Anthony E., author.

Title: The metaphysics of power : understanding the deep structure of ripening being / Anthony E. Mansueto.

Description: Eugene, OR : Pickwick Publications, 2025 | Includes bibliographical references.

Identifiers: ISBN 979-8-3852-1786-1 (paperback) | ISBN 979-8-3852-1787-8 (hardcover) | ISBN 979-8-3852-1788-5 (ebook)

Subjects: LCSH: Power (Philosophy). | Metaphysics.

Classification: BD438 .M35 2025 (paperback) | BD438 .M35 (ebook)

VERSION NUMBER 03/17/25

This work is dedicated to my wife and partner, who has been there even when I was not and who has helped me understand how to find joy in the limitations of contingent being.

Contents

1 What Is Happening to Us? | 1
2 What Is Political Theology? | 70
3 The Right | 82
4 Why the Center Cannot Hold | 123
5 What Was and Is Socialism? | 186
6 Communism as a Spiritual Project | 230

Bibliography | 291

1

What Is Happening to Us?

Framing the Problem

The Social Context

When we published *The Ways of Wisdom* (Mansueto 2016), the world was a very different place. The crisis tendencies which define the current situation were, to be sure, already very much in place. Already the planet was being rendered uninhabitable by climate change, resource depletion, mass extinctions, and the toxic waste generated by the combustion of the planet by industrial technology. Developments in robotic and information technology were rendering human labor power redundant while the commodification of labor power was destroying the social fabric and alienating humanity from its own deepest nature. Already we were witnessing, as the result of advances in information technology and globalization, the emergence of Capital as an autonomous intelligence independent of the historic bourgeoisie. The backlash against the election of the first US president of African ancestry and the growing media attention granted to police murders of African Americans had already demonstrated the depth of racism in a country which had leveraged that election to convince itself that "racism was a thing of the past." And the "me too" movement served as a painful reminder that the victories of liberal feminism were very far from breaking down the patriarchy which constitutes the deep structure of oppression.

Still, the presidency of Barack Obama, however hobbled as it was by Republican control of Congress for six of its eight years, had not only created an atmosphere of hope, but it was a period of modest and incremental but very real progress. Climate change was back on the agenda. The claims of the maximalist left aside, the Democratic Party turned decisively away from neoliberalism and returned to its social liberal heritage, however cautiously, intervening as best it could given the balance of power to support effective demand in the face of the deepest economic crisis since the Great Depression and succeeding where no one else had in advancing the cause of universal access to health care. And these were years of striking gains for the LGBTQ community, which won marriage equality and began to put the question of gender identity on the public agenda, chipping away at the same patriarchal deep structure of oppression which the "Me Too" moved unmasked.

This context shaped the theological position articulated in *The Ways of Wisdom* which, while profoundly critical of the capitalist *saeculum*, reflected a comfort with approaching the *longue durée* tasks of organizing and spiritual transformation which were and which remain central to our strategy for humanity within the context of a very broad *Convivencia* theology which continued to argue that, its hegemonization by Empire and Capital notwithstanding, Christianity could still be or a force for justice. More specifically we argued for engaging the spiritual and civilizational traditions which had emerged from the Axial Age (Jaspers 1953) in dialogue with each other and with the humanistic project to set the latter in a broader spiritual context and address its internal contradictions. And we did this in a context which was informed by our own very deep Catholic roots, affirming the Catholic doctrine of accidental *theosis* by means of caritative wisdom rooted in the supernaturally just act, even if it also built on our criticism of the inherently anti-Semitic character of core Christological doctrines (Mansueto 2002a).

Today the world looks very different. First, the global pandemic which began in 2020 and which shows no signs of abating has brought to light yet another fundamental contradiction in the human civilizational project. On the one hand, growing levels of global trade and interaction not only make it possible for the planet to support a much larger human population, but also promote humanity's ongoing deliberation regarding the aims of human life, and thus our spiritual as well as our civilizational progress. But epidemiologists have long known anything that increases the intensity and extent of human interactions—urbanization, trade, and now globalization—creates the context for pandemics which have not infrequently set back or radically altered the course of the human civilizational project (Wu et al. 2017). And it is increasingly clear that essentially *no* state on the planet has the political will and resources necessary to do what is necessary to contain the pandemic. The Right resisted mitigation from the beginning and spread destructive rumors about the origins of the virus, the efficacy of fake "cures," and the supposed danger of vaccines. The Center supported both cautious mitigation and income transfers to limit the impact of the pandemic on the economy—but then caved into pressure from the Right and is pretending that the pandemic is over. China, which for a long time seemed to understand the dangers presented by a virus which has long term disabling effects on up to half the people it infects, has now stood down as well, creating what could at worst be an extinction level event, and what will likely rank as one of the major disease driven turning points in human history.

At the same time, the pandemic has brought to the fore a new core constituency for communist project—and one the emergence of which sheds light on the limits of Marx's vision. As the pandemic progresses, now hidden by a consensus "return" to normality, the numbers of the disabled—and especially those with the often-occult disabilities which affect those with Long COVID and Myalgic Encephalomyelitis—increase, calling into question one of the foundational and constitutive decisions of the human civilizational project: the decision to forego opportunity in order to care for the sick and disabled and elderly. Marx's formulation of the communist project, which centers creativity as definitive of humanity's "species being," remains vulnerable the being hegemonized by capitalist productivism, which values people in proportion to their usefulness, a vulnerability which has been exploited by essentially all historic socialist societies in order to prioritize "the development of the productive forces" over the decommodification of labor power. The emergence of the disabled as political actors alone can heal this flaw in our movement.

Second, with the advent of "generative" AI, we have entered an entirely new phase in the development of information technology, as artificial intelligence moves into the terrain of creative intellectual labor and threatens the intelligentsia not just with proletarianization but with redundancy. This new development builds on advances in robotics which are increasingly rendering human manual labor, especially in manufacturing, redundant as well.

Third, entirely new powers have emerged, as capitalist magnates like Elon Musk, Mark Zuckerberg, and Jeff Bezos demonstrate their ability to act on a global scale, often with greater impact—and not generally for the good—than great powers and even the supposed global hegemon, the United States. Coming on top of the emergence of Capital as an autonomous intelligence independent of the historic bourgeoisie, this has further eroded the power and privilege of aristocratic lineages like the Kennedys and the Bushes, which find themselves increasingly marginalized. And even as state structures seemed to be in decline we have witnessed the resurgence of territorial empire as a political project across Eurasia in particular, in Russia, China, India, and *Dar-al-Islam*.

Fourth, as proletarianization is completed, the authoritarian personality structure which is the result of the alienation labor becomes nearly universal. The result is a resurgent fascism which threatens the liberal order—and, interestingly, also, a resurgent socialist Left which seems more than willing to collaborate with rising fascist powers such as Russia. This authoritarian turn has focused, at least outwardly, on overturning the gains made by and crushing ongoing resistance on the part of colonized peoples, women, and the LGBTQ community, trends which are reflected on the Left in both the overwhelmingly "white" character of the new democratic socialism and Left populism and the emergence of a very significant backlash against those who challenge gender essentialism on the part of many older feminists.

The Theoretical Context

It is in the context of these developments that we must consider the way in which the theoretical terrain has changed as well as ways in which earlier theoretical developments have now come more sharply into focus. Here the most important development and one largely ignored in theological scholarship is the emergence of the *Dark Enlightenment* (Moldbug 2008; Land 2013), an offshoot of fusionist libertarianism which links a Right accelerationist technocommercialism with traditionalism and "human biodiversity" theory arguing for the biological basis of white supremacy and traditional gender roles. Sometimes allied with this trend are the Heideggerian *Fourth Political Theory* of Alexander Dugin (Dugin 2021) and the more purely ethnoparticularist theories of the European New Right (Faye 1998/2000) and their North American Identarian allies. These trends all share an affinity for traditionalism, which invokes the centrality of sacrifice and violence as the foundation of society (Bataille 1949/1991, 1973/1989; Girard 1972/1977). This poses the question of why these ideas have so much salience among high technology capitalist magnates and their associated scientific/technical intelligentsia (Thiel 2007), something which will point to the way in which male identity has been forged for millennia—and reinforced in the milieu of the rising technology sector. At the same time, these three trends all advance different visions of the future. The *Dark Enlightenment* argues for a world of privately owned city states in which residents have the right of "exit" (i.e., they may leave the city) but no voice in governance—a way to ensure unlimited freedom for both capitalist magnates and, ultimately for Capital as an autonomous intelligence, which would inevitably regulate the relations between states. *The Fourth Political Theory* poses as a defense of ethnic particularism but is actually an argument for a restored Russian Empire. *Identarianism,* on the other hand, in its attempts to recover European pagan roots fantasizes about a return to a pre-(Roman and Christian) imperial Europe. And so, we will need to see how the common threads they share—the focus on violence and male identity—serve to bind them into an alliance, and also assess the limits of the alliance as global conditions change.

These developments on the Right, we should note, have been accompanied by the appearance of a significant scholarly literature on Empire which does not itself advocate a return to territorial or what it calls "civilizational empire" but which is increasingly invoked by forces on both the Right and the Left to add weight to their positions (Darwin 2007; Coker 2019; Jiang 2018/2020, 2020/2020).

What is especially interesting, however, is that we see parallel and convergent trends on the Left. The most important of these is what we call *Dark Liberation,* which is defined by the decision of a good part of the Left to trade Marx for Heidegger and other theorists of the "hermeneutic," "genealogical," and "ontological" turns. This impact is reflected in a resurgent deep ecology and anarchoprimitivism, in an indigenism which grounds itself in the ontological turn in anthropology—the claim that different peoples not only see the world differently but actually create their own worlds—and in a gender essentialism which invokes a feminist version of a pagan Old Europe of the Identarians. But we will also show that even those who profess to uphold Marx and profess the primacy of class over race and gender are not always immune to the Heideggerian virus. We will argue that these are all forms of fascist hegemony over the Left, which explains the resurgence of Red/Brown alliance patterns around the world.

Both the Right and the Left, we should note (and this will be fundamental to our argument) embrace the decisionist political theology advocated by Walter Benjamin and Carl Schmitt. And The Chinese Communist Party, and especially its leading theorist Jiang Shigong, embraces both Schmitt and the language of Civilizational Empire.

The rise of the Right and the (rather weaker) resurgence of the Left are matched by a relative decline of the political Center. We attribute this, among other things, to

- the theoretical incoherence and the political impossibility of the old Center Right "liberal conservatism" which tried to reconcile individual liberty with unlimited capitalist power;
- the underlying and ineradicable if implicit authoritarianism of Christianity, written in particular into the Pauline corpus, which ultimately undermined the Christian Left and Center, and to
- the role of professionalism and technocracy in persuading the more privileged (bourgeois and upper petty bourgeois) layers of humanistic intelligentsia to neuter itself, while the middle and lower strata succumbed to the Heideggerian virus and fascist hegemony.

Thesis, Method, and Outline

This changing context, while profoundly threatening to humanity, has helped us to clarify considerably both our strategic estimate and our political theological position. While there is much in *The Ways of Wisdom* which we continue to affirm—including our claim that theology is, at least in significant measure, a product of intercultural engagement and our argument for a theology which engages spiritual questions across as well as within spiritual traditions—we need to revise significantly our comparative historical analysis, our fundamental theology, and our political and pastoral strategy.

On the comparative historical front, we will:

- identify *Empire* as a distinct *way of being human,* something which will shed light on the *alterimperialism* which characterizes the present period (i.e., the resurgence of imperial ambitions in Russia,

China, India, and *Dar-al-Islam* and the resurgence of a territorial imperial identity in the United States, distinct from the latter's roles as guarantor of the Global Capital and the International Liberal Order—themselves distinct),

- nuance our analysis of the relationship between *Empire* and the axial *ways,* which will help us to address the emerging discourse around "civilizational empires" emerging in China and elsewhere,
- argue that Christianity, as shaped by Paul of Tarsus, with its doctrines of divine sovereignty and original sin and its divine command ethics is *the* ideology of Empire *par excellence* and also—building on but radically extending Weber and Agamben—the foundation for the primitive accumulation of Capital and indeed for the capitalist system as a whole,
- show that Islam is the principal heir of the revolutionary messianic option present in the Jesus movement and the Ebionite or Jamesian tradition (Eisenman 1997) (if not directly of these tendencies themselves) *and* show why, though far more progressive than Christianity, also inevitably becomes bound up with Empire, something which has positioned it so well as a vehicle for *alterimperialism* after the crisis of the Soviet bloc, and
- take a more critical look at the lineages of the humanistic project in its liberal, democratic, and socialist forms. On the one hand, it was interaction with Judaism which transformed the dialectical tradition—which was deeply compromised in its origins by its complicity in slave regimes—allowing it to emerge as a revolutionary force. At the same time, much of this interaction took place within a Christian context and Christianity, by putting entitative *theosis* on the table, in the person of Christ if not that of the Christian, led to the transformation of humanism from a tragic ideology which celebrated human capacities but lamented human finitude and contingency, into to a strategy for godbuilding, a transformation which becomes complete in Hegel and Marx.

At the level of our fundamental theology, we will make an argument for an *equivocal* metaphysics of *Esse,* as against the *analogical* metaphysics we have historically advocated. This argument will be set in the context of a systematic consideration of the relationship between metaphysics, political theology, social theory and social ontology. Our argument will center around the claim that in the process of demonstrating the reality of God we show that God acts as and only as final cause, luring things into Being, and that because of this God *is* in a fundamentally different way than the phenomenal universe. This in turn renders the concept of sovereignty incoherent because, while the ultimate cause of everything, even God does not exercise total control over a territory (in this case the universe) and its inhabitants. We also show, at the level of social ontology, that underlying networks ordered to ends (institutions) are distinct from and relatively more real than formal organizations, rendering the historic socialist focus on state power fundamentally misguided. We will then go on to show how similar results can be obtained in the context of a Buddhist metaphysics of interdependent origination, an *advaita* metaphysics in which Brahman and Atman are identical, and the syncretic Confucian-Taoist metaphysics of the *daoxue*.

Finally, at the level of political and pastoral strategy we will argue for a broad popular front against fascism which then leverages power to reduce the underlying source of the alienation which engenders authoritarianism: pressure to sell one's labor power in order to survive. But this must be complemented by *deep organizing and deep engagement* focused on rebuilding communities which can challenge and nurture humanity and cultivate human beings capable of communism.

We will begin by analyzing the current situation in greater depth, fleshing out and providing an argument for the analysis we suggested above. This analysis will conclude with an identification of the principal political actors and their alignment in the present period. From there we will go on to look systematically at the various tendencies on the Right, Center, and Left that we discussed above, before turning towards our positive argument. Revisions to our comparative historical analysis will be woven into our analysis of current political theological tendencies.

The Current Situation

Let us analyze the current situation in greater depth. It is fundamental to the dialectical sociology that we have developed and defended (Mansueto 2002a, 2010, 2016) that human societies are defined by:

- their material basis, i.e., the ecosystem in which they emerge, and by
- social structures which emerge on this material basis (technological, economic, political, and cultural) in order to pursue

- the end of human life, which is the power of Being as such, understood at different degrees (from mere survival through full *theosis*) and in many different ways, in accord with the cultural structures through which it is perceived.

Let analyze these various levels or dimensions of human civilization with a focus on the current situation.

Ecological Contradictions

Human beings evolved in a very specific ecosystem—the subtropical highlands of East Africa—which created just precisely the conditions which selected for our defining characteristics: hands which can make tools and the capacity for complex symbolic communication. That we were able to leave this relative paradise and adapt to other ecosystems which were vastly hotter or colder, wetter or drier or both is a result of the fact that the capacities which define us also enabled us to interact with different ecosystems in different ways by creating tools which further extended those capacities (including shelter and clothing) and eventually to effectively modify the ecosystems into which we migrated by forming symbioses with various plants and animals the flourishing of which we favored by creating a built environment with fundamentally new niches, by means of irrigation, roads, dwellings, villages, and eventually cities.

But the very developments which have made human civilization possible now threaten it in ways with which we have yet to come to terms. Over the course of the past 250 years, industrial production has transformed our planet's ecosystem in ways and to degrees that until recently we could not have imagined possible. Ancient communities which guarded the knowledge of how best to tend a planet already transformed by horticulture and agriculture from a wilderness into a garden have been dissolved by the corrosive power of primitive accumulation and proletarianization, while direct producers have been stripped of their understanding of how to unlock the hidden potential of matter for complex organization and transformed into instruments of the very tools they once used. The great liturgy of our species, ripening being, has given way to the accumulation of dead labor.

The Crisis of Industrial Production

Of the various elements in our argument that we are in a time of crisis, the most widely accepted is that we face a profound ecological crisis, rooted in a technological regime centered on combustion, i.e., on breaking down existing forms of organization in order to release energy that can then be used to do work. Combustion, by its very nature involves (1) the destruction of the underlying fuel source and (2) the production of by-products that alter the ecosystem in important ways. This in turn results in profound changes in the ecosystem including:

- climate change
- pollution, and
- resource depletion and loss of biodiversity.

That the climate is changing as a result of human activity is now beyond dispute. According to the *Global Climate Change* program at the National Aeronautics and Space Administration:

- Surface temperatures have risen 1.8°C since the late nineteenth century.
- The top one hundred meters of the ocean has warmed 0.6°C since 1969
- Greenland has lost 279 billion tons of ice per year since 1993, Antarctica 148 billion tons per year.
- Sea level has risen twenty centimeters in the past century and the rate is increasing.

This climate change is overwhelmingly anthropogenic and overwhelmingly the result of a technological regime based on the combustion of fossil fuels which have resulted in the highest carbon dioxide levels in 650,000 years, though methane emissions from cattle production and chlorofluorocarbons from certain chemical production processes are also significant. The result will be increases in sea levels from one to eight feet by the end of the century, more frequent droughts and heat waves, stronger hurricanes and other extreme weather events, and the effective elimination of the arctic ice cap. There are very strong reasons to believe that climate change, as it melts the permafrost and releases long dormant pathogens, will also further increase the frequency of pandemics. These changes will at the very least result in massive disruptions in the global economy and may, according to some of the more extreme scenarios, render the planet effective uninhabitable for humanity.

Climate change is not the only dimension of the ecological crisis. More than one half of the population continues to experience increased air pollution as a result of industrialization in Asia, Africa, and Latin America. About one third of the global loss of biodiversity can be attributed to water pollution and 2.4 billion people live without access to any form of sanitation. And economic expansion on a finite planet means that resource depletion is an ever present danger. Various estimates suggest the following dates for "peak" production and subsequent decline for the resources indicated:

- Petroleum (2023)
- Copper (2024)
- Zinc (2025)
- Aluminum (2057)
- Coal (2060)
- Iron (2068)

And these problems are all intertwined. Carbon dioxide production is a form of air pollution. And one of the principal forms of resource depletion—deforestation—makes it much more difficult to rectify the problem. The Food and Argiculture Organization estimates that the global forest carbon stock has decreased 0.9 percent, and tree cover 4.2 percent between 1990 and 2020 (FAO 2020).

Measuring levels of biodiversity is quite difficult (Duran et al 2020) but some estimates show that we have lost as much as 13.6 of all species on the planet since the beginning of the Industrial Revolution and could lost up to 17 percent by the year 2100 if we do not make drastic changes in our technological regime (Iberdola 2023).

The Pandemic

But climate change is not the only ecological effect of the current technological and economic regime. Economically and politically motivated claims by public health authorities to the contrary, the global pandemic of SARS-COV-2 or COVID-19, which has already infected 756 million people, killing between 7 and 28 million (Adam 2022; Economist 2022), is still very much with us. As many as 43 percent (Chen et al. 2021) may have contracted "Long COVID," amounting to 325 million people significantly disabled. It has become nearly impossible to track confirmed new cases since most governments have stopped reporting, but wastewater sampling suggests that infections have settled into a rhythm with high points every few months which, while well below the peaks early in the pandemic and in January 2022, have not decreased significantly below levels at other times through the first two years of the pandemic (CDC 2024). There is growing evidence that COVID ravages the human body, significantly increasing risk for a broad range of disabling and potentially lethal conditions, including cardiovascular problems, neurological changes (including a significant loss of intellectual capacity, cancer, and others) (PAI 2024). This is in addition to the broader disability caused by Long COVID.

Pandemics have played a very significant role in major historical transitions, including both the emergence of fundamentally new adaptations, such as the advent of horticulture, and the collapse of large urban civilizations. Bubonic plague twice killed what may have been as much as half the planet's population: during the Plague of Justinian (541–549) and during the Black Death (1346–1353)—and continued recurring for centuries. Smallpox killed between 23 and 37 percent of the Mexican population in 1520, only to be followed by the Cocoliztli Epidemic of 1545–1548, which killed between 25 percent and 50 percent of the remaining population (Wade 2021; Mordecai et al 2019).

At this point COVID-19 does not yet represent a major pandemic on the scale of the Black Death, Plague of Justinian, or the Cocolitzli epidemics. But we are only four years into the pandemic and many pandemics have lasted centuries.

The root of this dynamic is not difficult to find. *The development of human civilization, and especially the increasing density of the human population associated with urbanization and the growing interconnectedness of the planet's principal civilizational centers, create a fundamentally new challenge: pandemics which do not merely stress existing social structures, but which periodically annihilate a significant part of the population of the planet, and in some cases more than half of the population of a particular region* (Diamond 1997).

This should not lead us to simply displace other theories of social change with a "pandemic" thesis, but it does suggest an important correction to the dominant models of human history which tend to put scientific, technological and economic progress, and/or conscious political activity and ideological innovation at the forefront. Nor should it lead us to reject the human civilizational project as such, as do anarchoprimitivists. Humanity has in fact, recovered from past pandemics and gone on to build ever larger and more interconnected civilizations. But we do need to factor the dynamic into our strategy for the future. Living together and being globally interconnected is enormously enriching, but it is also hard and requires self-discipline and care for others.

It is precisely the lack of such self-discipline and care, especially for the most vulnerable, which has defined the global response to the pandemic, with the partial exception of China. As we will see, it is in fact a commitment to care for the ill and disabled *even when this requires significant sacrifice* which for many anthropologists marks the dawn of human civilization. And as we will see later in this chapter it is precisely such a commitment which is currently lacking as regimes across the political spectrum leverage the pandemic to purge what has become (from the vantage point of Capital) a very significant surplus population.

Technological Contradictions

Automation

It is fundamental to the dynamic of industrialization that human labor gives way to that of machines and that human beings, to the extent that we remain necessary, are ourselves reduced to the status of tools. This is, indeed, one of the presuppositions of Marx's argument that capitalism is internally contradictory. On the one hand, it depends on the success of capitalists in selling their products and thus realizing the surplus value they have extracted from their workers. But there is a long-term tendency of technological progress under capitalism to drive the value of labor power towards zero by progressively replacing human with machine labor. In earlier stages of capitalism this took the form of using combustion to generate energy to do the work which had formerly been done by human beings or our animal companions, while still using human beings for everything from planning and design through set up and tasks requiring fine motor skills. Increasingly, today, it is intellectual labor which is being automated. This is especially true since about 2022 with the public debut of "generative" AI, which use Large Language Models to generate text which is often indistinguishable from what human beings can produce, and which can also generate images across artistic styles.

Some remain skeptical of the claim that automation leads to a long term decline in wages. Harry Holzer of the Brookings Institution, for example, argues that:

> On one hand, automation often creates as many jobs as it destroys over time. Workers who can work with machines are more productive than those without them; this reduces both the costs and prices of goods and services, and makes consumers feel richer. As a result, consumers spend more, which leads to the creation of new jobs.
>
> On the other hand, there are workers who lose out, particularly those directly displaced by the machines and those who must now compete with them. Indeed, digital automation since the 1980s has added to labor market inequality, as many production and clerical workers saw their jobs disappear or their wages decline. New jobs have been created—including some that pay well for highly educated analytical workers. Others pay much lower wages, such as those in the personal services sector (Holzer 2022).

Holzer acknowledges that many high-skill jobs will, in fact, be automated, but argues that the problem can be addressed pressing our schools to teach high level analytic and creative thinking which can keep human beings ahead of the robots. The question, however, is whether or not there will really be significant demand for such skills within a globalized system with a global culture in which we all consume cultural products produced by a small number of creatives and in which key decisions are made by the marketplace.

Others, however, acknowledge that there is already significant downward pressure on wages.

> Between 1990 and 2007, the increase in robots (about one per thousand workers) reduced the average employment-to-population ratio in a zone by 0.39 percentage points, and average wages by 0.77%, compared to commuting zones with no exposure to robots, they found. This implies that adding one robot to an area reduces employment in that area by about six workers (Acemoglu and Restrepo 2020).

The net result of this process will, inevitably, be a tendency for the value of labor power to decline towards zero, since the average socially necessary labor time required to reproduce labor power itself declines towards zero. It is unlikely, to be sure, that we will even closely approach the zero-value point for labor power any time soon (and we may never get there), but we do not need to get anywhere close to that point for effective demand to drop so far as to make it impossible for Capital to realize the surplus value its machines create.

This dynamic is, furthermore, penetrating the artistic and humanistic intelligentsia. While global numbers are still hard to come by, the advent of text to image AI technology has led to a 70 percent loss of illustrator jobs at game studios in China and 40 percent increase in productivity (Zhang 2023). The threat to those who write for a living is sufficient that the issue became central to the recent Hollywood writers' strike (Zhang 2023b).

What seems most likely is that authentic creative activity on the part of human beings will become a luxury commodity which only a few will be able to afford, as the price of such labor suffers from Baumol's Cost Disease. According to Baumol, whose work originally focused on the performing arts, wages tend to rise in sectors which have *not* experienced significant growth in productivity at roughly the same rate as in sectors that do (Baumol 1965). This is why physicians' services and university level education have risen in cost so much more rapidly than manufactured goods. Eventually the vast majority of the population, even as they consume high technology goods which did not even exist a few decades ago, can no longer afford to attend a private university or even a concert. These activities become, as they were before the advent of social liberalism, the province of the very rich.

Economic Contradictions

Proletarianization

Closely associated with automation is proletarianization. It has long been taken for granted, even on the Left, that among Marx's many claims (Marx and Engels 1848), that concerning proletarianization was simply wrong. Marx argued that the classes intermediate between the bourgeoisie and proletariat—the petty bourgeoisie and peasantry—would gradually be destroyed by capitalist development, with a few ascending into the bourgeoisie and the vast majority falling into the proletariat. Since at least the mid-twentieth century, this claim has seemed to fly in the face of the reality of the rising incomes of the majority of the population in the advanced capitalist countries. And even though that progress largely stopped after about 1973, the strata in question have behaved politically more like the threatened petty bourgeoisie of the nineteenth and early to mid-twentieth century, gravitating towards authoritarian and fascist movements, than Marx's proletariat. For a long time, there was a tendency on the part of many Maoists and other Third Worldists to argue that the revolutionary torch had been passed to the workers and peasants of Asia, Africa, and Latin America, a view which has enjoyed some resurgent support in recent years, but in fact, even as economic inequality has increased in the advanced capitalist countries, it has begun to decline in many regions of the old Third World—and rural insurgencies with it.

The difficulty with this approach is that it radically misunderstands the nature of class and of proletarianization. Marx's critique of capitalism is not a critique of economic inequality and mass impoverishment in general, nor is it simply an attempt to explain why poverty and inequality continue in spite of the enormous development of the productive forces under capitalism. On the contrary, Marx's argument bears on poverty and inequality only indirectly. Social class, for Marx, is determined by our relationship to the means of production, not by our wealth or income, occupation, lineage or education. This definition is driven by Marx's understanding of what makes us distinctively human—our creative capacity—and the way this is affected by economic structures. And while our ability to cultivate and express our creative capacity was certainly affected by our economic situation in precapitalist societies, with the exception of slaves everyone retained significant control over *the way in which they did their work*, even if some had access to more opportunities for creative labor than others. And even the ruling classes *had* to do certain things which were not creative: i.e., engage in warfare. Under capitalism, on the other hand, there are basically three possibilities. We can:

- Have enough capital that we don't have to work, and if we choose to work can also choose what we want to do and employ others in realizing our vision,
- Have enough capital to work for ourselves, perhaps employing a few apprentices (literal or figurative) and support personnel, or
- Have little or no capital and be forced to sell our labor power to others in order to survive.

The first group is the bourgeoisie, the second the petty bourgeoisie, and the third the proletariat.

With these fundamentals in place we are now able to clarify what is meant by proletarianization. Specifically, we are looking primarily at a loss in control over work processes by the middle and lower petty bourgeoisie so that, even as their incomes may remain high or increase, they have less opportunity to determine the ends for which they work and the means they use to achieve those ends. They are, in other words, increasingly reduced to instruments of Capital, either in generating surplus, realizing surplus, or creating the larger social conditions necessary for generating and realizing surplus. Mostly this is coming about through the application of rationalizing management processes such as strategic planning, quantitative outcomes assessment, etc., which make it more difficult for professionals to set their own agenda and bend their nominal employers to that agenda.

It is, unfortunately, very difficult to come by data that supports (or challenges) a thesis of this sort. There are two reasons for this. First, there are very few scholars who understand class in this rigorously Marxist way. Most of them hail from the humanistic or Frankfurt School tradition, a tradition which, in recent years, has been more focused on theory than on empirical research. Second, it is very difficult to quantify and thus measure creative control over one's work. That said, there are certain well-established trends that document that members of the petty bourgeoisie are, in fact, losing this creative control. Consider for example the decline of the institution of tenure in the academy. According to the National Center for Education Statistics, in 1994 62.6 percent of all institutions had a tenure system of some kind. By 2019 this number had dropped to 57.4 percent (NCES 2021a). During the same period the percentage of faculty actually tenured dropped from 56.2 percent to 45.1 percent. (NCES 2021b). Significantly more men than women are tenured—53.5 percent as opposed to 40.5 percent. And this is on top of the long-term trend towards hiring adjunct faculty on a course-by-course basis rather than regular faculty of any kind, a trend which has slowed only because of a total contraction in the instructional workforce and a shift to other occupations in higher education. Roughly 50 percent of instruction is carried out by adjunct faculty with no security of employment from one term to the next (Lederman 2019).

The academy is not the only profession affected. While most of us are reluctant to shed tears for physicians, who are notable for both the extent and the abuse of their professional privileges, we also know that as physician independence declines, so does the quality of care and the possibility for care to take a more holistic and integrated approach. And according to various measures, only one-third to one-half of physicians are now in private practice. And morale is not good. Physicians have the highest suicide rate of any profession (Wallace 2023). Similar trends are affecting lawyers. Roughly 75 percent of attorneys the US work in private law firms. Of these, roughly half are solo practitioners and one third of those who work in firms with more than one member make partner, so only about 56.2 percent of attorneys are either independent practitioners or partners—i.e., petty bourgeois professionals. And it must be remembered that even partners are often subject to very strict norms governing the production of billable hours, etc. (Kane 2019).

The Emergence of Capital as an Autonomous Intelligence

Automation is not the only threat we face from a non-human intelligence. Indeed, there is a powerful case to be made that this planet is already largely under the rule of a nonhuman hegemon. I am referring to Capital. Let me be clear. I am not claiming that Capital has become self-conscious or a *person*, though in the absence a clear understanding of what makes something conscious and what makes *something* into *someone*, this also needs to be evaluated. What I *am* arguing, instead, is that as Hayek (Hayek 1978) has demonstrated, the marketplace functions as a sort of information processing system. Buy and sell decisions are the inputs and prices the outputs that then tell human beings how much of each commodity to produce. Indeed, a similar case can be made for all human institutions, though the mechanisms for accessing and processing information and delivering outputs are rather different for political or cultural institutions than they are for the marketplace. What has changed is the relative balance of power between these institutions and individual and collective human actors. The formation of a unified global market, especially in Capital, facilitated by electronic information processing systems, the withdrawal of the state from economic regulation as a result of the neoliberal reaction, and the emergence of Big Data and algorithmic trading has meant that Capital has become increasingly self-allocating in accord with a single norm: maximizing the rate of return on investment. And when this happens it becomes more and more difficult for individual and collective human actors to intervene and change outcomes, as under capitalism effective action *requires* Capital.

It might be argued that even if the global market *is* an information processing system, that it does not meet the classic test for intelligence: i.e., the Turning test, which requires that a human observer be incapable of distinguishing between the information processing system being test and a human respondent. Two points are in order here. First, the Turing test is exceedingly problematic because it rules out the possibility of an intelligence, natural or artificial, that is radically different from our own. We already know that artificial information processing systems can do some things far more effectively than human beings, such as making complex calculations very quickly, and cannot do other things at all, such as interpreting ordinary human conversation in its pragmatic context.

When we say that Capital is an intelligence we mean that it is capable of accessing and processing information in accord with a formally rational algorithm—and in fact that it can do this far more effectively than individual human beings or collective planning agencies. Specifically, it can decide what allocation of resources maximizes the return on Capital over a time frame determined by those of individual investors. What it cannot do, of course, and what makes it merely intelligent and not sapient, is to reason regarding ends or purposes. It cannot ask itself whether or not maximizing returns to Capital is the best end, nor indeed can it even *think* ends or purposes at all.

Second, we should not be so sure that Capital is *not* passing the Turing test, and indeed has been passing it for a very long time. As we have argued elsewhere, the sovereign God of Reformed theology, who predestines some to glory and others to damnation without respect to foreknowledge of their merits is an ideological reflex of Capital and of the mysterious workings of the marketplace, which behaves in precisely this fashion, rewarding a seemingly arbitrary set of talented hard workers and skillless sloths while punishing an equally arbitrary set of the same. Another way to frame this observation, however, is that most people, without benefit of economic theory, simply do not understand how Capital works, and imagine that there is an inscrutable divine sovereign operating behind the scenes. One might make the same point about conspiracy theories, which have also been around for some time, but which seem to become ever more prevalent and ever more bizarre as Capital grows in power.

Finally, we should point out that it in deciding the allocation of resources Capital effectively decides what happens on the planet. Capital *rules* even if it does not *reign*.

The net result of the emergence of Capital as an autonomous intelligence is that *even most of the larger bourgeoisie has been increasingly marginalized politically*. This is true in spite of the fact that we have *also* witnessed an increase in the number of capitalist magnates who *are* capable of acting effectively on a global scale, often with the assistance of imperial states which they have partly privatized under their own control.

The Rise of the Capitalist Magnates

Lest we assume too quickly, however, that individual capitalists are being rendered irrelevant, it is essential to take note of the emergence of a new stratum of capitalist magnates who are capable of acting on a global scale, often as effectively or more so than states, though not generally for the good. This stratum is a product of the information technology revolution, and its earliest exemplars, such as Bill Gates and Steve Jobs generally confined their global interventions into more traditional philanthropic and political channels. More recently, however, figures like Mark Zuckerberg, Jeff Bezos, and especially Elon Musk have begun to intervene in ways that raise questions about whether or not their motives are still primarily economic. Bezos, for example, purchased the Washington Post. Zuckerberg's *Facebook* provided, intentionally or not, a significant platform for Russian and other authoritarian disinformation campaigns. And Musk's purchase of *Twitter*, followed by his decision to open it up fully to Rightist political operatives and to destroy it as a platform for civilized public deliberation all point an entirely new sort of political activity. The same is true of the intervention of Musk in particular into the aerospace industry, which raises the prospect of powerful private capitalists effectively controlling access to space travel.

In order to get a measure of the wealth of these capitalist magnates, it is useful to compare them to longer established lineages such as the Kennedys and the Bushes are as families. Musk is roughly 200 times wealthier as an individual than the entire Kennedy clan and 500 times wealthier than the Bushes. This, coupled with an option for decisive, focused expenditure of resources on key targets (such as Musk's attack on Twitter) makes then capable of doing things that members of the historic bourgeoisie either couldn't do or would not because of potential long term repercussions to their relationships with other members of their class whose collaboration they required.

Political Contradictions

The emergence of Capital as an autonomous intelligence is simultaneously the crisis of *all* human political formations, which find their ability to affect the allocation of resources, and thus to organize and direct human activity, severely restricted. But this is especially true of the "nation-state" which emerged alongside the twinned process of capitalist development and the liberal and democratic revolutions, which presupposes some coherence between a group of people—generally an imagined or constructed community—which shares a common history and culture—and a state which is sovereign—both autonomous and exercising control over a territory and its people (Anderson 1991; Hobsbawm 1991).

This said, we need to understand approach the concept of the nation state critically. In reality most nation states were actually empires or attempted empires which attempted a legitimation strategy based on a shared (politically constructed) identity based on land, lineage, language, history, and culture. That most failed to reach subcontinental or continental status was largely due the balance of power between them—and perhaps also because of their insistence on creating a shared culture, which becomes more difficult the greater the territory and the diversity of peoples one is trying to integrate. Those which succeeded—the United States in particular—had to become radically multicultural and pluralistic in the process. In this sense the Westphalian System was very much like the periods during which China was divided into competing kingdoms after the collapse of the Han and Song dynasties. Nation state structures played a critical role in capitalist development because they provided a way of leveraging state power to protect emerging centers of capitalist development from "early adopters" and especially from the British. But Capital emerged in the first place through a process of conquest and colonization, which was a precondition for primitive accumulation. And ultimately, as Marx pointed out, the internal contradictions of capitalism and in particular the tendency of the rate of profit to decline the economy becomes more technology intensive, requires the export of capital and the construction of new colonial empires, whether territorial, mercantile, or financial.

A tippling point was, however, reached with the collapse of the Soviet Union and the subsequent formation of a unified global market in Capital which reduced the effective sovereignty of nation states to something like that of municipalities, which could attract investment and promote growth only by making concessions to Capital and which were powerless in the face of the power of Capital to escape rising wages or troublesome regulations simply by redeploying elsewhere. Thus, in the period after 1989, it was commonplace to hear discussion of the *crisis of the nation-state,* which was understood to be an inevitable result of globalization (Dunn 1995).

This said, there *are* countervailing tendencies—in particular the resurgence of territorial empire over the course of the past decade, a trend which we noted earlier in this chapter. More recently, however, the phenomenon of Empire has become a focus in its own right. John Darwin's *After Tamerlane* provided new tools for theorizing this reality by trying to define Empire as a global phenomenon distinct from European colonialism (Darwin 2007). With the idea of non-capitalist empire back in play, Darwin was both taken up and criticized by thinkers on the left such as Christopher Coker (Coker 2019) and Jiang Shigong (Shigong 2018/2020, 2020/2020). Christopher Coker leverages the idea of Empire to provide what he sees as the missing link in Huntington's analysis. Civilizations do not come into conflict, *civilizational states* do. Jiang, who is among the principal theoreticians of the Chinese New Left, finds the rehabilitation of the concept of Empire as a way of thinking about multicultural territorial states independent of the Leninist theory of imperialism quite helpful, but criticizes Darwin for not distinguishing between the brutal rapacity of European Colonization and the morally constrained empire building practiced by China and other "civilizational states." The result of this discussion has been an emerging distinction between the Liberal International Order—understood as (or rather, I will argue, partially misunderstood as) the network of political and military institutions which make the world safe for Capital—and Civilizational Empires (or, in language that some prefer, Liberal Empire and Civilizational States). This literature has been complemented by scholarship (Lin 2019) demonstrating that Leninism, by way of *narodnism,* shared with fascism roots in romantic nationalism and that leaders of the national liberation movements of the last century frequently admired and drew from fascist theory and practice.

This requires that we address the question of Empire directly, in a way which goes beyond the resources of existing historical materialist theory. Historical materialism has, at least for the past 100 years, tended to theorize imperialism as either a stage in or a permanent dimension of specifically *capitalist* development. Lenin (Lenin 1916/1963) argued that imperialism represented a specific stage of capitalist development associated with the export of capital to low skill, low wage regions in order to compensate for the declining rate of profit in the higher technology industrial sectors. Dependency and World Systems Theory (Amin 1978, 1879/1980, 1988/1989; Frank 1998; Wallerstein 1974, 1980, 1989), make imperialism foundational for the process of capitalist development itself, locating the principal sources of primitive accumulation in colonies established beginning around 1500. These two approaches to imperialism, while at the root of significant differences in political strategy in the final stages of the national liberation struggles, are not, in fact, entirely incompatible if treated as theorizing distinct stages in the relationship between Capital and Empire. Furthermore, to the extent that these two approaches, singly or in combination, have been questioned, or treated as out of date, it has been to argue that the global market has become so integrated and powerful as to overtake state structures of all kinds, so that it is no longer possible to talk meaningfully of "US imperialism" or other national imperialisms, but only of a deterritorialized "Empire" of Capital. This approach is also, interestingly enough, broadly compatible with the normative neoliberal claim articulated most clearly by Francis Fukuyama that the defeat of the Soviet Union represented a sort of "end of history" in which ideological conflicts would give way to the technocratic management of a global capitalist order of which unlimited freedom in the movement of capital was the foundation. The work of Darwin and Coker, furthermore, while useful, is primarily historical in character and Jiang's "theorization" on the basis of this work amounts to a slight of hand in which the great world empires of the Silk Road Era become "civilizational states" and the term Empire is reserved for the Liberal (i.e., capitalist) world order, moves which exempt China and the other "civilizational states" from the taint of imperialism of *any* kind and maintain a (superficial) consistency with historical materialist usage which reserves the term for capitalist formations.

We will argue, against Jiang's approach, that Empire in fact represents both an historic precapitalist social formation and a civilizational ideal or *way of being*. As a social formation, Empire uses tributary modes of exploitation (rents, taxes and forced labor), petty commodity production, and sometimes chattel slavery, to create and capture surplus which is then traded across what ultimately becomes a global market in luxury goods, which we call, with some oversimplification, the *Silk Road*. A portion of this is then extracted at a second level by imperial states using the mechanism of taxation. Economically, Empire serves as creator and guarantor of global trade routes but also as a direct means of enrichment for the imperial household and the section of the aristocracy involved in the imperial bureaucracy. As a civilizational ideal and *way of being* Empire aims at the systematic bureaucratic rationalization of human life in order to maximize material production and accumulation, often understanding this as in the interest of the vast majority of people. Empire as an ideal is reflected in a range of philosophical movements during the Axial Age, including Sophism, the *Caravaka* school and, most specifically, Chinese Legalism or *faxue*.

If the emergent Empires of the Silk Road Era used tributary means to profit from the petty commodity production which had led to the Axial Age and the Silk Road trade networks to begin with, the resurgent territorial empires of the present period attempt to use similar but more fully rationalized methods to profit from global capitalism. We will argue in succeeding chapters that elites within colonized or marginalized empires leveraged historic socialism to carry out state led industrialization efforts which are now allowing their states to re-emerge as major global players, sometimes while retaining significant socialist elements, as in the case of China, and sometimes not, as in the case of Russia.

We will examine resurgent Empire as a political project in the next chapter. For now, it is sufficient to point out that there is an organic relationship between alterimperialism and the rise of fascistic tendencies within countries ordinarily regarded as adhering to liberal norms. There are two reasons for this. First, most of these countries—the United States, but also Canada, Australia, New Zealand, the "nation states" of Europe, Japan, South Korea, etc.—are *also* territorial empires, fragments of territorial empires, or failed attempts to create a territorial empire. And so while their principal role in the global order is as political agents of Capital and guarantors of the liberal order, they harbor elements which envision *alternative histories* which are focused less an creating a global legal and institutional framework for the free flow of Capital, goods, services, and labor than on conquering and exploiting vast territories for the benefit of a dominant or settler population. In general, the smaller the state is and thus the less realistic any imperial ambitions, the "kinder and gentler" it appears, though there are exceptions.

Furthermore, precisely because these countries are relatively open, they are vulnerable to foreign operatives who in some cases expend vast sums of money to influence their internal politics. There is growing evidence that the alliance between Russia and the US and European Right, for example, dates back to long before the collapse of the Soviet Union, and reflects a long standing Russian geopolitical strategy focused on doing everything it can to undermine potential adversaries in order to compensate for its vulnerable geopolitical location.

The Broken Heart and Severed Head of the Revolution

The Social Basis of Racism and Misogyny

The final feature of the present period is the resurgence of fascism and other authoritarian tendencies, both racist and misogynistic, and associated with a perverse synergy between scientism and irrationalism among broad layers of the population and the decision of the humanistic intelligentsia, which Marx had identified as the "head" of the revolution, to disarm itself and withdraw from effective political engagement, or else to embrace positions which, like poststructuralism, are themselves profoundly deformed by fascism.

The idea that the resurgence of fascism and other forms of authoritarianism is the result of the "economic anxiety" of industrial workers in advanced capitalist countries displaced by globalization and/or automation is fundamentally flawed. First, "deindustrialization" is at least forty years old and the worst effects of the collapse of the steel industry in Western Pennsylvania, for example, came in the 1980s, not the 2010s. And while there certainly are "white working class" districts which voted for Trump in 2016 and in 2020, there are many that did not. Trump voters, especially core voters who are actually enthusiastic about Trump, tend to come from high income/low status groups, such as small capitalist and petty bourgeois business owners in fields like automobile retail (Mutz 2018).

What *does* define core Trump voters—and those who have voted for the far Right in recent years globally—is racism and misogyny. Indeed, the transformation of the Republican Party in the US from a liberal conservative party which, like many of its European counterparts, preferred a more cautious and fiscally conservative approach to the welfare state, into the fascist organization which it has become began back in the 1960s when it embraced Kevin Phillips "southern strategy," outlined in the book *The Emerging Republican Majority* (Phillips 1969) and to the sharp turn to the Right on the part of the Catholic Church, which moved from a cautious alliance with the Left in the 1960s and 1970s to a political stand which, in the US at least, made opposition to legal abortion the litmus test for fidelity to the Church. The Republican Party lured "white" working class voters away from the Democratic Party not by addressing any economic anxiety but by embracing white backlash and eventually embracing a very explicit white supremacy—and by a similar embrace of male backlash against the new wave women's liberation made possible by effective contraception.

This was, however, possible, only because of an underlying dynamic written into the structure of capitalism itself. Marx expected that the process of proletarianization would generate a revolutionary class which would, with little more than organizing and strategic leadership, struggle to transcend capitalism and decommodify labor power (Marx and Engels 1848/2000). This has turned out to be a fundamental mistake. The alienation engendered by the commodification of labor power is real and results in a radical de-humanization and de-moralization of the proletariat. In response to this, as Fromm and others have demonstrated (Fromm 1941/1994), people develop authoritarian personality structures centered on submitting to those above them and dominating those below them. This is, by itself, not confined just to "white" workers. It happens to everyone to the extent to which they lose creative control over their own labor, are ripped from communities of shared meaning, and are not able to find a way to resist at a spiritual level. But when it happens to white people, and white men in particular, the authoritarian psychological dynamics that take shape are expressed by way of racist and patriarchal ideologies, creating a massive strategic reserve for the Right. We see a lesser form of this playing out with Black and Latino men, who have actually turned *towards* Trump since 2016.

These contradictions are further exacerbated by *status* differences within the working classes. Status refers to the prestige, honor, or *mana* attaching to a person or thing, and Marx and his interpreters have ignored it at their peril, though Weber (Weber 1920/1968) analyzed it in depth, and Bourdieu (Bourdieu 1983/1986) considered it under the category of "cultural capital." First, there are sharp contradictions between those who have a university level education and those who do not, and especially between those who have a liberal arts education and those who do not. In the multidimensional status hierarchy which exists in the US, higher education generally has emerged as a substitute for older forms of ascribed status such as lineage and liberal education in particular confers nominal gentry status. Increased access to higher education has enabled both women and members of historically oppressed communities to gain status in relation to "white" men who do not have a university degree.

Indeed, the term "white working class" must be understood as referring not to an intersection of actual class and ethnicity—people of European descent who are forced to sell their labor power in order to survive—but rather to a *constructed identity*, and a racist and patriarchal one at that, that dates back to Kevin Phillips "southern strategy" for the Republican Party (Phillips 1969; Grosghal and Kruse 2019). Many so called "white workers" are not proletarianized at all but are small proprietors of low status but often very lucrative businesses such as automobile dealerships, sometimes making millions of dollars a year. And, of course, the symbols of "white working class" identity are not symbols of proletarianization or even, for that matter, of manual labor, but rather of racism (the Confederate Flag) and *machismo* (an oversized pick-up that allows one "to rule the road," or a large collection of rifles).

The basis for the formation of this sort of identity is spontaneous, a direct and inevitable result of the alienation of labor, but it is carefully cultivated, crafted, and mobilized by the Right, beginning with the theoreticians of the Southern strategy and continuing today with the interventions of the *New Axis* consisting of right accelerationist/transhumanist sectors of Capital (Peter Thiel) backed by the more usual members of the reactionary bourgeoisie (the extractive, agrarian, construction, transportation, and manufacturing sectors), along with reterritorializing state actors such as Russia. This Axis has determined that the "libertarian" policies they favor (i.e., policies which give them the right to do whatever they please, even if it harms others) will never be implemented in a democratic setting and have made the struggle against democracy, explicitly in the case of the Dark Enlightenment and indirectly, by undercutting the democratic claims of immigrants and those not of European origin among the ethnonationalists, their central priority. They have at their disposal a vast political apparatus including major media outlets such as Fox News and a network of alternative media sources, as well as large "sock puppet" farms around the world working to shape identities and mobilize political actors.

The Abdication of the Humanistic Intelligentsia

What about the abdication of the humanistic intelligentsia? Again, some context is essential. While Marx did not understand fully the impact of the alienation generated by the commodification of labor power, and expected that the working classes would spontaneously evolve in the direction of what we call social democracy, he did realize that they would not develop a *revolutionary* class consciousness on their own. He thus expected that the leadership for the communist movement would come from the humanistic intelligentsia, which he apostrophized as *Philosophy*, calling it the "head" of the revolution where the proletariat was its "heart." And this insight was extended by Lenin, Gramsci, and Mao in their theorizations of the need for a vanguard party.

This assumption that the humanistic intelligentsia, a social category which includes elements ranging from the highest reaches of the bourgeoisie down through the lumpenproletariat (albeit concentrated numerically in the middle and lower petty bourgeoisie of partially proletarianized professionals and salaried workers) would somehow be free from the alienation which affected everyone else is simply unsupportable. There is, to be sure, an argument to be made that *theory de-alienates*. But this presupposes that the individuals in question embrace theory and follow it into a practice which stretches them beyond their narrow social location and ultimately beyond their humanity. Theory de-alienates only when, in the context of community, it becomes spirituality. Lenin, of course, was aware of the danger presented to the communist movement by a leadership and cadre drawn from the bourgeoisie and petty bourgeoisie, and engaged in constant polemics against what he called "infantile disorders" and "petty bourgeois childishness." But in the end his solution to the problem was simply party discipline. Before he came to power this meant controlling the party absolutely and expelling those who ceased to be useful to him. After he came to power and especially after his death and the rise of Stalin, it led to a totalitarian nightmare.

It will be one of the principal aims of this work to address this problem in depth, showing that communism is a spiritual as well as a political project and one that Marx only partly understood. We will explain the role of theory, of practice—political and spiritual—and of communities which nurture us, challenge us, and hold us accountable. And while I will argue for both the necessity of a conscious leadership and for the role of the humanistic intelligentsia as a vitally important revolutionary social category, "us" here means everyone. We are *all* subject to alienation and the spiritual disorders it causes and we all need to avail ourselves of *all* of the means of de-alienation. It is not enough to read theory nor is it enough to take orders from whoever has seized control of the party apparatus.

This means that by and large the intelligentsia, rather than serving as a revolutionary leadership, systematically reproduces and refines the spontaneous ideology of Capital. This ideology is rooted in the experience of being at the mercy of forces beyond one's control (the marketplace), which allocates resources mysteriously, without respect to subjectively perceived merit. This experience results in a sharp distinction between fact and value, reason and affect and the production of a dual ideology, or a type of ideological schizophrenia, in which people simultaneously rely on the technological products of something called modern science in order to do nearly everything they do, while treating judgements of value as purely subjective—whether as matters of personal preference or matters of faith. *This is the default ideological setting for everyone in our society, even as we try to transcend it.* At the same time, the intelligentsia becomes divided between those with a mathematical and scientific and those with a literary and humanistic education, and the population between village atheists who are convinced that science teaches that the universe is meaningless and the idea not just of God but of the sacred ridiculous and suburban subjectivists who believe that the social embeddedness of knowledge implies that they create their own truth and their own reality.

This ideology also has an affective dimension. For those who feel successful, it is the facts that matter. This is, as will show, a secularized survival of what Weber (Weber 1920/1968) called the "Protestant Ethic," for which usefulness in society was a mark of election. For those who do not feel successful it is, on the other hand, affects that matter: giving your heart to Jesus . . .

This dynamic has significant implications for the subjective constitution of the intelligentsia. On the one hand, there is a section of the intelligentsia which accepts the bargain offered it by the bourgeoisie: that in return for offering value free technical advice they will be granted day to day autonomy in carrying out their work and a position of relative privilege in both economic and status terms. This is bargain is accepted by most of the scientific and technical intelligentsia, but also by a section of those trained in the humanities and social sciences. Accepting this deal is, generally speaking, a condition of employment on the tenure track at a major research university, with those who insist that their role as intellectual and moral, spiritual and political guides is fundamental relegated, if they are fortunate, to appointments as "teaching faculty" or positions at teaching institutions and if not, as is more likely, to adjunct hell. This is largely without regard to the actual quality of their scholarship. And of course those with a politically or ideologically controversial record are unlikely to find employment in private foundations, think tanks, or other nonprofit organizations funded by even the more progressive elements in the bourgeoisie, much less in the civil service.

There is, however, an exception to this pattern. A significant portion of the humanistic intelligentsia of the late nineteenth and early twentieth century bemoaned the ecological, social, and cultural effects of the industrial revolution, but would not ally themselves with the working classes. After the Russian Revolution and especially after the rise of Stalin, it became apparent that actually existing socialism was not going address most of the concerns of the humanistic intelligentsia. Some, like the Frankfurt School or the Right Opposition generally (especially Gramsci) mounted a criticism of the Communist Party of the Soviet Union which, whatever one may think of the details, remained faithful to the communist ideal. But others broke with the Left entirely and were lured by the hermeneutic ontology of Martin Heidegger, which we have shown and will again show in a somewhat different way later in this work is *organically fascist*. Indeed, there are thinkers who, like Marcuse, both embraced Heidegger and clung to Marx . . .

The multiple crises of socialism since then have led the vast majority of the humanistic intelligence to abandon the communist ideal and the commitment to an alliance with the proletariat entirely in favor of the range of ideologies generally known as "poststructuralist" and "deconstructionist." While most of the leading thinkers in this trend continue to consider themselves part of the Left, they are all, ultimately Heideggerians and their ideas ultimately (as we will show) organically fascist. This is why so much current theory on the Left, what we will call the *Dark Liberation* trend, draws on the political theology of yet another Nazi theorist, Carl Schmitt. But we will show that even most of the new "democratic socialist" and "Left populist" trends bears the marks of the Heideggerian virus and, more broadly, of a romantic anticapitalism which has abandoned the alliance with the proletariat and anything like a materialist analysis.

It is this trend which has, since the 1960s in particular, held a more or less complete monopoly on the very small number of prominent, research focused academic appointments in the humanities offered to those who insist on actually engaging fundamental questions. And most of these are in continental Europe: in the last generation, Derrida, Foucault, et al., in the present, Agamben, Badiou, and Žižek. We will argue that the reason they have been granted this privilege is very simple: *they are doing the work of their bourgeois masters, promoting an objectively fascist ideology.*

Meanwhile, however, the continued development of science and technology and especially the (temporary) opening of upward mobility into the bourgeoisie for highly innovative "tech" founders, coupled with growing monopoly rents for some scientists and engineers have created a situation in which this group believes itself uniquely superior to the vast majority of the population and especially to the humanistic intelligentsia and has taken it on itself to begin addressing philosophical and political questions which were historically the province of the humanistic intelligentsia. At first this group tended towards radical libertarianism, but after the election of Barack Obama and the failure of the "Tea-Party" insurgency against him, they began to argue that libertarian policies will never be consistently followed under democracy, and began to constitute what has come to be known as the *Dark Enlightenment,* a mélange of technological accelerationism, recalcitrant masculinism, scientific racism (under the banner of Human Biodiversity) and traditionalism (more often pagan than Christian).

The influence of scientism is not, however, confined to the right. On the contrary, in the 2000s, in response to the persistence of religious fundamentalism, much of the Left embraced the New Atheism of thinkers like Daniel Dennett and Sam Harris. This trend was always deeply problematic, and had the effect of cooperating with religious fundamentalists in destroying the religious left by claiming that attempts at anything other than a literalist hermeneutic was, in spites of millennia of tradition, intellectual dishonest. After the election of Barack Obama in 2008 this tendency began to gradually show its true ideological colors, conciliating scientific racism and "aiming the main blow" against "social justice warriors" and "wokeism." It is now a key strategic reserve (or perhaps more nearly a periphery) of the Dark Enlightenment.

Meanwhile, those who accept the terms of value free professionalism and technocracy and who succeed as a result, or who do the ideological work of the bourgeoisie by promoting what we will call the ideology of *Dark Liberation,* also imagine themselves objectively superior than their colleagues who are relegated to the lower ranks of the academy or public service or excluded altogether.

Political Actors

Contradictions are structural in nature, and in significant measure *define* the elements which are in contradiction and shape the trajectory of events. But politics unfolds through the action—conscious or otherwise—of individuals, networks, organizations, and institutions. How do we understand the way in which the contradictions we have identified above constitutes concrete political actors in the present period?

There is a tendency to think of political actors in terms of identity. This is true not just with respect to race and ethnicity and gender, but also with respect to class. This is because at the empirical level we have an array of actors who *identify* in a variety of ways: as Black Men, white workers, transwomen, etc. Identities in this sense are *constructed,* partly by those who *identify,* but primarily by where the individuals identifying are situated in the context of broader social networks and structural contradictions. There is some leeway in the ways in which individuals can construct their identity, but only so much. There are, for example no Black Whites, Bourgeois Workers, or Cis-Het Transmen. This is because, with very few exceptions, identities are constructed within the context of structural binary contradictions.

There is also a tendency, rooted in the currently fashionable *intersectional* theories of oppression (Crenshaw 1989) to treat class, race/ethnicity, and sex/gender as fundamentally autonomous realities and then to pose the question of how they are interrelated. This is by contrast with older debates between, for example, radical feminists who regarded the oppression of women as fundamental, socialists who privileged class, and cultural nationalists who privilege race or ethnicity.

We regard this approach as fundamentally inadequate. First, from a scientific point of view, it fails to adequately explain the construction of identities. Second, it fails to take seriously the possibility that class, race/ethnicity and sex/gender are all dimensions of a single dynamic of instrumentalization which emerged and evolved together and which remain so intimately bound up together that while they can be distinguished analytically they cannot be engaged politically except as an integrated complex. One cannot meaningfully address "class" for example, without addressing race and gender and one cannot meaningfully address race or gender without addressing class.

This default, empirical, identity based way of understanding political actors is layered over two competing ways of thinking about stratification. Historical materialism and functionalism have generally understood stratification as collective. Classes, and where they are considered sex/gender and racial/ethnic categories are empirical *groups* with definite shared properties. Thus, the easy default to intersectionality. One can be a man and a worker or a woman and Black but also bourgeois. Some combinations of identity may be more likely than others but except for those which, as noted above, are logically contradictory nearly all exist. Intersectionality is a matter of overlapping collectives.

Interpretive sociology on the other hand has considered stratification as individual and multidimensional. For Weber, therefore, class is a matter of what we bring to the marketplace in terms of skills, capital, etc. Status is a matter of the respect we receive based on lineage, achievement, etc. And power (less well defined by Weber, interestingly, given his greater interest in it) is our individual ability to mobilize others to help us accomplish something. Layered over this interpretive sociological framework intersectionality becomes a matter of highly individualized configurations of class, status, and power determined by the assets we bring to the market, the respect we get, and the extent and capacity of our social networks.

Here we propose a way of analyzing the constitution and alignment of political actors in the present period which takes seriously the structural (and therefore neither strictly individual or collective) and multidimensional (economic, political, and cultural) nature of class, race/ethnicity, and gender. Specifically, we argue that all three derive from the emergence of warfare and conquest as economic development strategies with the development of bronze technology, which simultaneously lead to conquering and conquered peoples, exploiters and exploited and which shifted power relations and thus access to assets and respect from women to men. The reality has, since then, become vastly more complicated, leading to what in reality is a proliferation of classes, strata, sectors, and fractions, a complex global caste system with different inflections within diverse local realities, and a multitude of genders, many of which actually lack a name or are even entirely hidden but which are relatively real nonetheless, *all of which involve inextricably intertwined economic, political, and cultural dimensions.* It is his near approach to this sort of analysis which has made Pierre Bourdieu (Bourdieu 1981–1986/2012–2016) so popular. But even Bourdieu continues to think in terms of individuals who *have* various amounts of economic, social, symbolic, and cultural capital, rather than in terms of individuals constituted at various points in economic, political, and cultural fields by the structures they inhabit.

In what follows we will try to elaborate this approach in the context of an analysis of the current situation globally and in the United States with an aim to seeing what light it can shed on the current situation for humanity.

Class, Status, and Power

Class

Marx's claim that class is the most fundamental social category and that "history is the history of class struggle" (Marx and Engels 1848/2000) is grounded in the recognition that we human beings are *defined* by our creative activity, which is a participation in the power of Being as such. Divisions based on our position in the relations of production are thus fundamental. This means, under capitalism, whether or not we must sell our labor power in order to survive. The result is the threefold division we noted above between:

- the bourgeoisie, which has enough capital to live off the labor of others,

- the petty bourgeoisie, which has enough capital to work for themselves or to negotiate formal employment arrangements which give them *de facto* autonomy and which do not involve the extraction of surplus, and

- the proletariat, which is forced to sell its labor power in order to survive.

In addition to these classes Marx identified what amounts to an *out-class*, the *lumpenproletariat* of those who are *unable* to sell their labor in order to survive and must therefore turn to alms, crime, or some other "unproductive" activity. Marx regarded this out-class with suspicion, but as will see, it in fact challenges Capital in a way that is even more profound than the proletariat itself. This is especially true of the disabled, whose inability to sell their labor power is, in many cases permanent and definitive of the social position.

Classes are further subdivided by:

- class fraction: which is determined by the way in which a group extracts surplus or the way in which surplus is extracted from them,
- sector: the part of the economy in which their assets are primarily located or in which they labor, and
- stratum: their relative power, in so far as it is determined by their access to Capital, before taking into consideration mana, relationships, etc.

Status

Labor is, however, from the beginning an intellectual act, not just in the sense of presupposing *techne* or skill and knowledge of the nature and structure of the "matter" on which one works, but in the sense of presupposing an end, a purpose or a *telos*. To put the matter another way, one of the things that human beings create in the very process of creating everything else is *meaning*. And creative activity is, furthermore, fundamentally social in character, and thus presupposes the capacity to organize people for a common end: it presupposes power.

This has profound implications for the way in which we understand the relationship between class, status, and power. Because finding or making meaning is one of the highest expressions of human creativity and because the meaning we find in things shapes their value, we naturally assign different values to different individuals and/or the social positions they occupy.

This means that we need a clear understanding of status. The historic definition is Weber's: status is the degree of respect or honor attached to a particular social characteristic (Weber 1920/1968), whether it is ascribed, such as lineage, ethnicity, or gender, or acquired, such as education and professional achievement, *habitus* or disposition, or objectified, in the form of ownership of prestigious real estate, works of art, etc. (Bourdieu 1977). While class and power have to do with access to the *means to the ends of human life*, status has to do with the degree to which people are *regarded* as *embodying realization of the those ends themselves*. And this in turn means that *status* is a function of what a society *values* which is, in turn a function of what it *believes*, i.e., of ideology.

Now as we have shown, the present period is defined above all by capitalism and in particular by a very advanced capitalism which operates across a unified global market in goods, services, capital and to some extent labor, and which is giving rise to Capital as an autonomous emergent intelligence. But Capital itself is the product of Christendom and in particular of the Crusades, the *Reconquista*, and the Conquests, which in turn led to the primitive accumulation of Capital, the formation of the modern state, the Reformation and the Scientific Revolution. It also emerged alongside of and intertwined with the liberal, democratic, and socialist revolutions and, as it became global, engaged and both affected and was affected by the whole complex of civilizational traditions and *ways of being* around the world (Mansueto 2010, 2016). This means that the meanings and values which define our society are at once profoundly capitalist and radically pluralistic.

Within this context I would like to suggest that the hegemonic ideological complex determining status in the present period remains what Weber called the *Protestant Ethic*. Specifically, as a result of the Augustinian Reaction which we analyzed above—itself a product of and catalyst for the Crusades and *Reconquista*, the age of Conquest and the primitive accumulation and state formation they engendered, Europe (and especially the Protestant Northwest) embraced the ideal of a sovereign God who chooses who would be saved and who would be damned "before the foundation of the world," and without foreknowledge of their merit—but with usefulness to society being a possible, though not definitive sign of election. The result was, as Weber (Weber 1920/1968) pointed out, an obsessive psychological drive to work, save, and invest that formed people intellectually, morally, and spiritually for capitalism. Even the temptation to rest or enjoy might be a sign of damnation.

This had a number of implications. First, while it gave the emerging bourgeoisie—and, in the English context, the economically "progressive" (if socially ruthless) gentry—an ideological lever to use against the hereditary aristocracy, these groups soon generated their own lineages which found their own scriptural justifications for hereditary privilege, spiritual as well as social. Second, it made the traditional petty bourgeoisie anxious about its status and inclined to interpret proletarianization as the product of personal failure, and thus inclined this class to cling ever more closely to Capital rather than to move in a revolutionary direction. The Protestant Ethic also made the emerging new petty bourgeoisie, on the other hand, which depended on gainful employment in order to exercise a profession, susceptible to cooptation. Thus the ideal of the professional scientist or scholar-bureaucrat who, even if their learning is in the humanities, professes value-neutrality and provides technical advice but not normative direction—a much safer stance that setting oneself up as the *"head of the revolution."* Those who step out of line are marginalized and no longer taken seriously as scholars. Third, economically marginalized populations were stigmatized as unproductive and (again implicitly, as secularization has hidden this ideological dynamic from sight) predestined to damnation. And so, the segmentation of the labor market which is an inevitable legacy of slavery and of colonialism generally is read in a way which results in the spiritual derogation of historically enslaved and colonized peoples.

What Weber misses, of course, is the fact that the Reformed tradition has split repeatedly as previously progressive groups have been left behind, and have had to search for other ways to claim election or at least salvage their self-esteem. Generally speaking, it was those further from ports and roads and thus opportunities for commerce who provided the constituency for mass movements such as the Salem Witch Trials (Boyer and Nussenbaum 1974) and evangelical as opposed to liberal Protestantism (Heimart 1967; Hatch 1974). Where the wealthy saw in the mysterious workings of the marketplace the predestining hand of God electing them to glory, those left behind saw the hand of Satan himself, and staked their own identities and claims to status on a personal conversion experience.

Weber could not, furthermore, have been aware of the incredible range of competing claims to superiority which would emerge both from within Capital's original Euro-American domain or out of its interactions with other civilizations at it colonized and globalized. There is thus prestige attached to being part of a lineage with a long history not only of wealth but of civilizational leadership and also prestige attached to being "self-made." There is prestige attached to membership in the dominant ethnoreligious communities—especially Anglo-American Protestantism—but also prestige attached to membership in competing elites which can claim many more centuries of civilizational leadership. There is prestige associated with conspicuous consumption but also with living a "simple life" or with "thrift" or "voluntary poverty." Competing status hierarchies persist, in other words, but are hegemonized by the Protestant Ethic. Thus Brahmin status claims are translated, to some extent by Brahmins themselves and even more so by the broader global arena in which they now operate, into claims to status based on education and professional achievement. The same is true of Chinese and certain other Asian lineages which historical claimed status based on scholarly achievement, a claim which has now shifted from the Confucian classics to mathematics, the physical sciences, and engineering.

The result is what amounts to a global caste system. And like any caste system, it produces outcastes. These consist first of all in the disabled, the no longer socially "useful" elderly, and in general those who are capable of neither exploiting nor being exploited. Women who do not want to become outcastes are required to be exploitable across a broad spectrum of arenas: as sexual "partners," emotional caretakers, mothers, and as contributors to both the accumulation of capital and the high consumption levels their partners demand of them. But, the Protestant Ethic is layered over a broader distinction determined by means of the what we have called the *Lockean Exception*. John Locke developed, in his *Two Treatises* (Locke 1690/1967) what appears to be a condemnation of slavery. For Locke property comes about by means of creative activity, and since human beings were created by God, we are God's property and ought not harm, steal, or restrain each other. This is the basis of our rights to life and liberty. Any property we own comes about by mixing our labor with the land, i.e., with raw materials, in the act of production, something which would seem to exclude slavery. Locke, however, makes an exception for cases in which someone commits a crime for which the penalty is death. If rather than executing this sentence the convict is instead set to forced labor, that is licit, because they always have the option of resisting and accepting the death which they already, in any case, deserve. While Locke never says this explicitly the implication is that, since he actually *wrote* the constitution for the Carolina Colonies, which allowed slavery, that those enslaved were in some sense guilty of a crime which would have merited death. This ideological dynamic persists in the phenomenon of mass incarceration of African Americans in the US and the broader ideological motif of African men as inherently dangerous as well as the subsequent extension of this hereditary criminal status to "illegal" immigrants and "terrorists" and those who sympathize with and aid and abet them.

What the Lockean Exception does is to define a group of outcastes who are denied not only respect but the minimal status of citizen, whether because they are migrants, because they are considered savages, or because they have been declared felons and stripped of their rights. As we will see this division plays a profound role in shaping the actual political dynamics both within nominal states and at the global level.

Power

Power in general consists in *organized money, organized people, and organized mana*. We have already analyzed the general dynamics of *organized money* and *organized mana* in the form of class and status. But in order to have a complete picture of the way in which structural dynamics constitute and align political actors, we need to consider how direct social capital or organized people, affects power dynamics. Here the distinction made with regard to *status* between *ascribed* and *acquired* is useful. The *Protestant Ethic* means that *lineage* does not operate *openly* as a factor at the level of status within most ethnoreligious communities in the US. We have no *recognized* aristocracy or gentry based on lineage, and questions of lineage tend to arise only in relatively private settings and in relation to decisions about marriages etc.

The same is not true at the level of *organized people* or pure social capital. Lineage relationships and networks between established families are real and those who come from prominent lineages enjoy a type of social capital that no one else does. It is relationships like this that give marginal *rentiers* access to employment "suitable" to their standing so that they can recover their position over a generation or two or which allow them organize the capital necessary for major entrepreneurial campaigns of the sort that create capitalist magnates such as a Bill Gates or Elon Musk. These same networks also operate at lower levels of the bourgeoisie, among families which are economically established but which are not especially high status, at least outside of a nonmetropolitan community or an economic niche of some sort.

In the US and most other advanced capitalist countries elite colleges and universities function as a kind of recruitment pool and proving ground for members of privileged families to recruit new "blood" both because they need people more capable and ambitious than their own coddled offspring to run the civilization and because it helps to preserve the myth of meritocracy. It must be remembered, however, that the most elite schools admit as much of 50 percent of their student body as "legacies," i.e., children of alumni, at much lower standards in a kind of aggressive affirmative action for the aristocratic, actually constituting a sort of just barely hidden nobility or gentry. And admission to and academic success at an elite school—*or even a lifetime of high-level professional achievements*—do not by any means guarantee admission to high status lineage networks. While universities can be forced to at least appear meritocratic and while, depending on the profession and the economic sector businesses, government, and nonprofit organizations *sometimes* actually require and thus reward good work, *families still play an enormous role in vetting which outsiders will gain access to economic and professional opportunities and who will be allowed to marry into a lineage. And even where they do not, they can effectively deny their in-laws access to the power and privilege which is theirs.*

Historically it was possible for members of relatively marginalized communities to build up their own networks and leverage them for access to capital or to shape public policy, though much less frequently to gain status. This is what organizing is all about. Labor unions represent the historically most significant example of this phenomenon, but urban political machines and institutionally based community organizations which leverage and build on existing networks in local congregations, civic organizations, labor unions, etc. have also, historically, been important. The erosion of the labor movement under the neoliberal regime, the destruction of historic ethnoreligious communities by white flight, suburbanization, and gentrification, the turn from precinct organization to mass/social media as the principal instrument of electoral politics, the decline of congregational religion, and now the COVID-19 pandemic with its lockdowns and mandatory social distancing have all served to undercut this dynamic, contributing to the political marginalization of all but the most powerful established networks. *Indeed, when we see the sudden rise of a new political movement, whether on the Right (e.g., Trump* and his followers) *or on the Left* (*Our Revolution*, the *Justice Democrats*, and the sudden explosion of *Democratic Socialists of America*) it should always make us suspicious that powerful existing networks are behind them. In this case the evidence points very clearly, in both cases, to the Russian intelligence/organized crime complex.

What this means is that while it is certainly possible to build power through intentional organizing, ordinarily organized money (class) and organized mana (status) *determine* the ease with which people can do this. Trying to build and exercise power if you are poor and/or low status is like playing with an enormous handicap—one the full extent of which Marx did not understand and with which historic socialist strategies, among others, have not reckoned. And for outcastes it can be all but impossible.

The Relationship Between Class, Race, and Gender

This analysis of the relationship between class, status, and power in turn allows us to clarify the relationship between class, race, and gender. As we noted earlier in this chapter, the origin of these three dimensions of oppression is the same: the advent of warfare as an economic development strategy at the beginning of the Bronze Age. This is what led to the first strict distinction between those who live or can live on the labor of others—the warlords who extract surplus from dependent peasant villages in the form of rents, taxes, and forced labor—and those who are subject to exploitation. But the emergence of warfare as an economic development also vastly increased any coercive advantage that men may have had over women due to different physical adaptations. And it created the distinction between conquering and conquered *peoples* which, while not yet racism, provided the basis in experience for the emergence of racist structures.

Now clearly the articulation between class, race, and gender differs from one social formation to another and from one period to another. Capitalism, in this sense, represents not just a new way of extracting surplus from direct producers, but also a new modality of the oppression of women and a new relationship between conqueror and conquered—the relationship which we call racism properly speaking. Understanding this is not just critical to a correct analysis of the oppression of women and of colonized people but of capitalism itself. The critical contribution in this regard belongs to Silvia Federici, whose *Caliban and the Witch* (Federici 2004) shows that

- the process of primitive accumulation was not simply about the separation of workers from the means of production and the conquest, pillaging and colonization of the peoples of Asia, Africa, and the Americas, but also the expropriation of women's bodies, and the transformation of the work of the reproduction of labor into utterly uncompensated labor power, and that
- capitalism requires for its reproduction and expansion the constant ongoing support of but also the continuing expropriation of a not-yet-commodified *commons* which alone can supply the creative capacity which commodification destroys.

Thus, while women belong to a given social class (bourgeois, petty bourgeois, proletarian) they are also superexploited through unpaid household and reproductive labor (biological and social). Colonized peoples also belong to a given social class but, precisely to the extent that they are colonized, experience the ongoing expropriation of their *land* in the broad sense of the ecosystem within which their not-yet-commodified social relations reproduce the creative capacity which capitalism requires for its existence, as well as imperialist exploitation through rape and pillaging, the export of profits, and unequal exchange (Amin 1978/1981).

These economic relationships are then reinforced by the status and power dynamics we analyzed above. Specifically, the *Protestant Ethic* devalues reproductive labor as unproductive, because being unpaid the value it creates is simply not recognized as socially useful in a fully commodified society. And this reproductive labor is not just that of women but also that of colonized peoples whose not-yet-commodified social relations don't just supply cheaper labor (by subsidizing wages which are below what is necessary for the survival and reproduction of labor with subsistence labor in the countryside) but also the creative content which Capital transforms into commodities and objects of consumption.

As Capital globalizes it claims to celebrate "soft skills," "people skills," or "emotional intelligence." But even though it actually depends on "native" practitioners of these skills who are overwhelmingly women and especially working class women and women from historically oppressed communities, it simultaneously formalizes, standardizes, and commodifies these practices and attempts to reproduce them through capitalist institutions, so that they never create an ecosystem in which resistance to Capital might emerge. As Capital globalizes it appears to celebrate "cultural diversity" and "multiculturalism," but actually commodifies the products of the cultures it claims to celebrate, uprooting them from the ecosystem of noncommodified relationships in which they emerged and cutting them off from the ends or purposes in service of which they formed people and reduces them to something to simply be consumed and enjoyed by the colonizer.

To put the matter differently, Capital is always identifying creative capacity, expropriating it from those who developed in the first place, devaluing them and assigning value instead to itself for seeing a "business opportunity," and then, once it owns the creative capacity, in the process of making it suitable for mass production and the mass market destroys it and denatures it—a process which culminates in the artificial "intelligence" we now see moving into the creative sector. This actually affects everyone, including not just workers from within colonizing peoples, but even intellectuals and creatives within the bourgeoisie. But women and colonized peoples, precisely because they have been marginalized and thus operated partly outside of the capitalist world system, have always been special targets of this process. And as peasant communities and artisan guilds and comparable precapitalist forms are gradually destroyed this becomes even more true.

Concrete Political Actors

We are now in a position to specify the principal political actors constituted by the structural dynamics we have analyzed. It will help, in this regard, to identify the following types of cleavages within social classes:

- fractions are defined by the way in which they extract surplus or are subject to its extraction
- sectors are defined by the broad area of the economy in which they work, generally a cluster of related industries, and
- strata are defined by the quantity of their total capital or, if they have none, of their income or other assets.

The Bourgeoisie

We begin with the fundamental classes defined by capitalist relations of production: the bourgeoisie, the petty bourgeoisie, and the proletariat and then look at how these groups are formed and divided by status and power considerations and by the underlying realities of patriarchy and colonialism.

The bourgeoisie includes the following *fractions:*

- Rentiers who have largely retired into luxury consumption and/or philanthropy but who continue to have fortunes that guarantee their continued independence and, if large enough, the ability to set in motion activities of significant scope and effect,
- Active investors who concentrate their efforts on increasing their wealth by investing in existing or emerging enterprises intended to generate wealth,
- Venture capitalists who invest in establishing new enterprises with the aim both of shaping the technological and economic direction of the society and of accumulating enough wealth to either retire as rentiers or become capitalist magnates.
- Entrepreneurs who establish new enterprises of various sizes with aims similar to venture capitalists, but generally relying in significant measure on capital provided by others, and either continue to manage them or who sell out to investors and go on to found other enterprises or achieve rentierization,
- Established capitalists who own privately held firms, often by inheritance, and live off the profits they generate. They may or may not be actively engaged in leadership and management, though they often are. While they may try to expand or diversify their business, they are unlikely to try to sell out and reinvest unless they are retiring without heirs, and
- State capitalists who leverage control of a state, often postrevolutionary, to gain access to business opportunities they would not otherwise have. This fraction often begins as part of the new petty bourgeoisie, a portion of which gains control of the state apparatus as the result of a socialist or anticolonial revolution, and then uses its position to enrich itself capitalistically as well as through what amount to neotributary means.

- Organized Criminal Syndicates. These exist everywhere but play an especially large role in postrevolutionary and postsocialist societies where, as disillusionment with socialism progresses, revolutionary vanguard parties degenerate into means of private enrichment.

With respect to *stratum* it is possible to identify:

- Capitalist magnates with wealth in the billions, tens of billions, or hundreds of billions of dollars whose economic decisions and political and cultural interventions can shape the fate of the planet on a large scale,
- large, established capitalist families with wealth into the hundreds of millions who are able to exercise very significant impact at the economic, political, and cultural level, generally over multiple generations,
- medium capitalists who are able to have impact beyond their own economic niche and local community, but who may have difficulty both significantly impacting the direction of society and passing significant wealth on to their heirs, at least across multiple generations, and
- small capitalists who may indulge in luxuries or contribute to their local communities, but who must use most of their capital to keep their business healthy if they hope to pass on their class position to their heirs.

With respect to sector we can identify the following:

- Architectonic sectors which focus on shaping the larger direction of the society, including
  - Philanthropy
  - Educational, Charitable, and Religious endowments,
  - Information
  - Finance
  - Many or most business and professional services such as accounting, consulting, engineering, architecture, etc.
  - Government
- Industry, which is often subdivided by technological level,

- Personal Services
- Agriculture
- Extractive activities such as mining, forestry, hunting, etc.

It should immediately be apparent that these divisions within the bourgeoisie have status and power implications as well as complex intersections with gender and race. Thus the *aristocracy*, while originally a *class* defined by land held by feudal tenure (i.e., in return for service, in either *frankalmoin*, in return for prayer, or *homage*, in return for military service), is now largely a status group which overlaps with but also shapes the bourgeoisie and to a lesser extent the petty bourgeoisie. Specifically, those with an aristocratic lineage are more likely to be *rentiers* than those without such a lineage, but an aristocratic lineage also assists in maintaining hereditary wealth both by credentialing those who have it and gaining them access to opportunities for investment and by providing a network of support and assistance not available to others. It is often assumed that countries that do not bestow or recognize noble titles lack an aristocracy, but this is not really accurate. Because of the global reach of Anglo-American imperialism the English practice of maintaining a sharp distinction between the titled nobility and the gentry has allowed much of the aristocracy to simply hide when it suits them, while maintaining their lineage relationships and their status with "those who know" as well as the pretense of being open to new blood, since in the English tradition, at least according to some authorities, the gentry *nominally* includes (at the lowest rank of "gentleman") everyone who earns their living by some means other than manual labor or trade, or sometimes specifically by the exercise of a liberal profession.

Those members of the bourgeoisie who are located in virtue of their investments and/or public activities in what we have identified as the "architectonic" sectors of the economy, similarly function rather like an aristocracy, though it is not unusual for someone with investments in a less prestigious sector to function publicly in government or philanthropy, for example. There is, similarly, a tendency for capitalist magnates, especially those who are active entrepreneurs or venture capitalists, to be less aristocratic than much of the large but not billionaire bourgeoisie, which holds wealth which, because inherited, has also been subdivided over the course of multiple generations.

Historical materialism has historically distinguished between *metropolitan* and *colonized* bourgeoisies, and among the latter between *compradors*, who simply buy up agricultural goods or the product of extractive activities and sell them to colonial powers, *dependent capitalists*, who engage in industrial production for the export market, and the *national bourgeoisie* producing domestically for domestic consumption. How relevant these distinctions remain is not entirely clear now that Indian and Chinese capital has assumed global significance. *But the fact remains that members of the colonized bourgeoisie, regardless of where they fall economically, are carriers of what they and their people experience as a foreign civilizational project.* This project may be welcomed as a liberation from historic forms of personal dependency and oppression and a door to opportunity or reviled as a profound betrayal of an ancient culture—or both. But it inevitably marks them as subordinate to the metropolitan bourgeoisie, regardless of fraction, sector, or stratum. This is not necessarily overcome by aristocratic lineage which will attract interest, or rather *fascination*, in the global context, but only as something to be consumed and not as a real object of respect.

Gender, finally, functions very differently for members of the bourgeoisie depending on the extent to which they have or are creating aristocratic lineage. Aristocratic women bear the burden of producing heirs and of managing lineage relationships—often on behalf of their husbands' lineages rather than their own—in a way that profoundly constrains and instrumentalizes them. It is partly the contradiction between extreme privilege and this instrumentalization which makes the stories of women like Diana (an hereditary aristocrat) and Meaghan (an upper petty bourgeois celebrity married into, in this case, a royal family) so captivating for those who are living out different but related dramas of lineage, gender, and race but who are only dimly aware of the dynamics involved.

What are the political implications of these distinctions within the bourgeoisie? With respect to *fraction* rentiers are generally concerned with the conservation of capital and may, therefore favor higher interest rates and other policies which make safe investments more lucrative. But for the same reasons rentiers may also be more open to economic regulation which conserves social stability. Active investors, venture capitalists, and entrepreneurs favor conditions which promote new business development—low interest rates and thus a strong incentive for equity investment, as well as state or state directed investment which subsidizes sectors in which they are invested. Owners of privately held established companies are, once again, concerned to conserve the value and viability of their companies, generally opposing any rapid social change or mobility and sometimes seek protection from foreign competition or emerging industries.

Broadly speaking, the bourgeoisie is divided politically by stratum primarily around the question of just how confident they are that capitalism will always serve their interests and the extent to which they are concerned that "socialism" or other breaks with capitalism threaten their interests. The more capital one has the more confident one is of the ability to shape the course of history in accord with one's will, so capitalist magnates are more concerned to influence the nature of state intervention than to eliminate it entirely—though this may be changing as the new generation of magnates who take Elon Musk as their model claim absolute freedom to do what they please with impunity. Those whose capitalist status is in question, on the contrary, will often develop quite strong anti-capitalist convictions, with petty rentiers whose freedom from the need to earn a living and still live comfortably breaking to the left and small capitalists engaged in running businesses in low status sectors or sectors threatened by global competition breaking to the right.

Sectoral differences are more important, with the architectonic and higher technology industrial sectors leaning a bit to the left, to the extent of favoring policies which protect the planet and promote a higher wage workforce which can buy their products, and generally favoring freedom of expression (including gender expression) and freedom of movement, which open up new market niches, while those in lower technology industry, services, agriculture, and extraction resisting these measures as they depend on the ability to engage in unfettered exploitation of the planet using vulnerable, low wage labor. This, at least, has been the general pattern. *But the leftward lean of the architectonic and higher technology sectors is not guaranteed. The advent of "generative" AI at least partly releases them from relying on a mass creative workforce and, by reducing costs, opens up the prospects of still being able to sell their products to a lower wage proletariat.*

Finally, as we have seen, there is a distinction between metropolitan and colonized bourgeoisies. With the development of a global market these distinctions have become less important, with both productivity and real wages rising in the old Third World, undercutting the basis of unequal exchange. Capitalists from China and India are now among the planet's leading capitalist magnates, though China and India remain underrepresented at this level in proportion to their population. At this point it probably makes more sense to distinguish between the international global bourgeoisie aligned with the project of a unified global market without borders, "alterimperial" bourgeoisies trying to leverage strong states to accumulate wealth even as those states leverage them in order to recover global superpower status, and authentic dependent and national bourgeoisies occupying subaltern positions in the international market or trying to catalyze domestic development for domestic consumption—with the last two represented primarily in the least developed countries and not in rising powers.

As a result of globalization, however, we have also seen the emergence of a distinction within the nominally metropolitan bloc between what we might call *cosmopolitans* and *provincials*. While the distinction between cosmopolitans and provincials does, to a certain extent, track the internal fractionalization and sectoral conflict within the bourgeoisie, it does not track stratification nearly so closely. There are "provincials" and "territorials" among the ranks of capitalist magnates (e.g., the Waltons or the Koch Brothers) and cosmopolitans among the small bourgeoisie (petty rentier "trust fund kids" who, freed from the burden to earn a living, monopolize and thrive in jobs in the nonprofit sector or the academy or even devote themselves to "the revolution"). The key distinctions have to do with, at the economic level, the degree of integration into global networks and resulting differences in both status and reference group. Cosmopolitans produce for the global market or, being *rentiers*, can invest globally. Provincials have capital which is closely tied to local or regional markets, such as the proverbial auto dealership, chains of family restaurants, gas stations, or liquor stores. But these economic differences have status and power implications. In addition to the prestige which comes from playing on the vastly larger field of the global market, cosmopolitans generally inherit or acquire the cultural capital necessary to engage globally and often multigenerational political networks which cross borders and industries and culture. The social standing and power of provincials is generally dependent on the smaller communities and regions they "serve."

We are accustomed to reading this divide as fundamentally binary, with cosmopolitans, colonials, and their retainers in the petty bourgeoisie forming a multiculturalist bloc and provincials tending towards . . . racism. But this gives too much credit to cosmopolitans, the vast majority of whom are involved in a vast project of instrumentalizing colonized peoples and cultures in order to sustain and expand Capital. This is the social basis of what has come to be called "corporate DEI" (Diversity,

Equity, and Inclusion), and the cosmopolitan bourgeoisie has drawn to its side an entire army of workers, both petty bourgeois and proletarian, mostly themselves form colonized peoples, to help them penetrate and control not just colonized markets but colonized societies as a whole.

All of this is further complicated by the fact that while much of the bourgeoisie benefits from and indeed draws most of its wealth, status, and power from the formation of an integrated global market in Capital, the emergence of Capital itself as an autonomous intelligence represents to the bourgeoisie an existential threat unlike any it has faced since its emergence in the late Middle Ages. The privilege of the bourgeoisie consists precisely in its ability to make its own decisions about what to do, whether this means creating a new liberal order with unheard of freedoms or simply satisfying basic urges to an extent unimagined by prior ruling classes. Understanding status and power is so important to the bourgeoisie because, like everyone else, it is in these realms that it reaps the greatest rewards of its social location and also experiences its greatest disappointments. The bourgeoisie can *buy* status and power—but only in part. One can buy a title, but not status as a member of a long and respected lineage. One can more or less buy office and become a dictator. But dictators are low status and always insecure. It is impossible to buy status as a monarch recognized as legitimate. And one can certainly buy a degree, but one cannot actually do creative, scholarly, or scientific work of which one is incapable.

What the emergence of Capital as an autonomous intelligence does is to radically undercut the power of the bourgeoisie to shape the planet in accord with its will. Rather than the market simply selecting which human beings—mostly men and mostly colonizers—will make the decisions which shape the future, the market *directly* makes these decisions as it spontaneously allocates resources in proportion to the anticipated rate of return on investment. This can imply anything from a decision to end production of some trust fund kid's favorite snack to a decision to which has the long-term effect of rendering the planet uninhabitable.

This, in turn, divides the bourgeoisie into three groups. There are, first of all, those who actually identify with and support the emergence of Capital as an autonomous intelligence. These generally embrace some form of transhumanism and imagine technological progress allowing them to upload what they imagine to be a superior consciousness to some new "platform" which will allow them to live, in effect, forever. We seen a variety of such ideologies from Frank Tipler's *Omega Point Theory*

(Barrow and Tipler 1986; Tiper 1994) to more recent forms of transhumanism. This is also, as we will see, the position of the *Dark Enlightenment* which proposes to privatize government into a network of privately held city states from which people are free to leave—if they can—but in which they have no voice. This has the effect of eliminating the state as we have understood it, which is the principal vehicle through which not only the people, but also the bourgeoisie, has historically exercised the freedom to act against the market. Second, there are those who oppose the emergence of Capital as an autonomous intelligence by doubling down on patriarchal ideas of personal authority and authoritarian concept of the state understood as reinforcing traditional gender roles and colonial hegemony. This position has a number of variants, from various religious fundamentalisms through national conservatism and fascism. Finally, there are those who reject the emergence of Capital as an autonomous intelligence largely in the name of the liberal ideal and who embrace elements of the democratic and socialist project in order to recruit allies against Capital while resisting measures which threaten bourgeois right—especially the wage relation—in a fundamental way. This is the liberal and especially the social liberal bourgeoisie which is in alliance with much of the new petty bourgeoisie and proletariat through the mechanism of social liberal and social democratic parties.

Even so, the distinction between metropolis and periphery remains significant in debates around who bears the principal responsibility for addressing climate change, with China in particular reluctant to forgo the growth necessary to catch up with and overtake the US and Europe in order to protect the planet, on the grounds that Euro-American wealth is the product of centuries of colonial exploitation.

The Petty Bourgeoisie

The status and power, gender and colonial dynamics which we identified in the bourgeoisie operate at the level of the petty bourgeoisie as well, albeit somewhat differently. The petty bourgeoisie is, first of all, divided by fraction, stratum, and sector. With respect to *fraction*, the most important distinction is between:

- The *traditional petty bourgeoisie* of small business people, independent professionals, skilled tradespersons, and independent peasants and

- The *new petty bourgeoisie* or *professional middle class* of salaried employees whose skills guarantee higher than average incomes and significant autonomy in their work. As we noted earlier, in post-revolutionary societies a section of this fraction gains control of the state apparatus and uses its position to enrich itself. This can be done capitalistically, if a significant market sector remains or if there is access to international opportunities, or it can be done through what amount to neotributary means. In either case the group ceases to be part of the new petty bourgeoisie and becomes either state capitalist or what amounts to a new aristocracy, whether hereditary or not.

These are fractions because while they all they live off of value they create, retaining all or most the surplus, they do so in different ways: because they own their own business and work for themselves or because their skills are in such demand that they can negotiate employment contracts which give them significant autonomy and significant monopoly rents, so that the wage relation and their status as employees is merely a formality—and in some cases even a source or privilege.

We can distinguish between the following strata in the petty bourgeoisie:

- An upper petty bourgeoisie which is distinguished from small capital largely in that their high incomes are generated by value they create or realize themselves, rather than by exploiting proletarianized workers. This includes highly paid professionals in the arts and sports and the very highest stratum of the traditional liberal professions such as medicine, law, the academy, and the clergy.

- A middle petty bourgeoisie with significant economic stability, a comfortable lifestyle, significant control over their own work, and the ability to pass on their petty bourgeois privilege to their children by means of elite education or significant staking or inheritance. Historically this consisted of members of the liberal professions. Today it also includes members of newer professions in technical or business fields whose skills are in sufficient demand to allow them to demand privileges comparable to physicians, attorneys, professors, etc.

- A lower, semiproletarianized petty bourgeoisie with low or declining income, diminishing control over their own work, and a compromised ability to pass on their petty bourgeois privilege.

Finally, two different types of sectoral differences turn out to be important and these include differences in the economic sector in which petty bourgeois individuals are located (and are the same therefore as those we identified for the bourgeoisie) and the nature of the skills they bring to the marketplace:

- members of the skilled trades,
- business professionals, including professional managers, accountants, and most consultants, etc. and those in the traditional petty bourgeoisie whose principal skills are in running a business and not in producing the particular good or service that business provides (e.g., an small entrepreneur owning a restaurant as opposed to a chef),
- scientists, engineers, and technicians, which we call the technical intelligentsia, and
- The arts, humanities, and social sciences (what we will call the humanistic intelligentsia)

The petty bourgeoisie is thus deeply divided as a class. Historically this stratum was both the original protagonist of the democratic revolutions and central to the socialist project but also profoundly implicated in fascism. Its underlying material interests—good conditions for developing small businesses and large wage differentials based on skill—can be arrived at in any of a number of ways: thus, the vacillating character of this class.

As we noted above many of the same status and power, gender and colonial dynamics play out in the petty bourgeoisie as in the bourgeoisie proper, but with some differences. Thus lineage continues to be extremely important for the petty bourgeoisie. Even if there is not a great deal of economic capital to pass on, social and cultural capital is the lifeblood of the class, as current discussions of legacy admissions to elite colleges and universities and "nepokids" in the arts, academia, and other fields indicates. While the lower petty bourgeoisie is relatively open to movement into and out of the upper strata of the proletariat, it is extremely difficult to secure a prestigious or even established and secure position in the academy or in an elite professional firm without both connections and the specific knowledge of "how things are done" which alone ensures "fit." And entry into the upper petty bourgeoisie requires *at least* the level of support which a middle petty bourgeois family can provide or else the sponsorship of someone with comparable connections and knowledge. Historically a university education, especially in the liberal arts, gave one the status of a "gentleman" and thus nominal gentry status, but this has become less true with the massification of higher education and the proletarianization of historically respected liberal professions such as law, medicine, and the academy. There is also sharpened status competition between disciplines, with those with STEM training claiming superiority on the grounds that their formation is more difficult and those with a humanities or social science background claiming superiority because their disciplines address more fundamental questions.

As we note at various points in this work, the principal means of controlling the new petty bourgeoisie is the idea of professionalism, which confers status and privilege in return for the offer of *value-free* non-partisan technical advice. This has the effect of essentially getting the entire class to opt out of politics, and especially disempowers the middle and lower new petty bourgeoisie which depend on formal employment for their livelihood. Bureaucratic understandings of fiduciary duty and limited jurisdiction similarly constrain the ability of even highly privileged professionals to use their position to challenge the system. We thus have the irony of people working very hard and still having to rely on lineage or patronage to secure coveted positions, only to find that they are effectively impotent to act on their convictions—or worse still to come to believe that they should not so act.

How does gender work here? Petty bourgeoisie women have much less pressure to produce heirs than do aristocratic women and there is generally a caution in this class about having more children than one can successfully "stake" at a level comparable to one's own. There is, however, still an expectation that women will manage social relationships both private and professional contexts, being responsible for nurturing children, for "institutional service" and informal office-based relationship management, and for cultivating a social life which supports the family's aspirations. In this sense, as women have gained access to professional employment, they have taken on an even larger burden of unpaid emotional labor than they bore previously. And like all labor gendered as female or "colonial," it is valued less than that gendered male—or not at all. Women who fail to perform these social duties will be driven out or made miserable. Those who do are much less likely to have the energy to do the things that earn professional respect and advancement.

The petty bourgeoisie, finally, is profoundly shaped by colonialism. On the one hand, the traditional petty bourgeoisie is continuously refreshed by colonized peoples for whom both expanding markets and home and, in the diaspora, open up new opportunities. Merchants in particular have always served as vectors for cultural diffusion and it is above all through the presence of lively business communities that cities in Europe, North America, and Oceana have become authentically cosmopolitan. At the same time, it is precisely the traditional petty bourgeoisie who suffer most from the penetration of capitalist relations of production, as corporate megastores undersell them and artisan production, if not eliminated, is restricted to the luxury sector. And it is the traditional petty bourgeoisie which is the principal victim of cultural appropriation, as members of the metropolitan and colonial petty bourgeoisie begin selling, often at luxury market prices, arts, crafts, and foods which were originally produced and sold cheaply to worker and peasants. This is nowhere more obvious than in gastronomy, where it is customary to take peasant food, serve it in small portions and at much higher price in a "fine dining" setting, and claim that it has been "elevated."

The Proletariat

The proletariat, finally, is distinguished by fraction more by the nature of the value they create than by the way in which that value is extracted from them, since the wage relationship is already definitive of this class. Nicos Poulantzas (Poulantzas 1968) distinguishes strictly between productive and unproductive labor, restricting the former to material production, and consigning those who do not engage in productive labor to the new petty bourgeoisie. This seems to us to be problematic. First, the concept of value should not be restricted to material goods. As we have argued elsewhere (Mansueto 2014) in our extension of the labor theory of value, value is a measure of the degree of organization of something: its complexity and the way in which those complex elements are brought together in a structure which serves an end. The average socially necessary labor time a commodity contains is a reasonable measure of value because *in general* it takes more time to produce more complex things or to perform more complex services, especially those which cultivate the development of human beings. Second, even if work is not productive—and some is not, such as capturing surplus produced elsewhere—those who must sell their labor power in order to survive share the proletarian condition. This said, it *is* meaningful to distinguish between:

- workers involved in producing the material conditions for civilization (the proletariat in the narrowest sense)
- workers who are not engaged in material production but create additional value out of the surplus extracted by the bourgeoisie by performing services which conserve and develop complex organization, and especially human life, including its biological and social, intellectual and moral dimensions (who we might call fully proletarianized new petty bourgeoisie), and
- workers who do not really create new value but simply assist capitalists in
    - realizing value as profit through marketing, sales, etc. (fully proletarianized traditional petty bourgeoisie) and
    - capturing value produced elsewhere, by means of exotic financial instruments (essentially a *lumpenproletarian* element, not unlike mob enforcers).

The following strata may be identified:

- relatively privileged workers, often referred to as the *labor aristocracy* who, while they must sell their labor power in order to survive, and while they have little or no autonomy in their work, receive a wage in excess of the value of that labor power, because significant skills or their degree of organization permit them to limit the extraction of surplus or even capture redistributed surplus produced elsewhere,
- workers who are paid roughly the value of their labor power, something which is determined by the cost of reproducing that labor power, which in turn is determined largely by their level of skill and by their position in the international division of labor, and
- workers who are superexploited, i.e., paid less than the value of their labor power due the existence of a surplus, generally but not always, of unskilled or low skill labor power.

As with the bourgeoisie and petty bourgeoisie the type of skills and the sector and industry in which they are deployed are also significant for shaping political action.

Status and power relations, gender and colonialism also play very significant roles in shaping the proletariat. Status for members of the proletariat can come both from work and from other engagements, but the status accorded skill in manual trades has declined enormously in recent years, with the completion of at least an undergraduate degree being regarded as the minimum mark of skilled labor. This is ridiculous, especially given the fact that most colleges and universities, including some flagship state universities, have acceptance rates of 75 percent or more whereas many skilled trades apprenticeship programs have rates around 10 percent—a bit more than the most selective elite research universities, but less than most of the "second tier" schools. The result is a sort of reaction formation in which many manual workers, skilled or not, polarize on the intelligentsia generally and the humanistic intelligentsia in particular, undercutting the key class relationship which was constitutive of historic socialism.

The principal power base for the proletariat has historically been the labor movement, which allows workers to leverage their key asset—labor power—to bargain for better wages and working conditions and to enter the broader political arena electorally or otherwise. The decline of trade unions over the last fifty years has undercut this power enormously, leaving the working classes in a weakened position, though there have been some signs of recovery in the past few years as unions adapt to the changes in the organization of labor. Other historic power bases included community organizations, especially those based in local congregations and political machines, which linked the interests of the working classes to those of the clergy on the one hand and those of smaller, often immigrant capital which controlled the machines. Both have declined with secularization, suburbanization and the growing political weight of the new petty bourgeoisie/professional middle class in the social democratic, social liberal, and centrist parties which have traditionally drawn support from these organizations. This has created a political vacuum into which authoritarian movements have been able to move.

These status and power dynamics overlap with gender and colonial dynamics. Thus women from proletarian families have been much more likely to pursue and succeed at higher education than men, moving from the industrial proletariat to the proletarianized petty bourgeoisie or the lower ranks of the new petty bourgeoisie/professional middle class. Women thus continue to carry the burden of unpaid reproductive and emotional labor we analyzed above, while finding themselves in an ambiguous class position and potentially in considerable tension with their partners, becoming the objects of a status resentment that fuels authoritarian tendencies—or, alternatively, finding little or no meaning in their supposedly "middle class" work, they may embrace patriarchal and authoritarian ideologies themselves, partly to keep the peace and partly as a fantasized escape from their own commodification.

Colonized workers experience their situation very differently from the proletariat of the metropolitan countries. In many cases even the most oppressive superexploitation in a factory seems like a liberation from the grinding poverty of the countryside. This does not mean that there is no resistance whatsoever, but in places like China it tends to be even more confined to the economic realm than in the metropolitan countries—a struggle over the distribution of the benefits of an industrialization and a new prosperity for which the Communist Party continues very largely to be credited. *Without the experience of the contradictions of the liberal order, in which workers are formally free to develop and express themselves but lack the resources to do so, the communist ideal is expressed in truncated form as mere egalitarianism rather than as a transition from formal to substantive liberation.*

Similar factors have led to rather different political results in countries where socialist revolutions either did not take place or were incomplete. Thus in India, the social democratic Congress Party carried out a preliminary industrialization but then ran into limits that were largely the result of a failure to carry out the kind of radical land reform that took place in China (Moore 1966; Amin 1982). This created room for the *Bharatiya Jana Sangh* (BJP) to move in and undertake a neoliberal "opening" to the global market which in turn led to rapid economic growth even if also to much greater inequality. The BJP has thus been able to build a base extending well beyond its historic stronghold among upper caste Hindus in the North, capturing a growing number of votes even among the Scheduled and Other Backward Castes (Rukmini S. 2019)—this in spite of the fact that the BJP supports their continued exclusion from both public life and the cult.

In all cases we should be clear that the pull of authoritarianism on the proletariat is nowhere due to economic insecurity but rather to the operation of gender and ethnoreligious status and power dynamics on a population already alienated from its underlying human creativity by the commodification of labor power.

The Peasantry

While in precapitalist societies the *peasantry* was a social class defined by the extraction of rents, taxes, and/or forced labor, under capitalism they are, strictly speaking, not a class, but rather a social category much like the intelligentsia which includes members from many different classes. It might broadly be defined as consisting of "non-exploiting agriculturalists" who rely primarily on their own labor and that of their family to work whatever land they can access. We consider them separately because until very recently some were still exploited by pre-capitalist means, such as sharecropping (and some still are), and because they are all located in one sector of the economy (agriculture). The following are technically petty bourgeoisie:

- "rich" peasants,[1] who own enough land that they need to employ at least some farm labor and who reliably produce a significant surplus which they sell on the market,
- middle peasants who have enough land to support themselves and their families and produce enough surplus only incidentally,
- lower peasants, who do not have enough land to support themselves and their families and who must also either rent land or sell their labor power.

Peasants who must rent their land are exploited not capitalistically but feudalistically, though again there are many different strata, including some who, at the top, are essentially prosperous farmers and others who, on the bottom, shade into the rural proletariat or slave populations. Feudalistically exploited peasants are, furthermore, divided by their degree

---

1. People of this group only identify as "peasants" where this is a broader social category including dependent and exploited agriculturalists who have not generally been reduced to the status of farm laborers. In countries like the United States, the term has generally only been applied to freed slaves and their descendants (though generally only by scholars on the Left and not by the people themselves) and members of Hispano land grant communities in the Southwest. Otherwise there has been a tendency to call all agriculturalists "farmers" or "family farmers" distinguishing between those producing for the market and subsistence farmers, and those who own land or rent an entire farm, and those who rent part of a larger plantation or former plantation, who are generally called sharecroppers.

of freedom, from those who are entirely free to those who are bound to the land and forced to perform a range of specific forms of labor service. Fully enslaved cultivators, finally, are not generally classed as peasants as here the workers themselves become commodities.

The peasant population of the planet has dropped significantly over the past few decades as urbanization has proceeded rapidly in Asia, Africa, and Latin America. This, together with the defeat of the socialist led national liberation movements in 1989 has moved peasant struggles away from center stage, but with roughly one third of the world's population still reasonably classed as peasants, this social category remains politically significant (Edelman 2012).

Peasants historically have demanded land reform ("land to the tiller") in the form of either partition or restoration of village land rights, depending on what was traditional in the particular region. These demands remain strong, but the freedom of the city and the possibility (however remote) of upward mobility are strong attractors and have, in recent years, undercut peasant movements and rural insurgencies, depriving the Left of its single most important strategic reserve. Where peasants do remain strong, we have seen a sharp tendency for peasants to pull away from the historic Left and towards populist movements of various kinds, even where as, for example, in the case of *Peru Libre,* they embrace Marxism Leninism.

The Global Alignment of Political Forces

We are now at the point of analyzing the global alignment of political forces which will form the context in which we assess the political valence of the various political theological trends which currently dominate the political debate.

Historically, at least since the French Revolution, political actors have been aligned primarily with respect to the humanistic secular project in its liberal, democratic, and socialist forms. Thus the Right has historically consisted of those who reject the project outright not just in its socialist but also in its liberal and democratic forms. Originally this space was occupied by Traditionalist representatives of the landed aristocracy, the absolute monarchies, and the Church, later by fascists who, while representing primarily sectors of the bourgeoisie, found that liberalism and certainly democracy were incompatible with their imperial ambitions, realization of which they believed required effective militarization of the population, legitimated by an appeal to religious, national, or racist ideas. The Center consisted of those who embraced the liberal and to some extent the democratic forms of the humanistic project. It represented the bourgeoisie and the petty bourgeoisie. The Center Right represented the older, more backwards sections of the bourgeoisie, consisting of liberal conservatives who upheld the liberal project of promoting the freedom of the rationally autonomous and/or property owning individual, with democracy functioning as a somewhat ambivalent and potentially problematic way of protecting that freedom from an overreach state. The Technocratic Center represented an attempt to unify the bourgeoisie and everyone else around policies which maximized economic growth. The Communitarian Center (e.g., Christian Democrats) embraced liberalism and democracy and sought to counter socialism largely by redistributional reforms, but was also, often, more conservative on Church/State questions, or questions of social policy such as divorce, abortion, and later LGBTQ rights. The Center Left was led by the more advanced sectors of the bourgeoisie who required state intervention to support effective demand, and generally embraced a social liberalism which argued that liberal freedoms were meaningful only if people hand the resources to use them. This left wing of the bourgeoisie operated in alliance with the broad elements of the new petty bourgeoisie and the more privileged strata of the metropolitan proletariat organized through social democratic parties. The Left, finally, presented the more proletarianized elements of the petty bourgeoisie (traditional and new), and especially of the humanistic intelligentsia, along with the less privileged strata of the proletariat and the peasantry.

The *concepts* of Left, Center, and Right, I will argue, actually remain quite valid, so long as we understand them in terms of orientation towards the humanistic secular project. But shifting political conditions have led to significant realignments. We cannot trace out here the entire history of these realignments, but we will only be able to understand the current alignment if we look back at least as far as the First World War. Up until this point political alignments tended to be nationally specific and while geopolitical alliances might attempt to take on the colors of a broader political project, global alignments were driven by more purely geopolitical factors and by interimperialist conflicts. Thus the Russian and Japanese Empires formed integral element of the Allied war to "make the world safe for democracy." With the end of the war and the Russian

Revolution, however, these basic geopolitical and economically driven forces were overlayed with the global political and ideological struggle between Capitalism and Socialism. Thus nearly all the rest of the world united in supporting the US and Western Europe in trying to break the power of the Bolsheviks and prevent what threatened to become if not a global then at least a European socialist revolution.

The united bourgeois-imperialist bloc was, however, quickly shattered as the late comers to capitalist empire building—Germany above all, but also Italy and Japan—embraced fascism as a way of militarizing their populations in preparation for a war of conquest. It took some time for an authentic popular front against fascism to coalesce, as there were significant elements throughout Europe and the US which were tempted by fascism as a way to contain the growing pressure from the working classes. At the same time, the Communist Party of the Soviet Union was focused on what it saw as the defection of social democrats and social liberals to the cause of reaction and was "aiming the main blow" against social democrats, who it equated with fascism. It was also, under Stalin, discovering the potential of socialism as a strategy for imperial restoration, something which gave it fascistoid qualities. But in the end the liberal bourgeoisie prevailed in Europe and the US, as the opportunities for economic growth through support for effective demand became apparent and Russia found that geopolitical considerations made war with Germany—and thus an alliance with the US, the UK, and France—inevitable.

After the defeat of fascism in the Second World War the principal contradiction in the global system ceased to be between fascism and the liberal order but rather that between the imperial metropoles and the national liberation movements. The Left, and Communism in particular, in other words, became increasingly identified with anticolonialism and anti-imperialism constituting the principal line of demarcation between the Center Left and the Left. This was reflected in the leading role of the Civil Rights and Black Power movements on the Left in the United States, and in the fact that new social movements, including ecologism, feminism, and the gay rights movement, as well as the student movement, which was fundamentally a movement of resistance to proletarianization among the younger generation of the humanistic intelligentsia, all gravitated to this global anti-imperialist Left, which the Center, including liberal conservatives, technocrats, Christian Democrats, social liberals and most social democrats united in resisting.

At the same time, the ideological and political character of the Left was gradually changing, as the humanistic intelligentsia increasingly abandoned its alliance with the working classes and looked increasingly to Heidegger rather than to Marx for guidance, undercutting the class alliance which had been constitutive of the communist movement. Antiimperialism, furthermore, was *from the beginning* also *alterimperialism* and the national liberation movements profoundly bound up with the attempt of elites in colonized and marginalized empires to restore their civilizations to their former position as great powers. And of course this sort of alterimperialism was actually more compatible with the romantic and culturalist orientation of Heidegger and the poststructuralists and deconstructionists than it ever was with historical materialism.

The result was that the dominant Center Left bloc represented by the popular front against fascism gave way to a Center Right front against communism and anti-imperialism, not unlike that which emerged from the First World War and the Russian Revolution. This in turn created a new space for the Right, which had never given up its resistance to the New Deal and the Welfare State or its fondness for fascism. Instead, it played a "long game," gradually cultivating a broad and deep movement of resistance to social liberalism and the welfare state which found a way to link a discourse around "freedom," which is always fundamental in the US, to racism and patriarchy, and to frame their critique of socialism in a way which appealed to the more technocratic elements of the intelligentsia. The result was "neoliberalism," especially as articulated in the work of F. A. Hayek (Hayek 1998) which argued human societies are the product of spontaneous self-organization, not rational planning, and that free markets, like language, the family, and religion has demonstrated its survival value. Their argument centered on the idea that the market is an information processing system which accesses information regarding supply and demand through buy and sell decisions and processes it into production directives in the form of prices. A planned economy (which is the way they defined socialism) could never access or process the quantity of information necessary to organize a complex society. Thus the contradictions of socialism and, they argued, of the welfare state.

While originally the work of a small group of capitalists largely in more backward extractive and low technology sectors of the economy, neoliberalism was able to build a base of mass support by appealing to the spontaneous racism and patriarchy of the masses, bringing to power Margaret Thatcher and Ronald Reagan just in time for them to claim "victory" in the Cold War and to deal a severe blow to the liberal bourgeoisie, which largely adopted a soft, moderate form of neoliberalism and began presiding over a massive retrenchment of the welfare state.

The collapse of the Soviet bloc and the decisive victory of neoliberalism suggested that this strategy had, in fact, actually worked and that Capital was the uncontested victor in (or rather over) the ideological struggles of the long twentieth century. Thus the claim on the part of Francis Fukuyama (a claim he has since retracted) that we had reached the "end of history" (Fukuyama 1989). The reality, however, turned out to be far more complicated. First, a new resistance to global Capital almost immediately took the place of the communist movement: Political Islam, which advanced a range of alternatives from the relatively moderate Islamic Republicanism of Iran, which limited democracy (and capitalism) by affirming the ultimate authority of Islamic legal scholars to a restored Caliphate under the rule of self-proclaimed religious authorities who embraced a variant of Islam (the Wahabi movement) with almost no continuity with historic Islamic Civilization. But this was just the first step. We have already seen that the present period is characterized by competing *alterimperialisms* which are the heir to socialist revolutions or developmentalist neocolonial states and which meld this recent history with appeals to ancient civilizational ideas. Second, the implementation of the neoliberal agenda had been left to liberal conservative, Christian Democratic, and social liberal or social democratic parties. The former found it difficult to let go of their attachment to liberal norms and tended to focus primarily on social austerity and tax cuts, rather than on implementing, for example, the socially conservative agenda which they increasingly advocated. What they actually delivered was one tax cut after another, a policy which led to the Great Recession. Social liberals and Social Democrats were actually more fiscally conservative, but in the process lost much of their base in the working classes and became increasingly parties of the liberal bourgeoisie and professional middle class and, to a lesser extent colonized minorities and immigrants. They had to balance their budget cuts with strong support for reproductive rights and immigration and an opening at least to the LGBTQ community.

Meanwhile, the development of new information technologies as well as neoliberal policies favoring the accumulation of wealth led to a new generation of capitalist magnates along with a highly privileged new upper petty bourgeoisie of scientific and technical intelligentsia earning monopoly rents on skill and innovation. While initially tending to the Left, in part because they rely on a prosperous population to create final demand for their products and in part because they had little tie to traditional social institutions such as the Church which promoted conservative social morality, their organic ideology was libertarian and individualistic and they believed profoundly that their success was due to their unique superiority. Around the time of the Great Recession they began to realize that libertarian policies would never be realized under a democracy, and began the articulate the political vision known as *Dark Enlightenment* which we have already mentioned and will analyze in depth in the next chapter. Focused at first pitting freedom against democracy, as the new decade brought increased pressure to address racism and sexism, they embraced the "race and gender realism" of the Human Biodiversity movement, i.e., pseudoscientific racism and sexism.

The precise way in which these developments have played out varies significantly from country to country due to the specificities of political structures and electoral systems which sometimes (as in much of Europe) favor the formation of new political parties and elsewhere (as in the United States) the radical transformation of existing parties. But globally we can identify the following principal political actors:

- The Right consists of:

    - Capital, as an emergent intelligence independent of the historic bourgeoisie, which has largely severed its ties with the liberal tradition—even with classical liberalism and libertarianism—in favor of a purely formal, market driven process of decision making focused on maximizing instrumentalization and thus return on investment.

    - The emerging group of capitalist magnates from mostly high technology sectors, along with their retainers among the higher strata of the technical intelligentsia, who have made it their business the clear the way for something as close to a purely economic regime of Capital as is possible for a human society. This is the group behind the *Dark Enlightenment*. This group imagines that it can benefit from a world ruled by Capital and other AI's, but this is ultimately just hubris.

    - *Alterimperial* powers such as Russia, India, those elements within *Dar-al-Islam* which are trying to recreate a unified Muslim

Empire, either as a restored Caliphate or along other lines[2] and, along with elements in the United States, Europe, and Japan and to a lesser extent nearly all nation states, aim to contain the both Capital as an emergent intelligence *and* the humanistic project, especially in its liberal and democratic forms.

- Smaller traditionalist and ethnonationalist elements representing residual aristocracies which resist both global Capital and Empire primarily because they do not believe they can compete on a continental or global scale.

• The Center includes the remains of the old liberal bourgeoisie, which remains dedicated to the idea that capitalism offers an authentic possibility of human self-realization open to everyone, along with residual aristocratic and clerical elements which have embraced the liberal and democratic projects and are committed to an alliance with the popular classes, as well as significant elements of the petty bourgeoisie and the upper strata of the proletariat which believe, for various reasons, that capitalism is still their best bet. This group is, in turn, divided between:

- What remains of the old Center Right, composed of what in Europe are called *liberal conservatives*. By liberal conservatives we mean those who embrace the liberal ideal of the rationally autonomous individual. Like libertarians they believe that this ideal depends first and foremost on individual property rights. Unlike libertarians, they embrace democracy means of holding leaders accountable and protecting against tyranny. They have historically been open to limited social liberal initiatives designed to expand the opportunity for members of the working classes to act on their freedom, but only in so far as this does not interfere with the rights of the established bourgeoisie and the privileges of and upper and middle petty bourgeoisie which

---

2. Many *alterimperial* states have, as we will see, a dual character. Thus China is at once more or less transparently a territorial empire with significant authoritarian tendencies *and* a society which retains significant socialist elements and which is the carrier of both Confucian and Taoist ideals from the Axial Age and of the communist project. The United States, the United Kingdom along with Canada, Australia, and New Zealand, and the European Union along with most other European states which are not yet fully integrated into it are guarantors of an Liberal International Order which at once creates the conditions for global capitalism and sustains the liberal and democratic ideals.

constitute their principal constituency. This group began moving to the right in the 1960s in the US and a bit later elsewhere, embracing racist and misogynist positions in order to mobilize support from members of the working class and petty bourgeoisie affected by the alienation generated by the commodification of labor power. In the US especially, this tactic backfired so that the liberal conservative Center Right has largely given way to a "National Conservative" tendency which is fascistic in all but name.

- A technocratic, self-declared "nonideological" center which embraces capitalism as an engine of growth but acknowledges the need for state intervention in order to address global challenges such as climate change, in order to manage the business cycle and maintain both investment and effective demand, and which is at least open to protecting and extending liberal rights. This group was very born during the postwar period among the value free technocratic social scientists and found a new base during the information technology revolution in the 1980s and 1990s. It found expression in a variety of governments, from Clinton and Blair through Macron, but is now losing support as the technology sector moves to the Right.

- Communitarian and social liberals who also embrace capitalism as an engine of growth but who believe that liberal rights are meaningful only if people have the resources to make use of them and who thus support a broad range of public investments and redistributional schemes designed to accomplish these ends. We use the term *communitarian* liberals to describe those who legitimate their policies by reference to religious traditions, such as the more progressive wing of the old Christian Democratic parties, and *social* liberals those who do so by reference to humanistic secular traditions. As indicated above, many social democrats are now indistinguishable from social liberals. This group was dominant during much of the postwar period, declined with the rise of neoliberalism, and made a comeback after the Great Recession, finding expression the Obama and Biden governments which, however, also represent a sort of power-sharing between technocratic moderate neoliberals and communitarian and social liberals.

- A broad and heterogenous Left based largely in the humanistic intelligentsia, from bourgeois and petty rentier elements through the middle, lower, and fully proletarianized petty bourgeoisie, with broader support outside the intelligentsia primarily among colonized peoples, workers active in strongly politicized unions, workers on the periphery of the world system, some peasants, and women and gender nonconformists pressing beyond liberal feminism. This Left has, outside of a few pockets, has largely abandoned dialectical and historical materialism in favor of a romantic anticapitalism which shares much common ground with the Right. This Left includes:

    - elements focused on the rejection of human civilization, in the sense of urbanism and especially industry, including *deep ecologists* and *anarcho-primitivists*,
    - *left identarians* focused on
        - conserving the identities of historically colonized peoples, including especially *indigenism, Afrocentrism, etc.*
        - resisting patriarchy and gender oppression, including various *feminisms* and the LGBTQ movement, now sharply divided over questions of the rights of transwomen in particular, and
    - various new socialisms including
        - the largely Latin American "socialism of the twenty-first century,"
        - the "left" populist formations of Europe such as *Syriza, Podemos,* and *Insoumise,* and
        - the resurgent "democratic socialist" tendency in the US, centered around *Our Revolution, Justice Democrats,* and *Democratic Socialists of America,* and
    - libertarian socialists such as the Neo-Zapatistas and the Kurdish Workers Party.

This new Left, we will argue, reflects the reality of a population so profoundly deformed by the impact of the alienation generated by the commodification of labor power that they believe that the only possible basis for resistance to oppression is the same as what grounds oppression itself: an arbitrary act of the will. Thus, their preference for Heidegger,

Schmitt, and Agamben to Marx and, when they do invoke Marx, their proclivity for doing so by way of Baidou and Žižek.

Alliances between these groups are complex and shifting,

- Capital as an emergent intelligence and the capitalist magnates of the *Dark Enlightenment*, which favors a network of privately owned city states linked, it would seem, only by market relations, are loosely but not strongly aligned with *alterimperial* elements in the US, Russia, Eastern Europe, and India.
- The Center Right vacillates between liquidating its support for the liberal ideal and aligning with the Right under the banners of "National Conservatism," on the one hand, and questioning its commitment to free markets and aligning with the technocratic, communitarian, and social liberals.
- The Center Left includes technocratic, communitarian, and social liberals and *part* of the Left—given the decline of historical materialism mostly the less ideologically driven and mass-based part.
- The remainder of the Left is isolated and in an objective alliance with *alterimperialists* from Russia and the Islamic World, which instrumentalizes it to undercut the United States both as an imperialist power and as guarantor of the Liberal International Order.
- China stands partially apart from these alignments as the single major *alterimperialist* power with enduring socialist commitments, focused on building support through investments in Africa and other parts of the "Global South," leveraging a quasi-alliance with Russia to contain the United States while in turn trying to reign in Russia's destabilizing and anticivilizational agenda.

It is also important to point out that there are very large elements of the population not really represented by any of these blocs. Many, including perhaps the majority of workers and peasants and much of the petty bourgeoisie, traditional and new, are entirely passive politically, not even bothering to vote. Others reluctantly support elements which do not really represent them and which they do not trust but which they see as less dangerous than the alternative. It is on our ability to engage this group while forging an alliance between the Center Left and China which the future of the planet depends.

And then there are the "unexploitable," the outcastes who are not really part of bourgeois society, who have only begun to speak . . .

2

What Is Political Theology?

The State of the Question

When interest in political theology began to emerge on the Christian Left and Center Left in the 1960s, those engaging the discipline were at pains to distinguish not just their specific claims but their entire set of questions and concerns from those which motivated the "Old Political Theology" of the Nazi jurist Carl Schmitt. This concern is reflected in the *status questionis* prepared by Francis Schussler Fiorenza in 1977 (Fiorenza 1977/2012), which makes it clear that the Schmittian problematic is simply one among many possible approaches, whether to a theology of the political or to what he and his associates call a "consciously political theology" as opposed to the unconsciously political theology which is created when theologians do not understand the social basis and political valence of their claims.

Specifically, Fiorenza identifies the following political-theological paradigms:

- The tripartite distinction between mythical, philosophical, and civic or political theology associated with Varro (cited in Augustine 427/1972),

- Augustine's own doctrine of the *Two Cities* (Augustine 427/1972),

- An Enlightenment doctrine centered around natural theology and civic religion (Locke 1690/1967; Rousseau 1762/1962),

- The political theology of the Catholic Restoration, within which he situates Schmitt, but which also includes the much earlier and somewhat different work of de Maistre and de Bonald (Bonald 1796; Maistre 1775–1821/1965),
- The German political theology of the 1960s and 1970s (Solle 1974), and
- Latin American liberation theology (Segundo 1985).

To these, even restricting ourselves to the limited historical and civilizational frame which Fiorenza analyzes, I would add, at a minimum:

- Thomistic political theology, in its original form, and in its Baroque and Social Catholic/Christian Democratic incarnations (Goerner 1965; Gilson 1968), which are quite different from what Fiorenza calls Catholic Restorationism, and
- An entire spectrum of Protestant political theologies including, at least, early Lutheran and Reformed political theologies, the competing liberal and Evangelical political theologies of the eighteenth and nineteenth centuries, Neo-Orthodoxy, and an entire sub-spectrum of fundamentalist political theologies, from Dispensationalism through Reconstruction and Dominion (Niebuhr 1951; Madsen 1980).

If we were to bring the typology up to date, we would need to add:

- The *Communio* theology which developed in reaction to Latin American liberation theology (Ratzinger 1984, 1986), and
- Radical Orthodoxy, which is distinctive in proposing the Church rather than the State as the architectonic political paradigm (Milbank 1991).

All of this, furthermore, presupposes that we addressing only *Christian* political theologies. It does not consider the vast range of Islamic political theologies which shaped *Dar-al-Islam* and which have informed the global political scene in recent years, or the various Jewish political theologies which have shaped Christian polities and which led, through the triumph of Zionism to the establishment of a Jewish State which has in turn become a significant point of political-theological interest to both Christianity and Islam (Levin 1971; Avineri 2017). Nor does it consider the Indian, Chinese, Southeast and Northeast Asian, Indigenous

American and African domains which make up far more than half of humanity.

We must, finally, include some of the political theologies which understand themselves as specifically *anti-Christian* which have emerged in recent years. The European New Right (Krebs 2012) rejects Christian universalism and indeed all monotheism as destructive of the unique ethnic identities it believes are the only context in which human capacities and be cultivated. And the *Dark Enlightenment* trend, represented by Curtis Yarvin (Moldbug 2008) and Nick Land (Land 2013, 2017), specifically polarizes against what they call the *Cathedral*, the complex of secularized Liberal-Christian cultural institutions which they believe dominate the planet.

This said, contemporary discourse around political theology in the broader academy has been dominated by precisely the Schmittian problematic from which Fiorenza was concerned to distance himself. Indeed, Schmitt's political theology, both as a *method* and as a *doctrine* regarding the nature of power, has become dominant not just on the Right, but also on the Left, as indicated in the work of Agamben, Baidou, and Žižek, and to a lesser extent Foucault and Derrida, among others, in a way which makes Fiorenza's Eurocentric typology seem quite cosmopolitan in character. As a *method* Schmitt's political theology amounts to the claim that secular political structures derive from religious, and indeed from specifically Christian theological concepts, the *genealogy* of which theorists like Agamben (Agamben 2011) have been charting in detail. Substantively, there are now really two theses on the table:

- Schmitt's original claim, following Walter Benjamin (marking this political theology as something that originated *on the nominal Left*), that political authority is constituted by violence or, as Schmitt put it, that "the sovereign is the one who decides the exception" and

- An additional claim advanced by Foucault and refined by Agamben that "modern" power is less political than economic and that the transition to economic power was mediated by Christianity and in particular by the doctrine of the Trinity, which integrates a divine "economy" of immanent action in the world with a divine politics centered on the unity and Being of God.

Schmitt's political theology has also profoundly influenced the thinking of the Chinese New Left and in particular of Jiang Shiqong (Shigong 2020) who has argued that:

- The Communist Party (which of course came to power by means of revolutionary violence, however legitimate) is the "deep constitution" of China, and thus its decisions (including decisions regarding a state of exception and thus unaccountable state violence) the standard against which the policies of the government and the actions of citizens must ultimately be judged, and

- Communism is not an actual social state to be achieved (a fantasy which he attributes to Christian political theology) but rather a "learning of the heart" (*xinxue*) which orients and regulates political culture.

With this in mind we need to look a bit more carefully at political theology as a *discipline*, and then ask to whether and how a global political theology, *beyond Christendom*, might be possible.

What Defines a Discipline?

What, if anything, do these various political theologies share that might help us define political theology as a *discipline*? Most obviously, of course, there is a common concern with the relationship between Church and State, something which—to the extent that the Church is a specifically Christian institution—helps explain why, beyond pure Eurocentrism, political theology has generally been done either from a Christian context or with reference to Christianity, something which allows us to understand the presence of Varro, Schmitt and Jiang on our list of definitive political theologians, though this does not mean that the problem does not exist in other civilizational traditions, just that it is going to be framed differently.

This said, disciplines are defined not just or even primarily by their *material* but also and primarily by their formal objects. The material object of a discipline is what is about; the formal object is how (in terms of what questions and using what sort of concepts) that subject matter is approached. And here we come upon a very interesting problem. It is possible for political theology to be treated as simply a branch of theology which is concerned with the problem of the State and especially the relationship between Church and State. Thus, the claim of Etienne

Gilson (Gilson 1958) that the relationship between Church and State can be understood only in the context of the relationship between reason and revelation, nature and grace. Thus, the fact that at the center of Milbank's political theology is a critique of the univocal metaphysics which he ascribes to Scotus and regards as the foundation of modernity. And this is almost certainly the way in which Christian political theology understood itself up until the work of Dorthee Solle, and might even encompass much Latin American liberation theology, which Segundo (Segundo 1985), for example, argues is the natural consequence of a certain understanding of the nature as already grace. Solle, however, suggested something different, something which is perhaps even the reverse of historic political theology, which is doing theology (i.e., considering God, as "material" object of the discipline) from the vantage point of the political.

This then raises the question of what constitutes the political. Here we will argue that the political is, at the highest level of abstraction, simply *power*. Thus, the *material* object of political theology might conceivably be *anything*, but its *formal* object is power understood theologically as either grounded in the divine or, in the case of an atheistic or nontheistic political theology, as something the ultimate ungroundedness of which is one of the principal results and core meanings of the absence of God. And, of course, this is coherent with many other definitions of the theology of liberation as theology done from the vantage point of the oppressed, engaged in struggles of liberation which are, among other things, political.

We bring a distinctive perspective to this problem. First, we will argue that at the most basic level Schmitt's *methodological* claim is trivially true. Religious ideas are *always*, as Durkheim demonstrated, a collective representation of social structure and *always* both reinforce social structure and (because social structures themselves have ruptures) challenge and transform them. "Secular" political ideas thus represent a secularization of religious concepts. All theology is political *in some sense* and all politics is theological *in some sense*.

Second, we will argue that Christianity, though not utterly unique in this regard, represents the principal form in which a new understanding of God, of Being, and of power was introduced, an understanding which much of historic Christianity, especially in its Orthodox and Catholic forms softened, but which was finally institutionalized and realized socially through the Reformation and ultimately embodied politically in Capitalism. Specifically, I will argue that along with various other doctrines which emerged during the Axial Age, including Sophism, the Caravaka School, and Legalism or *faxue,* Christianity understands Being univocally, with God as *a* being in the same sense we are, but infinitely powerful whose commands constitute the ethical and political order (though some of these other doctrines generally deny the existence of such a being). This is the point of origin of the decisionist political theology which Schmitt (and, ironically, Benjamin) embrace, and which Agamben, Badiou, and Žižek all, perhaps with some slight variations, all take for granted. And it is the religious reflex of Empire, of the attempt which emerged towards the end of the Axial Age to bring as much of the planet as possible under the rule of a single sovereign and, to the extent possible, to rationalize, bureaucratize and even militarize the population in service to the State (or, in its latter forms, Capital).

Third, this is why *After Christianity,* political theology inevitably becomes *the* architectonic discipline. Considering the Christian God, who is the first deity to be theorized as a properly absolute sovereign, against whom any act of disobedience or indeed even any deviation from absolute devotion, is a sin which merits eternal damnation, is considering God politically. And considering the world from God's perspective is a matter of theorizing God's political strategy, his historic work of "redemption" which makes effective in spacetime the sovereignty which is already established in eternity.

It might be argued that this God is something that Christianity takes over from Israel and is thus also the God of Judaism and that either or both then share it with Islam. Certainly, the God of Israel does a great deal of lawgiving and is constantly at pains to demonstrate his absolute sovereignty. And Islam is, of course, fundamentally about "commanding right and forbidding wrong" and thus making God's sovereignty fully effective. But this claim, we will show, is dependent on a Christian reading of the Hebrew scriptures. It is one thing to portray God *imaginatively* as a kind of cosmic monarch or emperor in myth, in which God cannot be anything other than *a* being; it is quite another to read that myth in a way which affirms conceptually the absolute sovereignty of God. And this is something which first appears with Paul, which is theologically elaborated by Augustine, and which is finally definitively formulated by Calvin and the Reformed tradition. Judaism, we will argue, is most consistent when it adopts an equivocal metaphysics in which God acts as and only as final cause, and because of this *cannot* be sovereign, as this would compromise the divine perfection. And Islam, as *After Christianity,* certainly carries elements of the Christian understanding of God as absolute sovereign. But it historically found ways to soften this, at least until the advent of the Wahabi movement and other fundamentalist tendencies which aim at "restoring" a Caliphate of a sort which never really existed. The same is true of the Catholic tradition which by and large opted for the middle ground of an analogical metaphysics.

Further, to the extent that the idea that "sovereign is the one who determines the exception" has any real roots in Roman Law, it is a product of the dictatorship being gradually transformed from a temporary measure under the control of the Senate into a permanent state of affairs. And this was more a *de facto* rather than a *de jure* development, and thus has no weight as precedent even for systems that depend on the Roman legal tradition. Nor is the transition from a political to an economic concept of power a consequence of Trinitarian doctrine, as Agamben claims, but of the Pauline innovation of a doctrine of absolute divine sovereignty which makes politics in the sense understood in the Hellenistic-Roman world, as deliberation regarding the nature of the common good among rationally autonomous individuals with different interests and perspectives essentially *sinful*, an act of rebellion against the head of what is not so much a *city* but rather a *household* of God. The result is inevitably some combination of allocation of Capital by the "invisible hand" of the market place and management of the resources Capital instrumentalizes by ministerial officers whose aims and methods are not open to deliberation—and the aims, not even among themselves. The accumulation of Capital is the only possible end. But the absolute negation of both the political and the economic which Agamben seems to be proposing simply rejects the alternative of submission in favor of an infantile rebellion which, covertly embracing Benjamin's messianism and antinomianism (Bat-Zvi 2017) simply prescinds from the realities of contingent being and material existence. *"Left" decisionism is not fundamentally distinct from Right decisionism.*

Where does this leave us? *After Christianity,* once a claim of absolute divine sovereignty has been advanced that claim must constantly be answered. We will show, however, that the political nature of theology and the theological nature of politics takes a very different form outside of Christendom and its successor formation, Global Capital. We reject unconditionally the claim that political authority is constituted by violence. This idea is simply an attempt to legitimate regimes which came into being as a result of violence, whether imperial or revolutionary *or* else a reflex of a market order the *telos* (accumulation) and the mechanisms of which are utterly occult and mysterious, and of the alienation of labor, which strips us of our humanity and generates an authoritarian personality structure for which power can *only* be coercion and domination, to which the only possible responses are submission or an infantile rejection of power as such. That it was suggested first on the Left and by an antifascist Jewish philosopher like Walter Benjamin of all people, and only later taken up by Schmitt to legitimate Nazi rule, shows the extreme poverty of Communism with respect to specifically *political* theory. We will also show that rejecting decisonism in political theology requires a rejection not just of a univocal but also of an analogical metaphysics in favor of an equivocal metaphysics which recognizes that God *is* in a way which is utterly different from that in which contingent beings exist, a way which is far superior, but which also renders sovereignty an illusion.

The real alternative to a decisionist political theology is already implicit in Marx's work but has only very tentatively been developed by his interpreters (Meikle 1985; Mansueto 2014). It is a natural law doctrine which grounds the communist project in rational knowledge of the Common Good, understood as the full development of human capacities, and the (real but limited) authority of the "party" grounded in its (far from infallible) ability to understand and apply that natural law. This is, of course, the correct answer to Jiang, whose insights regarding the deformation of the communist project by Christian political theology are insightful but who veers much too far towards the Legalist (as opposed to the Confucian and Taoist) pole of the historic Chinese ideological continuum. Natural law is the authentic deep constitution of every society, and while we will defend the necessity of a conscious leadership which, as Marx puts it, understands (better than others but still in a limited and partial way) the "conditions, line of march, and ultimate general result" of the historical process (or more humbly and accurately, which understands natural law in both the moral sense and in the sense of understanding how human history and human civilization work), the authority of this leadership is always limited to the value of its insight and the power of its arguments.

Whether or not communism is a state of affairs that we can fully achieve depends partly on how we understand it. The communist project has indeed been deformed by a Christian political theology which insists on a paradise whether in heaven and on earth. And we will argue that this is a false hope. Finitude and contingency cannot be transcended and lead inevitably to both natural evil (death, disease, disaster, etc.) and to humans and other rational animals (at least) pursuing their natural aim—Being as Such—in ways that involve exploitation and oppression. But if we mean by communism a society in which people are no longer forced to sell their labor power in order to survive—well that is not entirely unrealistic. And very significant progress in that direction is actually possible *even without state power*. So "communism . . . understood as the solution to the riddle of history" is indeed, ironically, a *Christian* fantasy. But communism as the decommodification of labor power (without the restoration of coercive forms of surplus extraction) is not just a "learning of the heart." It is a challenging but realistic political project.

Political Theology Beyond Christendom

It remains to demonstrate that political theology remains meaningful outside Christendom and its successor regimes. Here it is important to remember that different *ways* or traditions are not just *different* answers to the *same* question asked by Christianity, but ask *different questions* all together. Thus, in the context of Hellenic philosophy the foundational question is whether or not there is a first principle in terms of which the universe can be explained and human action ordered. The possible answers to this question are laid out in Plato's *Republic*:

- The Sophistic justifications of tyranny and democracy advanced by Thrasymachus and Glaucon, for whom Justice and the state are, in the absence of any first principle, simply a product of raw power or social convention and

- Plato's hypothetical aristocracy in which authority is grounded in knowledge of the Good.

For Judaism, Christianity, and Islam taken by themselves, apart from their syncretism with Hellenism, the fundamental question is about the nature of justice and how to achieve it.

- Judaism defines justice as "not driving a hard bargain with your neighbor" (Lev 25), i.e., not oppressing your neighbor, and embodies this principle in a Law subject to interpretation by prophets and legal scholars who extract the rational principles behind it and apply them to changing circumstances. Knowledge of God *consists* in doing justice. Judaism has historically been skeptical about claims to sovereignty. Israel accepted monarchy as a political necessity not a way of participating in the divine, and always regard monarchs as accountable to both prophets and legal scholars—who themselves, however, do not claim sovereignty either.

- Christianity proposes that justice is achieved only by the direct action of God both in the Crucifixion and Resurrection of Jesus and our baptism "into" Him, by which we are rendered individually just, and by the establishment of a posthistorical or spiritual "Kingdom of Heaven" in which God alone rules directly.
- Islam proposes to establish God's Kingdom on earth by building political power and using it to "command right and forbid wrong."

Practically speaking, however, Judaism, Christianity, and Islam exist only in syncretism with Hellenism. In this context the foundational question is about *both* God and Justice. *Does* God exist? And if so *how*? And how is the existence and nature of God related to the struggle for justice, both individual (our standing before God) and social? Do we understand God to exist in a radically different sense than we do (an equivocal metaphysics)? in a way in which we participate but which is nonetheless distinct (an analogical metaphysics)? or the same way we do (a univocal metaphysics)? The first is the classical Jewish position, and that of Islam when it is philosophically clearest and most consistent. The second is the Thomistic position and also of much historic Judaism and Islam. The third position is that of Augustinian Christianity and thus of most Protestantism, but also of some strains of Islam deriving from the Wahabi tradition. And both technocratic and humanistic secularisms fit well within this framework. Technocratic secularism, as we have demonstrated (Mansueto 2010, 2012, 2016), is the offspring of the Augustinian Reaction and assumes a univocal metaphysics. It simply regards God as (in the words of Laplace) an hypothesis of which it has no need. Our aim as human beings is to transcend the bounds of finitude by means of scientific, technological, and economic progress, i.e., in effect to build God. Humanistic secularism is the offspring of Hellenism and its syncretisms with Judaism, Christianity, and Islam, and most especially of Latin Averroism or Radical Aristotelianism. But it has only just returned to the question of the univocity, analogy, or equivocity of Being.

In the Dharmic traditions with roots in India, on the other hand, while the there is certainly a discourse about God, and there are certainly traditions which have a great deal to say about justice, the underlying problem is more nearly how we respond to the reality of finitude and contingency, which inevitably leads to suffering. The problems of Being and of God—as well as the question about justice—are set in this context. The most radical answer comes from Buddhism, which argues that *nothing* has the power of Being as Such and that suffering is a result of the illusion of permanence, self, and inherent existence. We overcome suffering by overcoming this illusion by means of various forms of right understanding, right conduct, and meditation. Political authority is legitimated primarily by the extent to which it demonstrates wisdom and compassion by both alleviating suffering and promoting enlightenment. In its most radical forms this favors what amounts to a monastic state of the sort which developed in Tibet, but it has also served to legitimate reformist monarchies on the model of Ashoka and the late Maurya Empire.

Other Indian traditions take very different approaches to the problem of impermanence and suffering. Vedanta approaches the problem through the related question of the relationship between Brahman and Atman (the creative power of Being as Such and the Self). The Jaina, Samkhya, and Yoga schools approach it through the relationship between *purusha* and *prakriti, jiva* and *ajiva*, roughly the conscious or spirit and the unconscious or material. The Mimamsa school grounds reality in the sacrificial act and the word of the priest, which *makes* kings and make kings *divine*. All of these tendencies have the effect of making political authority dependent on spiritual authorities of various kinds, whether ascetic virtuosi or establish priestly lineages. Still other school, such as the Caravaka, deny the reality of a first principle entirely.

In China and the Chinese sphere of influence, finally, the question of God recedes even further into the background, in the sense that the broad, abstract terms use to name the "first principle," such as *tian* (heaven), the *tao* (way) or *taiji* (great ultimate) are rarely defined rigorously and formally and also only rarely negated entirely (specifically by the *faxue* or Legalist tradition). The central concern is with restoring harmony between humanity and nature and within human society. How we do this is very much related to how we understand the first principle, though the key question is not so much its nature, but the extent to which it is knowable and to which its "mandate" can be formulated discursively and translated into laws and rituals. The Confucian tradition makes the emperor dependent for legitimation on scholarly advisors. The Taoist tradition rejects sovereignty altogether. The Mohist tradition, centered on the demand of a personal God that we love and serve all, is radically decisionist; the Legalist tradition is both atheistic and radically decisionist, grounding political authority in coercive power pure and simple, something we see reflected in the affinity of contemporary Chinese theorists such as Jiang Shiqong for Carl Schmitt.

What this analysis suggests, then, is that political theology is integral to *all* spiritual and civilizational traditions, but that it is integral in different ways, answering different questions.

* * *

How is all this playing out the present period? How are the various political actors we identified above articulating their claims in political theological terms? And how are the internal dynamics of political theology itself, which involves claims about the underlying structure of reality, shaping the alignment of political forces, facilitating some and making others more difficult? And what, in particular, do our conclusions about these questions say about our future? It is to these questions which we must now turn.

3

The Right

We are now in a position to begin considering the various trends and tendencies which have entered the field in the present period. We begin with those on the Right, understood, as we have noted, as those who reject fundamentally, the whole humanistic secular project in its liberal as well as its democratic and socialist forms. Here we can identify at least three distinct trends which, while they sometimes overlap and cross-fertilize each other, and are currently in at least tentative alliance with each other, in fact have fundamentally different social bases, distinct theoretical foundations, and incompatible visions for the future of humanity.

- a cluster of traditionalisms, internally divided among themselves between those that are Christian, those which are pagan explicitly anti-Christian, and those which profess an esoteric "perennial" wisdom,
- The *Dark Enlightenment*, with its periphery in the Human Biodiversity tendency, and
- the *Fourth Political Theory* of Alexander Dugin and other contemporary political manifestations of Right Heideggerianism.

Each of these trends, we will argue has a distinct social base or core constituency:

- Traditionalism finds its base in residual aristocratic elements, either temporal or religious, which have roots which reach back to the Bronze Age.
- The *Dark Enlightenment* represents a complex alliance of Capital as an emergent intelligence, a growing section of the stratum of capitalist magnates, especially but not only in the high technology sector, and the upper strata of the scientific-technical intelligentsia.
- The *Fourth Political Theory* and other manifestations of Right Heideggerianism (many of which are hidden behind various religious fundamentalisms and socialisms) is a manifestation of the phenomenon of alterimperialism or the resurgence of territorial empire both in marginalized or colonized regions of the world system: primarily Russia, India, and Dar-al-Islam, but also with significant reservations also China and many much smaller "imperial" formations around the world, and as an alternative path for the United States which, we must remember, is both the guarantor of the International Liberal Order *and* a territorial empire.

Traditionalism and the Sacral Monarchic Way

The Persistence of Aristocracy

What does it mean when we say that traditionalism is rooted in a civilizational ideal which emerged over five thousand years ago at the beginning of the Bronze Age? And what could it *mean* under the very different conditions of the present period?

Historically, the societies which traditionalists idealize emerged out of very specific technological innovations.

> In the course of a few centuries the villages of the plain fell under the domination of walled cities on whose rulers the possession of bronze weapons, chariots and slaves conferred a measure of superiority to which no community could aspire. (Watson 1961 in Lenski 1982)

The story was much the same throughout India, in the Mediterranean basin, and in Africa. As Gerhard Lenski puts it

> For the first time in ... history, people found the conquest of other people a profitable alternative to the conquest of nature.

> ... One might say that bronze was to the conquest of people what plant cultivation was to the conquest of nature. (Lenski 1982, p. 145)

Victorious warlords put the villages which they conquered under tribute, forcing the villagers to perform unpaid labor on their fields or to build temples, palaces, and fortifications. They imposed taxes, or distributed village lands to their retainers, who imposed rents. Warlords, meanwhile, continued to fight each other, with the strongest eventually emerging as monarchs and emperors. This new form of social organization, which we call tributary, represented the only way that the nomadic peoples of the steppes could gain access to—and participate in—the development of human civilization. Its emergence was neither a necessary evil, something required in order to extract surplus from indolent peasants who would otherwise have consumed it nor a mark of the intrinsic evil of human nature and something which marks the human civilizational project as inherently sinful and oppressive from the beginning. On the contrary, it represented an organic expression of the underlying drive of humanity towards ever higher degrees of participation in Being, simply under the less favorable conditions created by a difficult ecological niche. We begin to see how oppressive social structures and the ideologies which sustain them emerge *necessarily* out of the realities of contingent being.

But this is not how the emerging warlord states understood themselves. The way in which we understand the universe is largely determined by our position within it. And those who "create"—at least in the sense of creating new political entities, the earliest city states of the Bronze Age—by means of destruction—i.e., warfare—understand the universe itself as a process of creative destruction. Thus, the development in these societies of ideologies centered on deification by means of conquest and sacrifice, a pattern the intensity of which varies but which extends globally from the Vedas—in which the universe is created out of the sacrifice of the primordial human, Purusa, to the Aztecs, who taught that each "sun" or cosmic cycle required the sacrifice of one of the gods on a sacrificial pyre (Brundage 1985). Sacral monarchy exists and only exists in a reciprocal relationship of patronage on the one hand and sacrifice and sanctification by priestly lineages on the other.

But what do Bronze Age warlords and ritualists have to do with later aristocracies? And how in particular is the sacral monarchic ideal passed on, if perhaps also transformed, in the process? The Axial Age rationalized the aristocratic ideal, so that landed families—often the descendants of the founding warlords of small kingdoms or city states—which hoped to maintain their legitimacy had to engage in public liturgies, funding public festivals and building temples and baths, patronizing artists and scholars, and endowing temples and monasteries. The advent of Empire turned the vast majority of city state kings and patricians into generals and imperial officials. And both opened up avenues for upward mobility for artisans and merchants and citizen soldiers who proved themselves in battle, for artists and scholars, philosophers, prophets, and sages who created new ways of being human—and new means and standards of legitimation. Thus, Rome eventually had Senators who were of plebian birth, India had Sudra *rajas* and non-Brahmin religious virtuosi, and China had wave after wave of both military leaders and scholar-officials who rose to power with imperial insurgents who often emerged from the peasantry and were then partly or completely displaced by yet another wave of similar origins. This required the older families to at once broaden their portfolios and narrow the focus of their claims. Being warlord was no longer enough. One had to build temples and endow monasteries and patronize artists and scholars just as the emperor did. But one also had to claim something that the upstarts lacked: a lineage of ancestors who had done the same.

It is this focus on lineage above all which defines the *persistence of the aristocracy*. While the aristocracy as a social *class* living on large landed estates off of peasant labor exploited through rents and forced labor is all but extinct, *the aristocracy—or rather aristocracies—as lineages which constitute—individually and in relationship to each other—political networks and status groups persist.* The aristocratic status of these lineages is founded on the claim, recognized by other aristocratic lineages, to have made extraordinary and continuing contributions to the human civilizational project, to a degree which demonstrates a superiority which is attributed to "blood" (now generally glossed as genetic) and "breeding." *It should be noted that in authentically aristocratic circles the age of a lineage and its relative purity is more important than its nominal rank (e.g., the possession of titles), which are conferred by monarchs or other "fonts of honor" and which therefore, even when "merited" by the individual honored, and not simply a favor granted in return for political support, do not indicate anything about that individual's lineage.* The existence of aristocratic lineages, furthermore, does not require a "font of honor" which grants recognition. It is the informal recognition of other lineages which matters most and, as we will see, what amount to aristocracies exist even in societies which, like the United States, forbid titles of nobility. Indeed, one can regard such prohibitions as representing at least in part an assertion of claims to excellence on the part of the mostly "gentry" lineages which founded the United States against the confusion and corruption introduced by the conferral of titles in return for political support.

This focus on lineage, furthermore, implies both patriarchy and racism: patriarchy because the lineage is originally constituted by men, through their military or later business pursuits and because they must effectively instrumentalize women to ensure its continuity, and racism because lineage the purity of the lineage excludes marriage to the daughters of conquered and colonized—and therefore inferior—men. And it is here that traditionalism finds its mass appeal. Men, and imperial and colonizing peoples generally, especially when the commodification of labor power has stripped them of every other source of dignity and identity, take pride in their superiority to and power over women and colonized peoples.

This said, traditionalism comes in different varieties. We need now to explore these varieties and their social basis and political valence.

Variants of Traditionalism

Catholic Traditionalism

The term "traditionalism" has been used in a number of different ways by some very different historical tendencies and it is necessary to begin with to distinguish between these. The first wave of traditionalism derived from the thought of de Maistre and de Bonald (Maistre 1814; Bonald 1796) and was a reaction against the Enlightenment and French Revolution. Against the claim of Descartes and his followers to derive all knowledge from analytically self-evident first principles, the traditionalists insisted that human knowledge was a social product, based on concepts embedded in language, which constitute a sort of primitive revelation shared by all human beings.

At the political theological level, Traditionalism clearly affirms, along with the divine origin of human society, its roots in violence and sacrifice. Thus, while Traditionalism does not generally thematize the problem of univocal versus analogical or equivocal metaphysics it logically depends on both a univocal metaphysics and a divine command ethics. Because of this it can be seen as reflecting an attempt to preserve as much as possible of the sacral monarchic layer of the human civilizational project and was associated most strongly with the alliance which developed late in the *ancien regime* between the absolute monarchies, the aristocracy, and the clergy against the liberal and democratic revolutions. The effect was to put the kings and the warlord "aristocracy" on a par with the clergy as agents of God. This was the ideology par excellence of the Restoration regimes which put themselves forward as defenders of the Church and especially of the popes, but did so only at a price. Specifically, they claimed for kings not only the direct mandate from God which the Imperialist philosophers of the middle ages had claimed for the Holy Roman Emperor, but also a radical permanence which those philosophers had not.

The fact that the papacy was itself regarded as an institution established by divine revelation notwithstanding, this made traditionalism an unattractive option for the papacy, which had always claimed the right to depose unjust rulers, but it nonetheless had significant influence and probably a majority of the bishops present at the first Vatican Council had some traditionalist sympathies (Heyer 1969; Thibault 1972; Chadwick 1981). The doctrine of papal infallibility proclaimed by the Council can be read either as an attempt to construct a papal absolutism along traditionalist lines as a bulwark for the *ancien regime* (which is probably how most of its supporters understood it) or as an attempt on the part of the papacy to assert its authority vis-à-vis the traditionalists, which is how Pio IX understood it. Ultimately, however, the Council condemned the principal traditionalist thesis—fideism—which holds that knowledge of God is possible only on the basis of faith (Pius IX 1870).

We should be quite clear—contra Fiorenza—that traditionalism is radically different from even the most conservative variants of Neo-Thomism. Even as Thomism was pressed into service during the Counter-Reformation as an instrument against Protestant and liberal dissent, it could not help but defend the priority of conscience, arguing not that Catholics were obliged to simply submit to the magisterium, but rather that they had an obligation to inform their consciences by listening openly and respectfully to the teachings of their bishops. *Thomism, in other words, embraces the liberal ideal of rational autonomy, even if it insists that this autonomy be informed by revealed wisdom.* Traditionalist metaphysics, on the other hand, is the metaphysics of power and submission par excellence and seeks not merely to correct the individualism of the Enlightenment ideal, but rather rejects that ideal as such, arguing that social order is possible only on the basis of submission.[1]

To complicate matters, there is also a Center and Left Traditionalism which emerged out of this school and which became prominent in the early nineteenth century. These tendencies attempt to recover the religious and cultic dimension of the axial revolutions as a demand for universal access to cultic participation (Ballanche in Millbank 1990, p. 69) and which celebrates the role of the intermediate institutions of civil society as a foundation for a healthy democracy (Tocqueville 1835/2003). Center and Left Traditionalism are important sources of later Christian Democracy and Radical Orthodoxy respectively and of communitarian centrisms generally. Traditionalism of this sort, because it attempted to reassert the importance of the *social* over and against Enlightenment individualism became an important source for the development of sociology in the French tradition, by way of Auguste Comte and Emile Durkheim, both of who can be understood as, in a certain sense, center/left traditionalists, as can thinkers within the lineages deriving from them, such as Levi-Strauss and Bataille. This said, as we will demonstrate later in our critique of Radical Orthodoxy, it still bears the marks of its an origin which privileges sacrificial (and thus priestly) if not military (warlord) violence.

Perennialism

The second school to use the name *Traditionalism* is *perennialism*. Perennialism (Nasr 1989) is a philosophical and religious school which teaches that, behind their diverse exoteric forms, the world's great wisdom traditions, philosophical and religious, share a common esoteric and mystical core. It advances this claim in conscious continuity with Neoplatonic attempts to unify Hellenistic and Semitic spiritual culture, the Hindu concept of *Sanatana Dharma* or universal wisdom and the Chinese Buddhist *p'an chiao*. But the term itself derives from the Catholic Humanist Agostino Steuco (Delph 2006a, 2006b), for whom it represented the great

---

[1]. When the Dominican General Guidi offered the council a compromise text which recognized the infallibility of the pope's dogmatic definitions, rather than of his person, and under the condition that these definitions were consistent with the Catholic tradition, Pio IX responded by saying "*La tradizione son'io!*" (in Heyer 1963/1969, p. 191).

tradition of human wisdom which had culminated in Catholic Scholasticism, and which was then under assault by the Reformers. For Leibniz the idea of a perennial "philosophy of harmony" was at the center of a strategy to heal the religious divisions of Europe (Schmitt 1966). And the idea gained popularity as Europeans became aware of the significant common ground between their own mystical traditions and those of the peoples they had colonized. Advocates of the position include Huston Smith, whose introduction to world religions (Smith 1995) has promoted a moderate version of the doctrine among an enormous number of undergraduate students studying comparative religion, the Persian Islamic scholar Seyyed Hossein Nasr (Nasr 1989), Ananda Coomaraswamy (Coomaraswamy 1987), and Frithjof Schuon (Schuon 1992), along with Rene Guenon (Guenon 2007) and Julian Evola (Evola 1995), who we have already mentioned.

Perennialism has a complex and problematic relationship with the Right. Specifically, what it rejects is not so much the ideal of rational autonomy as such, but rather the idea of progress with which it is associated. On the one hand, it affirms that behind phenomenal reality there lies a rationally and mystically knowable first principle: Being, the Good, the One, Brahman or Tian. Humanity's end consists in understanding our unity and/or identity with this principle. On the other hand, perennialist cosmology is emanationist rather than emergentist. They see the phenomenal world, that is, as having fallen away from a primordial unity to which we must return, rather than as emerging out of the pure potential which is matter and reach towards Being as such. This inclines perennialists towards belief in a past rather than a Golden Age, though many embrace cyclical doctrines derived from Buddhism and Hinduism. The result is a social doctrine which is organically hierarchical. Integral to this conservatism is a failure to address the patriarchal expropriation of female generative power, though some members of the trend have been devotees of various goddess cults, especially those associated with the Hindu *mahavidya*. That said, it generally avoids the metaphysical moves which lead to a decisionist political theology. While perennialists have tended not to thematize the question of whether or not the term Being is used univocally, analogically, or equivocally, their emanationist cosmology and interest in mysticism tends to favor an analogical or equivocal approach. The idea of "a God" who governs the universe like an infinitely powerful version of a human sovereign is something that most perennialists regard as an artifact of the exoteric layer of religious traditions.

This, in turn has tended to pull most though not all perennialists back from support for fascism, with the principal exceptions being Guenon and Evola who include in the "tradition" they uphold preaxial, sacral monarchic as well as axial age doctrines.

Identarian Traditionalism

It is, however, a third school of traditionalism which interests us most as it has the greatest political salience in the present period. This school finds its roots in the European *Nouvelle Droite*, which has given birth to the ethnonationalism and identarianism of the second and third decades of the current century. If Catholic traditionalism was primarily a reaction to the liberal and democratic revolutions and the traditionalist wing of perennialism to the "iron cage" of capitalist rationality, the identarian right, while it resumes these other themes, is defined first and foremost by its resistance to *neoliberalism and globalization*. Associated with Alain de Benoist (Benoist 1977), Guillaume Faye (Faye 1998/2010, 2000/2016), and Pierre Krebs (Krebs 2012), this trend draws on a syncretic biological and cultural approach to identity and regards multiculturalism as a mechanism for destroying the distinct ethnic identities within the context of which alone it believes human beings can flourish—and doing this in the service of Global Capital and the American Empire, between which it does not really distinguish. These themes are joined to a radical masculinism or "gender realism" and a commitment to charismatic and authoritarian leadership as the only way to carry out systemic change. At the religious level, while there are Christian elements, there is an affinity for Neopaganism and polytheism as providing a theological foundation for ethnic particularism. While there is some common ground with alterimperialists such as Alexander Dugin (Dugin 2009), specifically the idea that liberalism and globalism destroy ethnic diversity, this trend differs from what we will call alterimperialism in favoring small ethnically defined states rather than multicultural empires and some element of anti-imperialism forms part of its discourse.

At the level of political theology, what sets Identarianism apart is its commitment to *polytheism* as the condition of ethnic pluralism. In this sense, the trend understands implicitly if not explicitly that the emergence of monotheisms during the Axial Age was *both* a reflex of emerging petty commodity production, which led people to experience the world as a system of quantitative relations and thus led to mathematical formalization, and the use of mathematical concepts such as the Infinite and the One to theorize the first principle, *and* a reflex of the emerging Silk Road Empires which at least aspired to global hegemony and thus constitute a social basis for the idea of a universal sovereignty. Identarianism, by rejecting monotheism, also implicitly rejects the idea of absolute sovereignty which depends on a monotheistic theology interpreted through a univocal metaphysics. But here the rejection of sovereignty is quite different from ourn own. Identarian traditionalism does not reject sovereignty because the power of God, which is the power of Being as Such, simply cannot be adequately expressed in the realm of finite and contingent Being, but rather because it denies that such a power exists at all, and in so doing fundamentally deny any universal principles by which human action might be ordered. This, of course, opens the way for unaccountable power even if it is not fully sovereign and does not aspire to universality.

Dark Enlightenment

Social Basis

We have already discussed the phenomenon of the *Dark Enlightenment* at some length (Mansueto 2017), and it might be argued that the topic is already *passée*, but in the light of the larger analysis being developed here, something like the *Dark Enlightenment* is likely to remain a feature of both the debate around what it means to be human and the larger global political dynamic. And elements of our analysis suggest a slightly different characterization of the social basis and political valence of the movement than we thought earlier.

In order to understand this situation, we need to understand the situation for Capital in the present period. The principal challenge facing Capital in the present period is not from the Left in any of its forms, but from the internal dynamics of its own evolution. Capitalism *depends* on the existence of a proletariat, not only in order to generate surplus value, but also to buy the products that workers produce. This allows the bourgeoisie to realize the surplus extracted from the proletariat in the work place as profit, as well as to capture and realize surplus generated through petty bourgeois self-exploitation, which can then be reinvested in further economic growth and development, or expended on luxury consumption or on noneconomic civilization building. There has always been a tension between these two functions, a tension which forms the basis of the principal contradictions of capitalism which Marx identified. As the economy develops technologically, productivity increases, driving down the value of labor power (which takes less labor power to reproduce) and thus wages, creating a tendency towards underconsumption. At the same time, as the economy becomes more capital intensive, the rate of profit declines (as it is living labor which creates value), and Capital redeploys itself to low wage, low skilled, low technology activities on the periphery of the system. But this redeployment of Capital itself sets in motion a process of industrialization which eventually eliminates peripheries and reinstates the declining rate of profit.

These contradictions have historically been ameliorated by collective bargaining, which can drive wages back up, income transfers which support final demand, and philanthropy and state investment in infrastructure, research, development, and education which, in addition to advancing human civilization, also create demand by way of the people employed in the activities which are thus funded and subsidize otherwise unprofitable high technology, capital intensive industries. The more progressive elements within the bourgeoisie have sometimes understood this, permitting extended periods of growth and stabilization such as that set in motion by the New Deal. But there have always been other elements which have rejected any restraint on their freedom to do what they please, even when it obviously harms others and even when it is obviously self-destructive.

The "neoliberal" assault on the so-called "welfare state" was not some sort of technocratic "course correction" designed to rebalance a playing field which, economically if not morally, had become tilted to the side of labor, with wages rising more than productivity and thus undercutting capital formation. It was, rather, the visible, public manifestation of a far Right assault on social liberalism, i.e., on the idea that in order to be meaningful liberal freedoms must be accompanied by the resources to exercise them. While this assault was generally framed in the language of classical liberalism or libertarianism, as in the work of Ludwig von Mises and the earlier work of F. A. Hayek, the underlying reasoning was ultimately evolutionary and utilitarian. Thus for Hayek (Hayek 1988) the marketplace functions as a kind of information processing system which takes supply and demand as inputs and provides information, in the form of prices, to producers. In reality, the only "freedom" that advocates of this trend ever cared about was that of the wealthiest to do what they please.

When this trend finally came to power at the end of the 1970s by way of the Thatcher and Reagan governments, it was dependent on a mass base mobilized around the defense of racism and patriarchy and had only very uneven support among the bourgeoisie, which really did see the turn to the right as a question of restoring balance to a system which had been rendered dysfunctional by mounting "entitlements" and a lack of respect for the "laws" of economics. Indeed, in terms of the success of the neoliberal project in the US, the UK, and Europe, the ability of the right to neutralize and even persuade members of social liberal and social democratic parties using pseudoscientific technocratic arguments was probably as significant as the ability of libertarians to leverage racism and misogyny to push liberal conservative parties to engage in draconian cuts to the social safety net and to cut levels of taxation well below what was necessary to maintain the infrastructure required by a complex capitalist society.

The new neoliberal regime, however, coupled with the collapse of the Soviet bloc, propelled rapid change, including the emergence of an almost entirely new information technology sector and the creation of vast new fortunes both in this sector and outside it. These capitalist magnates, especially in high technology sectors, and part of the technical intelligentsia, especially in information technology and quantitative finance and economics, have in turn provided the basis for a kind of "second wave" attack on social liberalism, especially as it became apparent, as we noted in the previous chapter, that they would not be able to implement their full "libertarian" program in an even formally democratic policy. This second wave began with the "Tea Party" reaction to Obama's victory in 2008, a movement which reprised the tried and true "Southern Strategy" which had been working for the Republican Party since 1968, but there were elements on the Right which wanted something cleaner and "purer."

Into this developing situation we must add the fact that the neoliberal turn coupled with the development of new information technology was sufficient to set in motion the emergence of Capital as an autonomous intelligence independent of the historic bourgeoisie. For some on the Right this led to a significant distancing from the globalist neoliberalism of the previous period and a turn towards what we have called *alterimperialism*. But others, and especially elements of the elite technical intelligentsia, began to think beyond capitalism and beyond humanity. This project is still in its early stages. We do not know for sure what would happen if those who advocate an end to regulation and income and wealth transfers which ameliorate the contradictions in capitalism got their way and/or if automation progressed until it rendered human labor obsolete, effectively liquidating the proletariat. But the result is no longer capitalism. Capitalism, in its moment of definitive victory, would become something else entirely. And capitalist magnates and their servants? Would their dreams of being "uploaded" to a "higher level of implementation" be realized? Or would they, more likely, be cut loose and abandoned like the rest of us? Many theorists of transhuman intelligence (Barrow and Tipler 1986; Tipler 1994) argue that such a "superior" intelligence would necessarily be benevolent. But we have very little evidence that the logic of Capital shows any care for "unproductive" human beings, for the human civilizational project, or, for that matter, for the planet.

This is the context in which the *Dark Enlightenment* has emerged.

What is the Dark Enlightenment?

The *Dark Enlightenment* is, fundamentally, a "next generation" offshoot of libertarianism—and in particular the fusionist libertarianism represented by Murray Rothbard and F. A. Hayek. This sort of libertarianism has had a strong constituency among the technocratic intelligentsia for some time. In the 1980s and 1990s, for example, Frank Tipler argued that humanity could, should, and would build God by re-engineering the universe into a massive supercomputer running off of the gravitational sheer created in the final instants of a closed universe which would run emulations of everything that was logically possible. And, following Frederick Hayek (Hayek 1988) he argued that free markets would get us to this point fastest (Barrow and Tipler 1986; Tipler 1994). But for Tipler and indeed for Hayek "right-leaning" meant free markets, not authoritarianism.

The turn towards a more authoritarian ideology came in the mid- to late 2000s as it became increasingly apparent that democracy and libertarianism were incompatible. Sometime around 2006 or 2007 elements within the technolibertarian trend, including Curtis Yarvin (aka Mencius Moldbug), Nick Land, Peter Thiel, and Michael Asimov began to realize that libertarian economics did not stand a chance in a democracy. A majoritarian electorate would simply never consistently vote to support libertarian policies which, advocates of this line of reasoning increasingly admitted, simply were not in their self-interest. And so they began to argue for abandoning democracy in favor of a network of autocratic corporate city states in which people would have the right of "exit" but no "voice." Anyone who wished to (at least anyone with the necessary resources) could, in other words, leave one city state for another, more to their liking. But within each city state, one would have to toe its line. The idea is that the owners of these city-states would be motivated to run them as well as possible and thus to attract the best and the brightest.

The question, of course, is how one builds the power necessary to carry out such a transformation. *Dark Enlightenment* theorists found their answer in the ideas of antidemocratic theorists from the first third of the twentieth century, including traditionalists such as Julius Evola (Evola 1934) and Rene Guenon (Guenon 1927), who had a quite different political-theological agenda, and more recent thinkers such as Hans Herman Hoppe (Hoppe 2001). They also began to attract around them a periphery of related trends which distinguished themselves from other currents on the right by the purportedly scientific basis of their claims: the "human biodiversity trend," which argues that there really are genetically determined races with distinct, if not necessarily superior or inferior biological adaptations (Frost 2015; Fuerst 2015), and the "androsphere" which argues for traditional gender roles on the basis of sociobiological and similar arguments.

What is the link between right accelerationism on the one hand and traditionalism, racism, and misogyny on the other? The answer is in an evolutionary understanding of human society. Here the intellectual heavy lifting was already done by Frederick Hayek (Hayek 1988) who argued that traditional practices, among which he included not only capitalism but also language, traditional family structures and sexual moralities, and religion, survived precisely because they promote survival. But Hayek was very careful to avoid *explicitly* racist conclusions, treating practices and not genes, individual organisms, or collectivities such as "races" (the very existence of which he denied) as the unit of selection. The *Dark Enlightenment* is not so cautious. For this trend, selection operates across practices, collectivities, organisms, and genes. And even if we were to call Hayek's commitment to democracy into question, it is fairly clear he always thought of capitalism as having to provide goods and services to very large numbers of human beings. The *Dark Enlightenment* points us beyond the mass market and thus beyond capitalism as we have historically understood it.

In other words, where Hayek argued that evolutionary theory shows that *capitalism* is superior to (more adaptive than) *socialism*, the *Dark*

Enlightenment is essentially arguing that some people are better adapted than others, as evidenced by their superior intellectual or entrepreneurial ability (and that of their ancestors who accumulated the capital required for their ventures) and that the body politic ought to, or rather must be forced, to get out of their way.

In what sense is this a political theology? We should note that the *Dark Enlightenment* is defined in part by polarization on what it calls "the Cathedral," by which it means the complex of hegemonic academic, cultural, and liberal religious institutions, including the mass media which, it argues promotes a more or less secularized version of liberal Christianity. The *Dark Enlightenment* is quite vigorous in pursuing this polemic, and in using Christian as a term of derision and attacking even militant New Atheists such as Dawkins and Denton as shills for the Cathedral.

The *Dark Enlightenment* associates the Cathedral specifically with the Puritan tradition. It is quite insightful, in this regard in tracing the specific cultural roots of what has come to be called liberalism (more properly social liberalism) in the United States. The spiritual shadow cast by Puritanism over the Center Left in the United States is evident in the fact that progressive politics are seen to be first and foremost a reflection of an innate spiritual superiority than an expression of definite social interests. This is one legacy of the Reformed Tradition, and especially its liberal variants, which looked to "usefulness to society," expressed through either economic productivity or (in this case) commitment to social justice, as evidence of divine election. And this pattern holds even for those whose Calvinism has become fully immanentized. Against this Puritan or "Roundhead" legacy, the Dark Enlightenment identifies with the Cavalier tradition and with its legacy in the Deep South, and indeed with traditionalist trends generally.

This might seem like evidence against our argument that Christianity is, in fact, at once the ideology of Empire *par excellence* and the deep source of capitalism. But this is not the case. The *Dark Enlightenment* argument against Puritanism and its identification with the Cavaliers is, first and foremost, a defense of *absolute* monarchy against *constitutional* monarchy and more especially against representative government of any kind. While Yarvin and others make the argument that unlike a temporary elected leader a King, as permanent owner of his kingdom, has more incentive to care for it and will thus govern well, the real concern here is against *any* limitation on the freedom of the largest magnates. In Yarvin's "neocamerialist" world of privately owned city states, individuals have the freedom of "exit" but no voice. If they don't like the policies of the state they live in, they can leave, but that is all. The owner gets to do and to rule as he pleases.

Furthermore, while less central to the *Dark Enlightenment*, it should be noted that among the key theorists of the Cavaliers was Richard Filmer, Locke's adversary, who argued that kingship was based on *paternity* and that a king's subjects were like his children and thus unconditionally subject to his authority. This amounts to a complete negation of the political and a reduction of human social existence to the *oikos* or *familia* in which wife and children (here everyone except the king himself) are fundamentally chattel to be disposed of as he sees fit.

It is in this context that we must understand the political valence of the Right's discourse around freedom. It long appeared that this was a rather paradoxical appropriation of US popular political culture to opportunistically leverage support for authoritarian policies, and it *does* operate at this level. But we must understand that when the Right talks about freedom, it is not the freedom of even classical liberalism, limited by the comparable freedom of others, but rather absolute freedom to do as one pleases.

What is distinctive about this political theology is that unlike pure Traditionalism which either accepts the superior authority of God and the King (in its Catholic form) or rejects Christianity in order to be freed of universal moral norms which limit freedom of action, the *Dark Enlightenment* actually proposes a world of kings, and has its mass constituency among those who actually believe that they could become kings. Thus the peculiar fondness for what seems like rather niche political theology: that of the early Anglican Jacobites, in which the King is free of the Church and the Pope, and is thus the sole arbiter of God's will. It is not so much that the theorists of the *Dark Enlightenment* affirm the *existence* of God as that the *image* of God is crucial for capturing the terrible freedom to which they aspire.

From this point of view, we can see the *Dark Enlightenment* as an attempt to withdraw from *Empire*'s compromise—driven by the need for legitimation—with the Axial Age and indeed from the surrender of would-be emperors generally to the One Emperor capable of ruling them all. Instead Yarvin and his allies propose a world of petty magnates. The only legitimation Yarvin and his allies propose is the vacuous claim that such magnates would be better rulers because they would own their realms and would take care of their property. There is, of course, no historical evidence to support this claim. And Yarvin is not, so far as we know, proposing slavery. As the value of human labor power declines to zero, the vast surplus population which contributes nothing to the magnate's pleasure will at best be left to rot and at the worst simply exterminated.

Another way of looking at this is that where traditionalism promotes the superiority of a collective founded on mutual recognition, the *Dark Enlightenment* proposes to be done, once and for all, with human interdependence. Its constituency is thus limited to those who imagine that they can survive and prosper in a war of all against all. This constituency is, unfortunately, far larger than one might imagine.

The Dark Enlightenment and the Dark Elf Strategy

It should be apparent, at this point, that the *Dark Enlightenment* is ultimately quite different from the rest of the alt-right. Specifically, while the rest of the alt-right is focused on ethnic particularism or on building, conserving, or restoring territorial empire, the *Dark Enlightenment* prefers a network of autonomous city states. The *Dark Enlightenment's* critique of the Cathedral, furthermore, sets it off from much of the rest of the alt-right which embraces or at least uses various forms of conservative Christianity. Just as the alliance between the extreme neoliberalism of Hayek, which is organically atheistic in character, and religious social conservatism, was mediated by the distinction which Hayek made between substantively rational, planned forms of organization and the spontaneous self-organization which characterizes language, the family, markets and religion, the link between the *Dark Enlightenment* and the rest of the alt-right is mediated by evolutionary theory which here, however, is applied to individuals, "races" (which are taken to exist in essence and to be biologically defined) and cultures as well as specific practices. And to the extent that the *Dark Enlightenment* draws on older Right ideologies, it is on traditionalism and not on the Heideggerian tradition which motivates at least some elements on the alterimperialist right, such as Dugin (Dugin 2009).

This said, there is currently a strategic alliance between the *Dark Enlightenment* and *Alterimperialism* centered on their shared rejection of democracy. Neither Capital as an emergent autonomous intelligence nor the bourgeoisie nor resurgent territorial states can match the power of organized people—*so long as human labor power remains necessary for the creation and realization of value.* For this reason, the defense of democracy, as imperfect and as subject to manipulation as it is, remains fundamental to any credible strategy of resistance. But where most of the Right presupposes the nominal persistence of democratic institutions and relies on ideological manipulation and voter suppression to ensure acceptable outcomes at the polls, the *Dark Enlightenment* envisions a future in which democracy has been "transcended," initially because political power has become the private property of capitalists who effectively own city states and ultimately because, without benefit of trade unions, transfer payments, etc. the great masses of humanity, lacking sufficient skills even to be exploited, will gradually die off, leaving material and much intellectual production to machines, and the remainder to highly skilled scientific and creative retainers who have been reduced to little more than servants of their capitalist magnate overlords.

More recently however, key *Dark Enlightenment* theorist Curtis Yarvin has begun to advance what he calls a *Dark Elf* strategy (Moldbug 2023). He argues that most of the political new right in the US—including both Trump and his allies in the Republican Party as well as Fox News and the whole universe of even more extreme outlets—is composed of "grifters." Using the various "races" of Tolkien's *Middle Earth* as metaphor, Yarvin argues that those who, like himself, want a "hard reset" of our social order should stop trying to mobilize the lower middle strata, who he compares to "Hobbits" who "just want to grill in their backyards and be left alone" and instead focus on turning liberal intellectuals (who he compares to Tolkien's Elves) to the dark side.

This may seem like a minor point advanced by a theorist who, despite some currency among a certain sector of the technical intelligentsia, is still quite marginal. It is not. Yarvin himself, with his direct appeals to dissident members of the *Cathedral*, may not be successful implementing a *Dark Elf* strategy. But others are. The clearest example of this is sharp turn to the right on the part of the Biden government with respect to its COVID-19 policy. How does a president who proposes what are without question the most progressive extensions of the welfare state since at least the 1960s and possibly since its inception under FDR effectively abandon COVID mitigation in order to placate a bourgeoisie anxious to return to "normal"—even when the move may well leave them with severe labor shortages and a much larger dependency ratio as the numbers disabled by the virus rise? The answer is Jeff Zients, known as the

"Obama-Whisperer" for his ability to get Barack Obama to abandon his most deeply felt convictions when serving under the former President, who also served as Biden's first COVID response coordinator. Social liberals, especially when they are dependent for support on members of the bourgeoisie who, even when they recognize both the economic necessity and moral value of redistribution and public investment, are reluctant to part with their wealth and especially reluctant to reduce market pressures on the working class, are always vulnerable to technocratic arguments that they are letting their admirable moral sentiments triumph over what *actually* serves the common good. And then there is Ezekiel Emmanuel, the center of the firestorm over "death panels" during the 2008 presidential campaign, who covers his arguments for the rationing of health care with references to communitarian and civic republican concerns about the common good, rather than even evaluating the possibility of rigorous cost controls and demarketization of health care, coupled with confiscatory and punitive taxes on the richest . . .

What is even more remarkable is the fact that so much of the Left—not the genteel Center Left which Yarvin calls the Cathedral, but those discontented enough to support spoilers such as Bernie Sanders and to denounce Obama, Biden, and Pelosi as "neoliberal shills" even when they are doing the right thing—have succumbed to precisely this Dark Elf strategy, embracing eugenics and the euthanasia of the aged and disabled as simple the price to be paid *Their Revolution* . . .

I don't really expect to see Peter Thiel crowned King with Curtis Yarvin as his prime minister. Nor do I expect to see socialism any time soon. But the *Dark Elves* are everywhere, working their mischief.

AlterImperialism

The third, and politically the most important, element on the new Right is what we call Alterimperialism. This is a phenomenon with deep roots extending back into the nineteenth century, but one which has only become a major trend shaping global politics over the course of the past decade or two, as the full implications of the crisis of socialism and the collapse of the Soviet Bloc became apparent. The first sign of the development was the emergence of Islamic Fundamentalisms, which attempted to take up the struggle against "Western" Imperialism as the global appeal of socialism faded. The second key development was the very explicit movement to restore the Russian Empire which was always latent in post-Soviet Russia but which became explicit and hegemonic with Putin's rise to power in the 2000s. The third development was the re-emergence of China as a global power, and especially its self-conscious ownership of this aim since the rise of Xi Jinping in 2012. But in addition to these key developments we see alterimperialist elements in the rise of Hindutva in India, in Trump's attempt to refocus US policy inward, on what amounts to its territorial as opposed to its financial empire, and in numerous other elements worldwide.

In order to understand this development we need to reconsider the whole question of Empire as a *way of being*, something which is facilitated by the emergence of a whole new literature on the question, a literature which we will bring into dialogue with our own earlier analysis of the relationship between the Axial Age and the emerging empires of the Silk Road Era (Mansueto 2010, 2016). Second, we will have to evaluate the claim that "Western" Empire, whether Hellenistic, Christian, or Liberal, is fundamentally different from other imperialisms. Finally, we will need to examine the way in which the socialist project was transformed into—or perhaps actually always was, at least in part, a project of imperial restoration. This will in turn require us to look at alterimperialisms which are not postsocialist, whether in the "West" or elsewhere on the planet.

Empire as a Way of Being

We begin with a consideration of the concept of *Empire*, something which, oddly, has not really been theorized with much rigor. Historical scholarship has, for the most part, treated empires empirically as "things with properties," and specifically as any formation which is, given its historical context, relatively large in scale and which results from the conquest of many peoples by one or by an alliance of conquering peoples. In this sense there is no clear line between larger sacral monarchies and smaller empires or between the Roman or Sassanid Empire and the British Empire or "US Imperialism." Empires may vary in their economic system, there political structure, and the degree of cultural integration.

The one exception to this pattern has been historical materialism which has, at least for the past one hundred years, tended to theorize imperialism as either a stage in the development or a permanent dimension of specifically *capitalist* development. This is true both of the Leninism

(Lenin 1916/1963), which argued that imperialism represented a specific stage of capitalist development associated with the export of capital to low skill, low wage regions in order to compensate for the declining rate of profit in the higher technology industrial sectors, and of dependency theory (Amin 1978, 1879/1980, 1988/1989; Frank 1998; Wallerstein 1974, 1980, 1989), which makes imperialism foundational for the process of capitalist development itself, locating the principal sources of primitive accumulation in colonies established beginning around 1500. These two approaches to imperialism, while at the root of significant differences in political strategy in the final stages of the national liberation struggles, are not, in fact, entirely incompatible if treated as theorizing distinct stages in the relationship between Capital and Empire. Furthermore, to the extent that these two approaches, singly or in combination, have been questioned, or treated as out of date, it has been to argue that the global market has become so integrated and powerful as to overtake state structures of all kinds, so that it is no longer possible to talk meaningfully of "US imperialism" or other national imperialisms, but only of a deterritorialized "Empire" of Capital. This approach is also, interestingly enough, broadly compatible with the normative neoliberal claim articulated most clearly by Francis Fukuyama that the defeat of the Soviet Union represented a sort of "end of history" in which ideological conflicts would give way to the technocratic management of a global capitalist order of which unlimited freedom in the movement of capital was the foundation.

It is this context that we must situate the work of Darwin and Coker, who attempt to extricate the concept of Empire from its Leninist and post-Leninist context and approach it in at least a comparative historical if not a fully theoretical way, something which then points towards Jiang Shigong's more rigorous formulations. Coker in particular, whose aim is to respond to Samuel Huntington's *Clash of Civilizations* thesis (Huntington 1993) argues that while clashes between civilizations are not inevitable, clashes between what he calls Civilizational States are. This in turn leads to a sharp distinction between the world empires which emerged from the Silk Road Era, which he calls Civilizational States, and the Liberal International Order for which alone the term Empire is reserved. Jiang then picks up on this argue that China's re-emergence as a global power is free from any taint of imperialism.

Our own approach to the problem of Empire differs from Coker's—and Jiang's—in a number of respects. First, we believe that Empire must be considered as a type of *social formation* integrating multiple modes of production or economic structures. What Marx called modes of production, do not exist in isolation but rather in complex articulated combinations (Amin 1978/1980). Thus, the emergence of the tributary mode of production at the beginning of the Bronze Age did not entirely displace the communitarian mode which preceded it, but rather superimposed itself on the earlier communitarian mode and instrumentalized it. Similarly, during the Axial Age, petty commodity production rarely existed in isolation, but was combined with communitarian and tributary structures and with chattel slavery which, in so far as it treated human beings as a commodity, was compatible with petty commodity production, but which, because human beings are a kind of capital investment, represented a departure in the direction of capitalism.

The large "world" Empires of the Silk Road Era emerged, as we have argued (Mansueto 2010, 2016) in response to the internal contradictions of the petty commodity production which emerged during the Axial Age. The emergence of specialized agriculture and crafts production (wine, oil, pottery, and wool in the Mediterranean Basin, spices in India, and silk and tea in China) allowed early centers which exploited these new technologies to grow rich on monopoly rents. It is this which allowed the "room" for the revolts which led to land reform and elements of democracy in Greece and the critique of sacral monarchy nearly everywhere which defined the Axial Age. Soon, however, others adopted the new technologies and markets became saturated. The only way to support a significant privileged stratum which could participate in the new ways of life which had emerged during the Axial Age, whether the pursuit of enlightenment, democratic citizenship, or a life of advising rulers, was by building an Empire which could tax trade between centers of luxury production and redistribute the resulting wealth to an enlarged privileged stratum. Empire is, at the economic level, a social formation which integrates petty commodity production, often supported by slavery or by the exploitation of dependent peasant labor, with tributary mechanisms which centralize and allocate surplus.

Second, at the political level, we see at least an *attempt* to develop uniform, instrumentally rational systems of administration—more so in the more advanced formations, such as China, and less so in peripheral formations such as Rome.

Finally, we believe that Empire faced profound legitimation problems emerging as it did during the Axial Age. There *were* organic ideologies of empire which generally emerged out of the schools which trained rulers and would be rulers in the art of building and exercising power. The most important of these were the Chinese *faxue* or Legalism, the Caravaka school, and Skepticism. But simply telling people that they need to become instruments of the state is rarely effective, and attempts on the part of the Qin and the Mauryans to legitimate their empires directly on the basis of such ideas rapidly failed. The Qin fell and the Han took over their structural innovations but legitimated it by way of what was gradually becoming a synthesis between Confucian and Taoist ideas. Thus, the *Tianxia* ideal, the claim that "all under heaven" is ruled by the emperor who is the Son of Heaven and bears its mandate, so long as he serves the people and maintains social harmony. Ashoka, after completing the brutal conquests his father began, turned to large scale land reform and patronage of Buddhist, Hindu, and Jaina monasteries, giving birth to the Cakravartin ideal of a "wheel turning king" who leads his people to liberation and enlightenment. Rome, meanwhile, never really attempted direct legitimation of Empire, but rather simply pretended that the Republic was still intact and that Rome's conquests existed to make possible a life of philosophical self-cultivation and civic engagement whether at the level of the empire as a whole or at the level of the *polis* or *civitas* which, officially, remained the principal social unit. In this sense all three became what Coker and Jiang are calling "civilizational states" in the sense that their imperial structures were formed by and to some extent served civilizational ideals which had emerged in the Axial Age. But they were no less empires because of this and thus I prefer the term *Civilizational Empire* and insist on its application to Rome as well as to India and China. This is not to say that Rome many not have been both more backward and more brutal than the others, but the world is not divided neatly between good guys and bad, but is, rather made up of human beings who are entirely capable of building brutally oppressive structures but who cannot live without meaning and who ultimately do everything, good, evil, or indifferent, in the pursuit of Being.

Kingdoms of God

Judaism Is Resistance

Where do Christendom and *Dar-al-Islam* stand with respect to the emergence of Empire as a *way of being?* In a very paradoxical position, to say the least.

If we are going to understand the relationship between Christianity, Islam, and Empire, we must begin with the fact that both emerged ultimately out of Judaism which was the anti-imperial movement *par excellence*. Israel had its origins in a peasant revolt in Late Bronze Age Canaan (Gottwald 1979) and as a result developed a distinctive spirituality centered on meeting God in the struggle for social justice—or at least in ethical conduct. Even after it was forced to restore the sacral monarchy it had initially rejected, as the condition of retaining its independence, under changing geopolitical conditions, and even after it ultimately lost its independence, its prophets reminded Israel that doing justice was, fundamentally, authentic knowledge of God.

There were a range of different responses in Israel to the reality of a word dominated by Empire. Some argued that Jews should accept that the military balance of power and leverage the Empire's civic humanism to mount a challenge for hegemony. The critical figure in this regard was Philo of Alexandria. Other tendencies had a more complicated relationship with Hellenistic Roman culture. While embracing aspects of Hellenism, the Sadducees remained focused on maintaining the sanctity and purity of the temple cult, even if this meant (generally unenthusiastic) collaboration with the Roman authorities. They argued against the Oral upheld the existence of free will, and rejected the resurrection of the body. They articulated the interests and perspectives of the priestly families and large landowners dependent for their prosperity of the Temple and the pilgrimage economy it created. Still others engaged in active resistance to Rome. Messianic revolutionary movements aimed liberating Israel by means of armed struggle under the leadership of one or another claimant to the throne of David were a dime a dozen in the first century, and by 66 CE a broad spectrum of Jewish parties had been won over to the revolutionary project. Ultimately it was only the overwhelming force of the Roman legions which crushed the Jewish uprising of 66–70 CE and the Bar Kochba revolt of the next century and which convinced Israel that liberation and restoration were not on the agenda.

The result of this process was the emergence of the Pharisees, who had been merely one of many political-theological tendencies in Second Temple Judaism, as the branch out of which most later Judaism—what we now call rabbinic Judaism—emerged. The Pharisees, while not rejecting the temple and while certainly sharing a long-term hope in liberation and restoration, had focused the bulk of their attention on adapting the legal traditions of Israel to the new realities of imperial rule, petty commodity production, and insertion into the Silk Road trade. But as Jacob Neusner (Neusner 1975) has pointed out, however, there is more to this way than simply adapting Jewish law, with its historic focus on social justice, to new social circumstances. The Talmud also suggests a new model of leadership and a new spirituality. While the Jewish communities in Palestine and Babylon, and indeed in other cities as well, often had an official leadership recognized by the political authorities, and while in some cases, as in Babylon, there was even an Exilarch claiming descent from David, real authority belonged to the rabbis. But it did not belong to the rabbis as an officially sanctioned body, the judgments of which were taken as legitimate in virtue of office. Rather, authority belonged to which ever rabbi was able to make the most logically convincing argument regarding the particular point of law in question. While earlier opinions might, furthermore, serve as a point of reference or departure, there was, in principle, no point which was not subject to criticism and re-evaluation. And the dominant approach to interpretation in rabbinic Judaism was, in fact, intensely rationalistic. The task of the legal scholar was to abstract the principle behind the written law and apply it freely in a contemporary context. The people of Israel became, in effect, a *logocracy*, where neither law nor persons but rather legal argument and scholarship alone ruled.

The result of this was to transform the Jewish people, deprived though they might be of land and king and temple, into one of the leading forces—in fact *the* leading force—in the development of "Western" society and the reason we call it Western rather than Christian or European. They became practitioners of "a ruthless criticism of everything existing" (Marx 1843/1978), a criticism grounded in a primordial experience of divine justice. It was, above all, the deliberative practice of the rabbis which shaped that of the Islamic *ulema* and through them that of the Christian scholastics (Makdisi 1989). And everything authentically critical in the European tradition (as opposed to what is merely messianic) bears this same rabbinic seal.

The destruction of the temple, similarly, and the postponement of any attempt at reconstruction to an indefinitely distant messianic future, also meant that the *sacred*, previously encountered in a privileged if not exclusive manner by the High Priest, in the Holy of Holies, was now encountered equally in all aspects of life to which the Law might be applied. *Everything*, in effect, was regarded as sacred.

What we see here is the emergence of a new political theology, one in which authority is invested not in a divine person (sacral monarchy) or even in human beings who cultivate virtue with such success that they come to be godlike (Aristotelian aristocracy) but rather in a *process* by which human beings deliberate around the nature and requirements of justice. This is, on the one hand, itself a spiritual practice, forming us intellectually and morally in the image of God, and thus fully compatible with Aristotelian aristocracy. But it also makes God present in the city in a fundamentally new way, in what happens *between* people, adding a new layer of meaning to civic humanism or, rather, situating it in a new, much broader, spiritual context. This will, as we see, as it flows together with the dialectical tradition, open up new possibilities, include a polity which is open to participation and even leadership from communities with diverse religious traditions. Rule takes the form of a cultural hegemony embedded in the practice of deliberation, and is *constituted* by the exclusion of any ideological or religious monopoly.

This political theology, furthermore, points towards a specific metaphysics. God is present in the community not by representation by rather by enactment. This is because God does not exist in the same way as other things, indeed does not ex-ist at all—is not outside of Being as a contingent thing which might be represented by another contingent thing. God is, rather, the power of Being as such, which makes all things possible, and is enacted in generativity of any kind, but especially in the struggle for justice, which is simply the struggle for a society which nurtures and ripens being.

An Historical Jesus? The Jesus Movement

If Christianity emerged out of Judaism it must be anti-imperial, right? It is not that simple. Arguments regarding the political valence of the Christian tradition always come down to arguments about Jesus. And regardless of where we situate the historical Jesus in the Jewish political-theological spectrum, no credible scholar could possibly make him out to be an agent of Empire. On the contrary, the current debates place him somewhere between Pharisees (Pawlikowski 1982) and the leadership of the Jewish War (Eisenman 1999).

Increasingly, however, it seems to us that the entire question of the historical Jesus is problematic. This is because in order to determine what the historic Jesus was like, or even if there *was* an historical Jesus, we need first to know what we are looking for. In a social context in which crucified messiahs were a dime a dozen, we need to know which individuals or even types might have contributed to the stories about Jesus. And this already involves setting parameters on "possible historical Jesuses." Is it possible, even likely, that there was a central figure whose life formed the basis for the stories which make up the Gospels and the later cult of the Risen Christ? Of course. *But even asking the question is a theological statement.* The question, or at least the importance granted it by all sides in biblical scholarship, already presupposes that *whatever* this individual was like, his life and teachings are somehow normative for us. *And this itself constitutes Christianity as a religion of abject submission to a single revelation of the divine, in advance of our knowing the content of that revelation and whether or not it is even reasonable—something which is in contradiction with at least historic Catholic teaching, which holds that any possible revelation, while it may stretch us beyond what we know by reason, can never contradict reason.* This is not to suggest that nothing of interest might come from continued scholarship around the question of the historical Jesus. But it will be in spite of the fact that the question itself is incoherent.

This said, there clearly *was* a "Jesus Movement" which predates Pauline Christianity. This movement was, furthermore, powerful enough to warrant persecution and quite possibly a very sophisticated ideological operation aimed at containing and co-opting it. This, in turn, imposes some constraints on what the movement was like. Given the fact that Pilate was ultimately removed by the Roman authorities for being *too* repressive, it is likely not necessary that the movement have been engaged in armed struggle in order for Pilate to crucify its leaders. On the other hand, while many of the teachings attributed to Jesus do, as Pawlikowski demonstrates, fit within the boundaries of a slightly radicalized Hillel School Pharisaism, others have a marked eschatological dimension, and the gospels themselves depict Jesus as engaged a triumphal "march on Jerusalem" in which he is clearly depicted as a messianic pretender. Furthermore, if we are trying to characterize a possible Jesus Movement, as opposed to *the* historical Jesus, then the claim that it might have become involved in armed struggle is actually rather unremarkable. This is because a very large section of the Jewish leadership was, eventually, won over to this position by the time of the Jewish War in 66 CE, including not only the majority of Pharisees, but also many Sadducees. Indeed, Eisenman suggests that the execution of James, who he identifies with the Teacher of Righteousness who figures so prominently in the Qumran documents, may well have been the catalyst for the Jewish War. Along with Maccoby he sees the Ebionites as the survivors of this original Jesus Movement, and argues that they may have flowed into the tradition which eventually gave birth to Islam.

These claims are difficult to verify definitively, but they are consistent with the evidence. In this context the synoptic gospels are best understood as a kind of bridge between Pauline Christianity, which we will analyze shortly, and this revolutionary messianism—an attempt to at once identify with and domesticate the radical ethical demands associated with the revolutionaries Jesus and James, and bring the communities which carried this theology into the fold of the emerging mystery cult of the dying and rising God.

Pauline Christianity

While is nearly impossible to produce a pro-imperial reading of Jesus of Nazareth, it is very difficult to derive an anti-imperial reading of Paul.

Who was Paul of Tarsus and how does he inflect syncretistic mystery cult which was already developing around the collective memory of Jesus? We know, first and foremost, that Paul *was* a Roman agent, or at least an agent of the Herodians, in persecuting the Jesus Movement in the period between the crucifixion and his own "conversion." Second, we know that he remained in significant conflict with the older Christian communities led by Peter and James, who not surprisingly doubted the sincerity of his conversion and rejected his theological innovations. There have been suggestions that Paul was in fact not the Pharisee that he claimed to be but rather a Herodian and that he may have had ties to Herod's family (Maccoby 2003). And it is difficult to imagine that a well-known enemy of the Jesus movement could have "turned" and then operated openly across the eastern part of the empire for several years without support from the imperial authorities. Thus, the claim that Paul was, in fact, a Roman agent, leading a complex ideological operation designed to subvert the Jesus movement and transform it into not just an ideology with which the Empire could live, but into an actual ideology of Empire (Voskuilen and Sheldon 2008), is at least a credible conjecture, even if it cannot be established rigorously.

Furthermore, the fact remains that Paul's gospel is something radically different from any of the main varieties of Judaism which a hypothetical Jesus movement might have taught. Specifically, Paul introduces concepts of divine sovereignty, radical depravity, and universal damnation which are fundamentally alien not only to Judaism but to *all other spiritual traditions on the planet*. Paul begins his letter to the Romans by identifying himself as a *slave of Christ* (Rom 1:1). He then proceeds to frame the problem of sin as primarily one of disobedience to God. Because humanity fails to acknowledge God, God actually *makes them evil* (Rom 1:21–29). As a result, *everyone* merits eternal damnation.

The solution which Paul proposes to this problem is, furthermore, that everyone is made righteous by their faith in Jesus Christ—i.e., in effect by *submission* to the divine sovereign or at least to his representative.

> But now the righteousness of God has been manifested apart from the law, although the law and the prophets bear witness to it, the righteousness of God through faith in Jesus Christ for all who believe. For there is no distinction; since all have sinned and fall short of the glory of God, they are justified by his grace as a gift through the redemption which is in Christ Jesus, whom God put forward as an expiation by his blood, to be received by faith. (Rom 3:21–25)

This reading of the Christian mysteries also has definite political consequences. We have already noted in our earlier works some of the problematic elements of Pauline political theology. First of all, Paul liquidates completely the Jewish aspiration for national liberation. For Paul "there is no distinction" between oppressed Jew and Roman oppressor. The fact that Paul looks forward to the eventual salvation of the Jews (Rom 9–11) does not change this. Their salvation is no longer a *Jewish* salvation no longer a restoration of the people of Israel to the land of Israel to live under Jewish law, but rather just another specific application of the generalized Christian salvation and thus a negation of Jewish national identity.

Second, because justice is done by the merits of another—i.e., Jesus—this reading as well requires no fundamental social transformation. Paul is quite clear that "there is no authority except from God. Therefore, he who resists the authorities resists what God has appointed, and those who resist incur judgment" (Rom 13:12).

Paul does not command the wealthy members of his Corinthian congregation to share their wealth with the poor, as was the custom in the Jerusalem community, but only to refrain from turning the Eucharist into an occasion for conspicuous consumption (1 Cor 11:17–22;

Theissen 1982, pp. 145–74). He does not command Philemon to manumit the Christian slave Onesimus, but only to treat him as a brother in Christ. How one does this to a person one is keeping as a slave may be a bit obscure, but Paul's interest is clearly more in the subjective motive than in the objective relationship. "I preferred to do nothing without your consent so that your goodness might not be by compulsion but of your own free will" (Kyrtatas 1987, pp. 63–71; Phlm 1:14).

Gerd Theissen has characterized Paul social ethics as a kind of "love patriarchalism."

> In these congregations there developed an ethos obviously different from that of the synoptic tradition, the ethos of primitive Christian love-patriarchalism.... This love-patriarchalism takes social differences for granted, but ameliorates them through an obligation of respect and love, an obligation imposed upon those who are socially stronger. From the weaker are required subordination, fidelity and esteem. (Theissen 1982, p. 107)

We have embraced this reading in the past, in large part because it helps to explain how Christianity helped solve at least one of the internal problems of the Roman Empire. After about the second century, as the Empire could no longer expand due to the difficult in fielding and supplying armies across the Sahara, beyond Mesopotamia, and in the dense forests of Northeastern Europe, the supply of prisoners of war and thus of slaves declined, creating a labor shortage in the West. Christianity helped legitimate a transition from slavery to non-chattel labor tied to the land but settled with families. But we are now inclined to see this not so much as inaccurate but as excessively generous. Specifically, *Christianity is able to legitimate the transition from slavery to the colonate because it rejects the civic humanism on which the Republic had been founded and which the Principate at least pretended to defend.* If this civic humanism was profoundly flawed by predicating the freedom of the few on the slavery of the many, Christianity "resolves" this contradiction by *rejecting the ideal of the free human being and engaged citizen entirely. Everyone* under the Dominate, which becomes Christian very quickly, is a servant of the Empire, required to perform the services associated with their rank. Thus, the decurions, members of the local city councils of what under the Principate at least pretended to be autonomous cities protected by Rome were reduced to the status of tax collectors.

Paul, in other words, is the author of a new ideology centered on the absolute sovereignty of a God who demands unconditional submission, under penalty of eternal damnation. Everyone deserves this damnation and we are saved only by God's own sacrifice—read torture and execution—of his Son. This ideology, then, in addition to hegemonizing and neutralizing whatever revolutionary tendencies were present in the messianic enthusiasm which we now associate with the "Jesus Movement," also created a road map for an absolutist Empire unlike any in human history.

We should, perhaps, pause at this point to address what will likely be the two principal objections to our analysis of Paul. First there is the claim advanced by Alain Badiou (Badiou 2003) that Paul is the prophet of a new vision of subjectivity and universalism—of a subject which grasps the Truth independent of both philosophy and the Law, on the basis of a defining "event," i.e., the Resurrection and his own initiation into it on the Road to Damascus. This claim, while presented in the context of an attempt to reground a post-Maoist communism is in fact quite typical of historic Protestant readings of Paul and ignores the fact that Paul's "universalism" is a liquidation of the Jewish *way* of fulfillment of the Law. If baptism into Christ is necessary for salvation then the Jewish way is both unnecessary and insufficient. This is, in fact, the foundational anti-Semitic claim of Christianity. The idea that subjects are constituted by events or rather in response to them, furthermore, and not by reason, is essentially an adaptation of Heidegger's claim that peoples are constituted by events—by various unveilings or advents of Being. And as Michael Millerman has shown (Millerman 2014) it is a focus on the event rather than on difference which divides the Heideggerian Right from the Heideggerian Left. This essentially marks Paul as a precursor—and Badiou as a follower—of the fascist philosopher.

Second, there is the claim advanced by John Dominic Crossan that by assigning to Jesus the titles of God, Lord, and Son of God, Paul the Roman Emperor of them, something which constitutes Paul's movement, like that of Jesus, as a nonviolent revolutionary movement of resistance to Empire. This is simply untenable. We know that even when reassigning divine authority to a rival claimant did unleash a revolution with a popular valence—a common phenomenon in pre-capitalist societies—this way of theorizing the new leadership kept the "revolutionary" society which emerged firmly within the boundaries of sacral monarchic civilization supported by the tributary mode of production. Here, furthermore, the Pauline theorization of the divine as absolute sovereign and the proper human response as radical submission, gives the move a distinctively authoritarian note. This is, in other words, much more reactionary than, say, Chinese peasant movements which identified an imperial pretender as the Son of Heaven *on the condition that he actually cultivated virtue and ruled justly.* This is why, as we will see, as Christianity spread it did not undermine but actually strengthened the Roman Empire.

Christianity and Biopolitics

We have traced out the complex evolution of Christianity and its rise to the status of the official religion of the Empire elsewhere (Mansueto 2016). Suffice it here to say that while there are many Christianities, and while many of them attempt in various ways to reintroduce at least the ethical and sometimes even the political content of the teachings attributed to Jesus in the synoptic Gospels, *the underlying theological problematic of Christianity was defined by Paul and refined by Augustine.* Historic Orthodox and Catholicism with their various syncretisms between Christianity and Hellenism, *Latinitas*, and Celtic and Slavic paganism all soften this dynamic, but they never escape it. The Reformation attempts to purge these syncretisms in favor of an attempt at a "pure" Paulinism, though it was, as we have argued elsewhere, formed profoundly by the core structural dynamic of Germanic society—the relationship between a lord and his retainers—and by the experience of life under emerging capitalism, which meant being at the mercy of an entirely inscrutable sovereign: Capital. But this much is clear: while Catholic and Orthodox Christendom, with their syncretic Christianities, might claim to be Civilizational Empires, Protestant Christianity—along with all of the more Augustinian and Pauline movements within Catholicism—have shown themselves to be organic ideologies of Empire a new kind. Where Sophism and the Caravaka School counseled would-be rulers on how to instrumentalize their populations and *faxue*, under the Qin, actually attempted such a total, instrumentalizing rationalization, *Christianity demands that the individual render himself radically instrumentalizable from within.*

It is here that our analysis connects with but also corrects Agamben's in *The Kingdom and the Glory* (Agamben 2014). Agamben's work is an attempt to "correct or at least complete" Foucault's analysis of power and his claim that in the "modern" world power takes the form of not of sovereignty, control of a territory, but rather of biopolitics, control over people. Where earlier kingdoms and empires claimed a right to exact tribute, taxes, or even the lives of those over whom they exercised sovereignty, modern governments intimately regulate the day to day lives of their subjects.

For Foucault, a "profound transformation" of the "mechanisms of power" in the West is the eclipse of the political by the economical that occurred in the transition from the classical age to modernity (Foucault 1979, p. 136). According to Foucault, the transition marks the transformation of the forms of power relations, from sovereign power to biopower. In the pre-modern world, sovereign power was characterized by a king's right over the life and death of his subjects. Yet, there was no serious attempt by kings to regulate the people who lived in their domains. Sovereign power was "essentially a right of seizure: of things, time, bodies, and ultimately life itself" (Foucault 1979, p. 136). Whereas sovereign power was the power of the king to appropriate property, labor, or the lives of his subjects (a juridical-political form of power), biopower in modern times is characterized by the governance of specific populations as objects (an economic-administrative form of power). In the modern period, governments take an active interest in the lives of the people (i.e., biopolitics) and people have turned from constitutive political body into population: a demographical biological entity (Agamben 2005b). Biopower aims to regulate, manage, and administer the life of the people who live in a nation state. It is a regulatory mechanism of power that allows the state to administrate and monitor the nation through institutions such as health care, education, tax collection, and military drafting (Beltramini 2020).

Agamben's "correction" of Foucault consists in arguing that this transition was mediated by the Christian doctrine of the Trinity, which encodes in the idea of God both an ontological moment, God's *Being*, which represents transcendent, sovereign power, and an economic moment—the relationships between the various members of the Trinity—which represents immanent, economic power.

> There are "two broadly speaking political paradigms," both . . . derive from Christian theology . . . in a broad, antinomous but functionally connected way: political theology, which founds in the one God the transcendence of sovereign power, and economic theology, which substitutes for this the idea of an *oikonmia*, conceived as an immanent order—domestic and not political in the strict sense—as much of the divine life as of the human one. From the first derives political philosophy and the

modern theory of sovereignty; from the second, modern biopolitics up to the current triumph of economy and government over every other aspect of social life. (Agamben 2011b, p. 13)

This is an interesting claim and at one level it has some merit. The doctrine of the Trinity is fundamentally a way of theorizing just how God can be One in Being (Being can only be One) and at the same time integrate the difference which the doctrine of the Incarnation presupposes. In the fully developed form of the doctrine, the three persons of the Trinity share a common essence, which is Being as such, but different relations. But whether or not this doctrine leads to what Foucault calls biopolitics depends on one's Christology and Soteriology. If one upholds the historic Catholic doctrine as explained by Thomas *and follows its internal logic consistently,* which even Thomas did not, the doctrine of the Trinity need not imply biopolitics. For Thomas the incarnation does not involve any change on the part of God, but rather a change in the way humanity relates to God—first and foremost in the person of Christ (Aquinas 1272/1952, 1.39–43). Specifically, Jesus, by fulfilling the Law (loving God with God's own love) Jesus becomes connatural with God and thus undergoes *theosis.* But this is only an *accidental theosis* and thus no different from that promised to human beings who cultivate successfully the theological virtues. *But then Jesus is not "True God from True God," not the Power of Being as Such and the Incarnation is really no different than any other form of divine presence, such as the Shekinah in Judaism.* This is why Thomas could not follow his own logic consistently. It would have resulted in an obvious departure from the historic teachings of the Church.

It is this contradiction which Augustinian theologians exploited and which led ultimately to the Reformation. Thus, Luther teaches that Christ lives in the believer in such a way that the believer is not more. Thus, the demand of some High Calvinisms, such as that of Samuel Hopkins, that in order to be saved one must be willing to be damned for the greater glory of God. And so it is not, strictly speaking, the doctrine of the Trinity itself which leads to biopolitics, but rather the doctrine of radical Divine Sovereignty which has as its ideal a man who is so utterly inhabited by God as to not really exist anymore, and which understands salvation as requiring that Divine Sovereignty to so utterly hegemonize humanity's interior, subjective life as to obliterate it entirely.[2]

2. It is often claimed that Augustine introduced the whole idea of human subjectivity and interiority as we understand it (Brown 2000). But if that is the case it was only in order to create a new domain for divine sovereignty to conquer. While previously it

If this understanding of God sounds suspiciously like our account of the current trajectory of Capital, which seeks to liberate itself once and for all from the proletariat . . . well then, our argument has been successful.

Dar-al-Islam

Dar-al-Islam presents us with an entirely different set of issues. In Islam we see realized the potential which at least a portion of the Christian Left wants to see in the Jesus Movement, so much so that some elements in the Muslim community have begun to identity Eisenman's "Jamesian" Christianity as one of the sources on which emerging Islam drew.

Contemporary scholarship (Cook and Crone 1977) argues that Islam emerged as a form of Arab resistance to Roman hegemony, which had the Arabs from access to trade roots, undercutting one of the few economic strategies open to the arid and inhospitable Arabian Peninsula. Still organized largely on a tribal basis, with the majority engaged in pastoral nomadism supplemented by trade, the Arabs lacked a cohesive political structure which might have allowed them to unite and resist Roman power. Working largely off of Greek sources, they argue that the initial preaching of Mohammed, whose historicity they do not question, was essentially a Jewish-influenced messianism aimed at uniting all of the Semitic peoples to throw off Roman (Byzantine) hegemony and to liberate Jerusalem. Because of the centrality of the idea of a common Abrahamic heritage, they call this early movement Hagarism, after Sarah's handmaid who was the mother of Ishmael, legendary father of the Arabs. Some historical sources suggest that Mohammed lived much longer than Islamic tradition acknowledges and actually participated in the liberation of Jerusalem. That done, however, the Arabs soon fell out with the Jews and began trying to carve out for themselves an independent religious identity, drawing on elements of Jacobite and Nestorian Christianity, Samaritanism, and Persian and Greek philosophical traditions as well as the Rabbinic Judaism which formed their point of departure. "Islam" emerged only gradually as various groups vied for leadership. These included varying types of religious scholars on the one hand (*'ulemma* or

---

would have been inconceivable to think that we would not only obey our sovereign, but actually will what the sovereign wills, now it is required that we will against our own will and ultimately, in the fully developed Hopkintonian version of this theology, find salvation precisely in willing our own damnation.

jurists, *mutakallim* or theologians, and practitioners of *falasafa* or philosophy) and generals on the other, as well as groups claiming descent from or designation by the Prophet or his kin and/or companions according to varying tribal traditions.

Whether or not we accept the details of this account, the broad outlines make sense. For one thing, had the movement not had a strong apocalyptic tone, it is difficult to imagine that the problem of succession, which drove later Islamic politics, would not have been better resolved, given the otherwise highly effective and pragmatic character of Islamic political strategy. More broadly, as one moves through the plethora of socioreligious movements and political-theological tendencies we meet during the first centuries of Islam, all of the various influences identified by Cook and Crone can indeed be identified, as Crone points out in her later book on Islamic politics, *God's Rule* (Crone 2004).

This said, it seems to me that Cook and Crone miss, or perhaps merely understate, the distinctive feature of Islam by comparison to the other Semitic monotheisms. Where Judaism grew up in an environment of political disenfranchisement, and thus had to find a way to realize the law without political power, and where most variants of Christianity traded the gave up early on the idea of actually building the Kingdom of God on earth, and redefined messianism in an otherworldly direction, thus laying the groundwork for an alliance with the Roman Empire and its successor states, Islam actually joined, from the very beginning, a religious orientation centered on realizing the law with the political power necessary to actually do so, or at least to attempt to do so. In this sense, the defining feature of Islam is no so much its radical monotheism but rather *al-amr bi'l-ma'ruf wa'nahy 'an al-munkar*: commanding right and forbidding wrong.

It is not surprising, therefore, that both some contemporary Christian biblical scholars, such as Eisenman (Eisenman 1999) and some Muslim thinkers (Ismaili Gnosis 2019), make a connection between emerging Islam and "Ebionite" or Jamesian Christianity, which affirmed Jesus as *moshiach* but not as divine and which rejected the entire Pauline mystery cult out of hand. This does *not*, to be sure, imply that we should overlook the other factors which Cook and Crone identify as feeding into emerging Islam: indigenous Arab monotheisms, direct Jewish influence, Persian influence both from the vantage point of theology and that of politics. Nor should we underestimate the extent to which Islam emerged as a way to unite the Arab tribes against Byzantium, or the extent to its success in this regard led rapidly to the emergence of what can only be called an empire. *All* sociohistorical formations are multiply overdetermined and polyvalent both politically and theologically. But Islam *did* capture the political theological niche which Christianity abandoned when it was hegemonized by the Empire by Paul and the Church fathers.

In this sense, *Dar-al-Islam* can make a much better and cleaner case for itself as a *Civilizational* or even as a *Revolutionary Empire*. But this there are still contradictions which emerge from the embrace of divine sovereignty. The struggle over the succession to the Prophet opened up into a struggle between the relative importance of having a leadership which was actually just and pious, and of being able to build and exercise power effectively enough to command right and forbid wrong. Two positions emerged. The first is, very broadly, the Shia position, the second the Sunni position, though there are countless overlaps and crossovers between them. The dominant Sunni position logically entailed Empire and even global Empire, even if the resulting structures were vastly more just and progressive than almost any others in human history. And when Christendom and then Capital won the struggle for global hegemony, many within *Dar-al-Islam* blamed the syncretism between Islam, Hellenism, Persian culture, and other traditions for their failure. The result has been the emergence, beginning with the Wahabi movement, of a fundamentalist Islam which effectively mimics Protestantism in purging everything except what it understands as the core of Islam: submission. The Shia, on the other hand, have had difficulty building enduring states of any kind. This is not surprising when on allows the only possible legitimate ruler is the Imam of the Age, who must be effectively infallible and without sin. When they have it has been by becoming more Sunni—as in the case of the Islamic Republican movement, which extends legitimacy to the *ulema,* moving from the advisory role they have in most Sunni states to effective dictatorship. Where they have remained true to their core convictions, they have ceased to be a state, as in the case of the Nizari Imamate, which functions more nearly as a global philanthropy than as a state and is even less state-like than the Catholic Church.

Alterimperialism

The question, of course, is what these historical forms of empire have to do with what we are calling alterimperialism: the resurgence of territorial empire under late capitalism, just when it seemed that territorial states of any kind were fading from significance. Here Lukacs's analysis of the political trajectory of Capital is very helpful. Early on it allied itself with the humanistic project, especially in its liberal and democratic forms and argued for capitalism as a force not just for growth and development, but also for freedom. But after about 1848 democratic demands came to the fore and the working classes attempted to take the field on their own. The contradictions of capitalism, meanwhile, began to manifest themselves, requiring a turn towards imperialism in the Leninist sense—building colonial empires to which they could export capital and receive a higher rate of return than they could in higher technology sectors at home. At this point the bourgeoisie retreated into what Lukacs calls the "indirect apologetic form capitalism: the irrationalist ideology centered on the will to power of the sort developed by Nietzsche and perfected by Heidegger" (Lukacs 1953/1980).

We will, however, argue that Lukacs's analysis needs to be modified and extended in a number of respects. First, Lukacs assumes, with the communist movement of his time, that Empire can only be imperialist in the Leninist sense and that under capitalism it is fundamentally a European phenomenon, as it certainly was in his time. England, France, and the United States had successfully colonized most of Asia, Africa, and the Americas; Spain and Portugal were looking to protect what remained of their once vast empires, and Germany, Italy and Japan were looking to militarize their populations in order to gain the empires they needed in order to manage the internal contradictions of their developing capitalist economies. Second, Lukacs assumes that socialism is by its nature antiimperialist, as again appeared to be the case during his time. The Communist Party of China had proved itself in the struggle against Japanese imperialism and after the Allied Victory and the collapse of the Popular Front, the Soviet Union turned its attention to aiding the national liberation movements struggling against British, French, and US imperialism.

It is in this context that he quite correctly reads Nietzsche and Heidegger as part of a broader irrationalist tradition leading to the emergence of fascist ideologies. For Nietzsche morality, especially the sort of egalitarianism which defined the liberal, democratic, and socialist movements was itself just a manifestation of the will to power which as the underlying driving force in the universe, holding back the few and the superior from the full realization of their potential. For Heidegger the whole project of an explanatory deductive theory which he labelled "metaphysics" or "ontotheology" was simply a mechanism for exerting technopolitical control over the planet as a whole. And socialism, however antimetaphysical and antitheological it claimed to be was part of this ontotheological tradition. Heidegger's theory of history as a series of spontaneous "unveilings" of Being as different peoples found their "god" put the rise of Hitler on essentially the same level as that of Moses or Buddha and effectively legitimated the Nazi state for which Heidegger, misunderstanding the way in which cadre parties work, aspired to be the chief philosopher.

What Lukacs missed was that many of the colonized peoples—who were, really and truly, suffering under European colonialism—were themselves historically part of large territorial empires: what Coker and Jiang call Civilizational States. And what the Communist Parties of the Soviet Union and China and other countries liberated from colonialism during the postwar period did overlapped significantly with what fascist parties did: leveraging nationalism broadly understood in order to win support for rapid industrialization and militarization in order to defend, acquire, or this case restore Empire. This is not to say that there were no differences. Socialism liquidated any independent bourgeoisie and partially absorbed it into the state. Fascism retained this bourgeoisie while both relying on it for support and trying to contain any independent initiative on its part. Hitler committed intentional genocide; Stalin killed millions as well but did not *aim* to do so. The vast majority of his victims, as of Mao's were "collateral damage" in the struggle for rapid industrialization. Those actually imprisoned and executed were those who posed a direct political threat.

It is for this reason that we maintain a distinction between Left and Right Heideggerianism and consider the Left form in a later chapter. Here we want to draw attention to the principal Rightist forms of the ideology. Of these the most important is Alexander Dugin's *Fourth Political Theory*. Dugin distinguishes his theory from liberalism, communism, and fascism based largely on the way in which it defines the subject of political action. Where for liberalism the subject of political action is the individual, for communism the class and for fascism the race or nation, for the Fourth Political Theory it is *Dasein* itself. On the one hand this is simply an opportunistic move to allow him to distinguish a position which by nearly all definitions is fascist from historic fascism and from Nazism in particular. But it also reveals the sharp distinction between alterimperialism and the other ideologies of the new Right which we discussed above. Specifically, by theorizing politics in terms of a *subject* Dugin already situates himself within the humanistic secular tradition he seems to want to reject. This tradition, we will remember, is defined by the aim of creating a political subject which can make humanity the master of its own destiny, whether as individual, *demos, ethnos,* class, etc (Dugin 2012, p. 34). He also identifies *space* as one of the principal defining features of *Dasein* and thus of any politics which has *Dasein* as its subject.

Despite Dugin's attempts to distinguish his Fourth Political Theory from fascism, however, we need to remember that for Heidegger Being unveils itself to various *peoples* as they discover their "gods." It may shift the role of subject from the people as *ethnos* to the Being that reveals itself through various peoples, but the result of this move is, if anything, to shift the resulting ethnopopulism in an even more authoritarian direction.

While Dugin's Fourth Political Theory is the most theoretically developed alterimperialist theory, we can cite at least two other movements which reflect a similar orientation. First, the *Hindutva* movement shares roots in German Romanticism. Narendra Modi's development of *Hindutva* is a strong cultural nationalism which attempts to strengthen Hindu identity in order to hold together an Indian state which is subcontinental in extent and the peoples of which share very little in terms of a common culture or experience (Patnaik 1993; Casolari 2000; Leidig 2020).

Second, Islamic fundamentalism shares similar roots. This is apparent especially in the ideas of thinks like Mohammed Rashid Rida and Sayyid Qutb. In both cases we see a turn towards what has come to be known as Islamic Fundamentalism primarily as a way of coming to terms with European imperialism. Rashid Rida was among the first in the Islamic world to attribute the decline if Muslim power not just to European imperialism and the military and economic power which came from European science and technology, but also to Islam's syncretism with Hellenic philosophy and to the spread of Sufism and Shiism. He turned to the emerging Salafi trend not primarily by theological conviction but rather because he saw it as a solution to the problem of Muslim decline. Qutb, similarly, moved from a strongly secular identity by way of influence from French physician and Nazi sympathizer Alexis Carrel, who argued that Western civilization was decadent and favored the machine over "soul and spirit," and argued for the euthanasia of criminals and of the criminally insane (Calvert 2000, 2009).

We should point out that this orientation is sharply different from both the *Traditionalism* and the *Dark Enlightenment*. For Catholic Traditionalism, if we were to insist on using the humanistic language of subjectivity, the subject of politics would be God as absolute sovereign, with the King as his representative, For Perennialist Traditionalism it would be Being (*not* Dasein, or the "being-there" which Heidegger identifies with humanity) or the One, or Brahman or the Tao or Tien. For Identarian Traditionalism it would be the people as *ethnos,* but in a radically particularist rather than imperial way For the *Dark Enlightenment* the subject of politics is the unit of natural selection: gene, organism, collective, practice.

The question remains, however, why the Right has had such an appeal over the past decades, and why that appeal is growing. Part of the answer lies the fundamental contradictions between Capital and the human civilizational project generally and the humanistic ideal, in its liberal, democratic, and socialist forms, in particular—contradictions which the Center has tried—and failed—to resolve.

4

Why the Center Cannot Hold

It is quite impossible to explain the rise of the Right apart from an analysis of why the political and theological "Center" which was hegemonic during the postwar period has entered a crisis nearly as significant as that of the Soviet Bloc in the 1980s and is no longer able to defend itself against attacks from both the Right and the Left.

By the "Center" we mean that section of the political spectrum which accepts the humanistic secular ideal—creating a political subject which can make humanity the master of its own destiny—in its liberal and to a certain extent in its democratic form, along with (on its Left-leaning side) some elements of the historical materialist critique of capitalism, while rejecting the need to transcend capitalism entirely. At one level this already explains why the position of the Center is *ultimately* untenable: human self-determination is incompatible with the requirement that we sell our labor power in order to survive. At the same time, this Center was hegemonic for a very long time. It is, indeed, possible to argue that the entire lifetime of the United States as an independent state was dominated by a politics of the Center, even if it was mostly that of the Center Right. And the same is true for most of Europe since the latter part of the nineteenth century. Social liberalism, furthermore, which accepts *de facto* some elements of the socialist critique of capitalism, furthermore, was dominant for much of the middle part of the twentieth century. And the underlying contradiction in the position of the Center expresses itself differently depending on what particular tendency we are considering. It is thus worth analyzing in some depth "Why the Center Cannot Hold."

We will begin by tracing the genealogy of the humanistic secular ideal in its liberal, democratic, and socialist forms. We will then look at the principal trends which have made up the political and theological center over the course of the past two centuries, each of which represents a particular way in which core variants of the humanistic secular ideal engaged the realities of capitalism and, in some cases other *ways of being*. We will conclude with an assessment of the prospects for the Center in the present period, and will argue that social and communitarian liberalisms do in fact have a future, but only as part of a *longue durée* strategy for transcending capitalism.

The Genealogy of the Humanistic Secular Ideal

Liberalism

Radical Aristotelianism

Humanistic secularism in its liberal, democratic, and socialist forms has, like capitalism, roots in the Middle Ages, and more specifically in the teachings of the "Radical Aristotelians" or "Latin Averroists"—Almaric of Bena, David of Dinant, and Siger of Brabant. In order to understand this claim it is necessary first to clarify the principal doctrines of this school. First, they upheld, along with Aristotle and most of his non-Christian commentators, the eternity of the world, a conclusion which flowed quite naturally from the Aristotelian doctrine of the unmoved mover. If the unmoved mover was eternal, and drew the world into being by its attractive power, then the world must naturally have been in existence as long as the unmoved mover itself—forever. Even Thomas conceded that this claim could be rejected only on the basis of revelation. Second, they upheld the unity of the Agent, and in some cases the Potential Intellect. As we have seen above, in our analysis of the Islamic commentators, this doctrine radically undercuts human individuality and undermines the philosophical basis for belief in anything like personal immortality. Individuation comes exclusively as a result of our materiality, which is precisely what are charged with overcoming. For followers of Ibn Sina, we might obtain a kind of union with the Agent Intellect in—a very imperfect—contemplation of the divine as it is reflected in the material reality of the sublunar realm. For followers of Ibn Rusd, even that seems difficult to imagine. Material civilizational progress represents not only our natural *telos* but the outer limit of our potential. Human beings are, in the end, simply information collection devices and manual laborers for the Agent Intellect, sharing in its work of creation, and then dying. As individuals, we mean nothing. Third, lacking a coherent doctrine of connatural knowledge Latin Averroism cannot trust that ordinary people can achieve wisdom, and so casts itself in the role of an esoteric truth reserved for the elite—or revolutionary vanguard—while the people are led to an approximate truth by means of the imaginative language of religion. We will see this spirit replicated in modern dialectics—both that of Hegel and that of Marx, Engels, and their interpreters. Finally, we see in the Radical Aristotelians a bit more variation in terms of the way in which they understand the nature of God than we do in earlier Jewish, Christian, or Islamic commentators.

> The primary, unformed matter contains potential forms as "seeds." Forms are therefore not extrinsic to but immanent in matter. If the forms were to come to matter from the outside, this would be a sort of *creatio ex nihilo*. The forms are as eternal and uncrated as is matter. God creates neither matter nor form. The task of the "prime mover" is to convert possible forms into actual forms, i.e., to develop the seeds contained in matter . . . Prime matter is universal potency that hides the seeds of the forms; the prime mover does nothing but turn potency into act. (Trachtenberg 1957, p. 66)

Among the Latin Averroists, this position is documented for Siger of Brabant, and later by Giordano Bruno. Most, however, developed interpreted Aristotelianism in a much more radically pantheistic way. For some this meant idealism. Almaric of Bena, for example, reasoning that it was form, not matter, which characterized actual being, Almaric argued that in a very real sense everything is form, and thus implicitly, at least, everything is God (Dahm 1988, p. 94). David of Dinant, on the other hand, argued that since God is the source of all things, God must *be* prime matter.

> The philosophy of David of Dinant is . . . a materialist pantheism. . . . The basic ground of this philosophy is the pantheistic unity of the material, spiritual, and divine principles . . . this unity lies not in the empirical world, and not in the reason of the individual, and not in the matter of single things, but in a higher realm, where reason *as such* melds into God and "prime matter." (Trachtenberg 1957, pp. 96–97)

From Averroism to Liberalism

Radical Aristotelianism points forward toward dialectical materialism, but it does so by a circuitous path. The Augustinian Reaction effectively destroyed Radical Aristotelianism as an independent philosophical tendency, though it survived, interestingly enough, at the University of Padova. Many of its concerns were, however, translated into the Neo-Platonizing Humanism of the Renaissance. And there was, in fact, a direct line between the Jewish Aristotelianism of Moshe ben Maimon and the rationalism Benedict Spinoza, who conserves and advances the concerns of this trend in a new ideological context. And ultimately, of course, Spinoza's project leads to that of Hegel, Marx, and their interpreters.

Initially, the humanistic intelligentsia was forced to take a step back and abandon any sort of global political project in the Gramscian sense (Gramsci 1949c) and instead try to protect its interests within the context of what remained of the city-state commune. This was made possible, in large part, due to the unusual cluster of social conditions which existed in Renaissance Italy. The stalemate between the Papacy and the Empire had created a context in which networks of autonomous city states could develop governed largely by powerful merchants and bankers but sometimes with significant participation of the artisan class. These cities were inserted into the Silk Road trade networks in a fairly privileged way. The papacy maintained its legitimacy in this context in large part by positioning itself as a patron of human self-cultivation and civilizational progress (especially when viewed against background of the much darker visions of Luther and Calvin). This structural configuration in turn served as the basis in experience for a focus on meaning and human self-cultivation without, however, clearly defining the relationship between human self-cultivation either popular power or humanity's ultimate spiritual aims. The Renaissance humanist, in effect, left latent and implicit any claims against secular or spiritual monarchy. Even so, those Renaissance humanists who pressed crypto-Averroist themes most consistently—e.g., Giordano Bruno—did not fare well in spite of the support of powerful secular patrons.

This said, many of the broader themes of the Latin Averroists were taken up by the Renaissance humanists. This is true first of all with respect to method. Like ibn Rusd, the humanists of the Renaissance devoted themselves to careful textual scholarship, and developed an "originalist hermeneutic" which privileged the author's meaning over that of commentators. On the one hand, this tended to diminish the importance of ibn Rusd himself, and of the other Islamic and Jewish Aristotelians, as a source for understanding Aristotle. But it represented the first step towards the development of the historical-critical method which has dominated religious studies in the modern era and which has certainly favored rationalizing interpretations with a broadly Averroist flavor.

But the substantive concerns of the Averroists also found expression, albeit in a very different philosophical vernacular, within the context of Renaissance humanism. Specifically, Renaissance philosophers such as Pico della Mirandola and Giordano Bruno, translated the Averroist focus on human self-cultivation and civilizational progress into the language the Neo-Platonic revival. This represents, in many ways a development parallel to the reorientation of scientific activity towards mathematical formalization following the Condemnations of 1270 and 1277 which set the stage, as we have argued, for the Scientific Revolution.

The most direct line between Radical Aristotelianism and modern dialectics, however, by-passes Christian philosophy entirely. Idit Dobbs-Weinstein (Dobbs-Weinstein 2001, forthcoming) has traced out the lineage linking Spinoza to the Radical Aristotelians by way of Gersonides. Yirmiyahu Yovel (Yovel 2001), for his part, has stressed the *converso* milieu as the context which nurtured this tradition. It is not hard to see how the cross fertilization of Jewish inner-worldliness and the Christian focus on divinization would trace a pathway from ibn Rusd through Spinoza to Hegel and beyond.

It is, furthermore, clear that Spinoza, despite his fascination with the results of the scientific revolution, had deep roots in the medieval Aristotelian and specifically Averroist tradition. Spinoza frames the question of God not quantitatively, as perfect being, in the manner of Descartes, but rather qualitatively, in terms of the problem of substance, which for Spinoza is that which can exist on its own—i.e., Necessary Being. At the same time, he makes a very subtle move which opens up the way for a secularist transformation of the Aristotelian tradition. Human beings are but modes of this one substance, the product of intersecting networks of relationships. Our only hope for beatitude consists in identification with the whole, i.e., with God. This can be read in the manner of a very sober philosophical spirituality in the manner of Maimonides or ibn Rusd, for whom human beings found fulfillment in identification with the Agent Intellect, simply adapted to the realities of a post-Copernican cosmology, in the context of which the idea of the Agent Intellect no longer made much literal sense. But it can also be read as a challenge: to develop to or at least towards the point at which we are in fact identical with the single substance.

It is instructive in this context to consider the difference between Spinoza and two liberal philosophers who operated within a broadly Christian problematic: Locke and Kant. Indeed, the comparison makes clear the sense in which Christianity distorted the humanistic ideal—and in two different and contradictory ways: one which transforms liberalism from a step on the road from metaphysical dialectics and civic humanism to historical dialectics and communism into *the* bourgeois ideology *par excellence,* and another, even as with imprisons the claims of justice within the prison of bourgeois right subtly introduces into the dialectical tradition a messianism which, when justice escapes that prison, turns around and enslaves it to an impossible utopianism.

Liberalism as the Heir of Radical Aristotelianism

But first let us look at Spinoza. Spinoza begins with a number of definitions and axioms and—skipping over the *cogito* entirely—proceeds through analysis of the idea of substance (something which can be conceived in and through itself, independently of any other conception) to a proof of the existence of God and of the identity between God and the universe. All particular systems are simply modifications of God; thought and extension are those two of the infinite divine attributes of which we are able to conceive (Spinoza 1675/1955). This is, in effect, an attempt to draw out fully the implications of the Avicennist and Thomistic distinction between Necessary and Possible Being for the Aristotelian concept of substance. Ultimately only Necessary Being—i.e., God—exists in and through itself.

How do we know that "substance" exists at all? In one place, Spinoza seems to depart from the Aristotelian tradition, which argues from existence and motion and presents instead an analytic argument which reflects the spirit of modern rationalism: that existence belongs to the notion of substance (Spinoza 1677/1955, 1.7). Later, however, he acknowledges that we know that something exists because our bodies are modified in certain ways by other bodies (Spinoza 1677/1955, 2.18). Our knowledge of the universe, in other words, derives from sensation of finite particulars, from which we infer the existence of God.

Contrary to the claims of Deleuze and others who have followed him (Deleuze and Guttari 1987; Deleuze 1994), Spinoza's doctrine of Being is not univocal but rather equivocal, along with the rest of the Jewish tradition. When Spinoza says that everything that exists is a mode or modification of a single Substance, which is God he is not saying that both God and the modes are beings, but rather that, as Stephen Houlgate has argued (Wolfendale 2009) that God is Being and the modes are something radically different from Being.

Spinoza's *Ethics* is first and foremost an ethics of seeking Being. "To act absolutely in obedience to virtue is in us the same thing as to act, to live, or preserve one's being (these terms are identical in meaning) in accordance with the dictates of reason on the basis of seeking what is useful to one's self" (Spinoza 1677/1955, 4.24). Lest we read this as a kind of hedonism or ethics of power, we should note that the highest expression of this drive is the intellectual love of God. "The highest endeavor of the mind, and the highest virtue, is to understand things by virtue of the third kind of knowledge" (Spinoza 1677/1955, 5.25). By the "third kind of knowledge" Spinoza means an intellectual intuition in which we grasp the very essence of God. "The intellectual love of the mind toward God is that very love of God whereby God loves himself" (Spinoza 1677/1955, 5.36).

This is, of course, very close—at least in the language used—to the Thomistic concept of connatural knowledge of God. But for Spinoza this is possible on the base of natural reason alone.

There has been considerable debate regarding the political implications of this vision—and this in spite of the fact that Spinoza left not one but two political treatises: *Theological-Political Treatise* and *Political Treatise* (Eckstein 1944; Den Uyl 1983; Feuer 1987; Negri 1991; Prokhovnik 2002; Garrett 2003; Rosenthal 1998, 2003; Miller 2012). This confusion is largely because the political context within which Spinoza wrote was rather different from those which informed most liberal political philosophy. Spinoza wrote in the context of the exiled Sephardic community of the Low Countries and more specifically in the context of his own excommunication from that community, which coincided with the brutal repression of the Arminian or Remonstrant Party by the Calvinist majority there after the Synod of Dordt. Within this context, his fundamental concern is the same as that of the Latin Averroists who sided with the Holy Roman

Emperor (a monarch but not their own) against their local bishop (an ally of the French state) in an effort to secure the freedom *of the philosopher* against the authority of the clerical intelligentsia (in this case the Calvinist clergy of the United Provinces).

The result is a political philosophy which is often compared to that of Hobbes, with perhaps a bit more opening to democracy and a stronger argument for religious toleration. But Spinoza himself is clear that his politics differs from that of Hobbles in at least one important respect.

> With regard to political theory, the difference between Hobbes and myself, which is the subject of your inquiry, consists in this, that I always preserve the natural right in its entirety [*ego naturale jus semper sartum tectum conservo*], and I hold that the sovereign power in a State has right over a subject only in proportion to the excess of its power over that of a subject. (Spinoza 1674)

This position is dictated by Spinoza's metaphysics.

> By the right and order of nature I merely mean the rules determining the nature of each individual thing by which we conceive it is determined naturally to exist and to behave in a certain way. For example fish are determined by nature to swim and big fish to eat little ones, and therefore it is by sovereign natural right that fish have possession of the water and that big fish eat small fish. For it is certain that nature, considered wholly in itself, has a sovereign right to do everything that it can do, i.e., the right of nature extends as far as its power extends...since the universal power of the whole of nature is nothing but the power of all individual things together, it follows that each individual thing has the sovereign right to do everything that it can do, or the right of each thing extends so far as its determined power extends. (Spinoza 1677/2007, p. 16)

One might also add that when Spinoza defends the right of every being to build and exercise power to the full extent of its capacity, he is does not envision as a result of this a Hobbesian war of all against all, but rather an imperfect approach to an ideal in which everyone realizes to a greater or lesser degree their potential for the intellectual love of God. But it is, above all, for Spinoza, the freedom of the philosopher, who most closely approaches this ideal, that matters most. Religious authorities are to be subordinated to the civil authorities, and the civil authorities counseled to respect the freedom of conscience, not so people can get on with the business of making money unhindered by spiritual concerns, but so that the higher spirituality of the philosopher can be defended against interference by backward and superstitious clerics.

This is, clearly, an ultimately untenable position. Philosophy, which is always and only a minority movement, has no hope for autonomy unless it is able to find allies, either within the clergy or among the people (or both). The next step in the development of humanistic secularism will be precisely this search for allies.

This said, we should note that it is Spinoza, more than any other philosopher, who makes the strongest claim for *rational* autonomy. There are others who claim more for reason, and others who claim more for individual autonomy, but no one claims that the rationally autonomous individual on the road to full realization through intellectual love of God retains full sovereignty in proportion to their actual power. In this sense Spinoza represents the most advanced expression of the liberal form of the humanistic ideal.

Bourgeois Liberalism

Locke and Kant, on the other hand, chain liberalism to the bourgeois project which is, ultimately, autonomy for those who have capital and instrumentalization for those who do not.

Let us consider Locke first. Locke must be understood in the context of the distinctive Anglo-American Road to capitalist development. The development of capitalism in England and North America proceeded along what, from a global perspective, must be regarded as very unusual lines. Throughout most parts of Europe, the peasant revolts of the late tributary period were put down, and a long period of feudal reaction ensued. Much the same was true throughout most of Asia, Africa, and the Americas, where European conquerors put down local revolts and strengthened indigenous tributary structures as a mechanism of surplus extraction and social control (Anderson 1974). In England, on the other hand, the peasant revolts, particularly the revolt of 1381, led to a partial victory, and by the end of the fourteenth century, the peasants had succeeded in eliminating most strictly feudal obligations, and in significantly increasing their total share of the social product. In response to this situation landowners began a long struggle to rationalize agricultural production. Many converted from grain production, which was relatively labor intensive, to wool production, which required fewer hands. Others began to implement new and more sophisticated techniques for cultivating grain. Implementation of these techniques required a smaller and more disciplined work force, with the result that in grain growing areas as well peasants were run off their land. Over a period which lasted nearly four hundred years the greater part of the English peasantry was gradually driven from the land, and transformed into a massive agricultural and industrial proletariat.

When the English conquered North America, they continued this process. The indigenous peoples of the continent actively resisted the imposition of forced labor, and so they were driven off their land, pressed westward, and eventually exterminated, opening up the continent to capitalist development. In the Southern part of the continent, they imported African slaves. The northern part of the continent, on the other hand, served as an outlet for English, and later European peasants, displaced by the penetration of capitalist relations into the countryside.

The result was the famous "triangle trade," a powerful engine for the primitive accumulation of capital. English traders captured or purchased slaves from Africa, which they sold to the sugar, tobacco, and later the cotton planters of the Caribbean basin. These planters in turn sold them agricultural raw materials, which the traders then carried to the industrial centers of England, or later the American northeast. The finished goods—rum, tobacco products, textiles—as well as guns and other manufactured goods were then resold to African slave traders or Caribbean planters. Grain farmers in New England, and later in the Northwest Territories, kept workers and slaves alike supplied with cheap food, and provided a secondary but growing market for manufactured goods. Capital was accumulated primarily by the industrialists, plantation agriculture being resistant to rationalization, and the planter culture oriented towards high levels of luxury consumption.

It is in the context of this distinctively Anglo-American experience that Locke's theory emerged. Locke's political theory builds on a moderate empiricism which allows inferences from sense data, something which in turn allows us to demonstrate the existence of God using something like a cosmological argument (Locke 1690/1995). Human beings, because we are created by God, are His property. We must not, therefore, harm others or restrict their freedom. Indeed, we cannot even dispose freely of our own lives and freedom. *Our very condition of servitude towards God thus defines our liberty with respect to other human beings.* God also created us with the capacity to make things ourselves. By mixing our labor and thus our lives with the soil (or any other raw material) it becomes our own, subject to no higher claim but God's. Government is instituted to protect and defend these fundamental rights to life, liberty, and property, and may do nothing for any other purpose. It is to natural rights theory, and not to natural law, which most US "conservatives," who use natural law language, such as Supreme Court Justice Clarence Thomas, actually owe their allegiance (Locke 1690/1967).

Two points are in order here. First, for Locke, freedom is something that exists only in relationship to property. Were we not God's property— i.e., God's slaves—it is not clear that we would enjoy any rights at all. And while there are rights to life and liberty which derive from our status as theodules, freedom is clearly ordered towards the accumulation and enjoyment of property. Second, while nominally excluding the enslavement of some human beings by others, Locke actually defines an "exception" which, while it seems small and technical is actually fundamental to legitimation strategies for the enslavement of essentially all colonized peoples. Locke says that anyone who commits a crime worthy of death can instead be enslaved for whatever term the offended party (in the state of nature or in a state of war between two peoples) or the government (in civil society) sees fit. While Locke never specifically draws out this implication, he did help draft the *Constitutions of the Carolina Colonies*, which permit slavery, so we can only assume that he regarded that slavery as legitimate and those enslaved to be in a state of hereditary criminality and thus subject to *hereditary penal servitude in perpetuity*. Thus the effective outlawing of African Americans, which is one of the principal ways in which racism works to this day in the United States. And, since crime and the state of war were not, in this context, rigorously distinguished, it being assumed that a liberal state would wage war only in defense of natural rights and thus against natural rights criminals, *all* of the global adversaries of the liberal state were, at least potentially outlawed. Thus the *de facto* criminalization of slaves, ex-slaves, and their descendants, indigenous peoples resisting conquest, undocumented migrants, revolutionaries, etc.

It is easy to see Locke's doctrine as a development of the Hellenistic Roman attempt to ground the freedom of some in the slavery of others. But actually it is much worse. Slavery, for Locke, is the normative condition for human beings, the natural product of our status as creatures. At the same time, those who, by their submission to radical instrumentalization themselves become participants in God's creative activity, subduing the earth and improving it, stand in the place of God in relation to those who do not so submit or who are even less productive. This is, as we noted above, fundamentally to constituting a global capitalist *caste* system, and specifically to defining at least one group of outcastes.

* * *

Kant was working in the very different context of the emerging Prussian Empire which, especially under Frederick the Great, encouraged freedom of conscience and expression as well as education, but which remained well behind England in the pace of capitalist development, which would take place only a century later on the direction of the unified German Reich. Rejecting the historic arguments for the existence of God, either as a source of divine commands or as a *telos* to which we are ordered, Kant had to seek some other way in which to ground ethical judgments. As with his attempt to reground the sciences, Kant turned here to *a priori* reason. Like science, ethics is grounded in the *a priori* structure of human reason. Just as the mind unifies experience under the forms of the intuition and the certain definite categories of the understanding, so it seeks to unify our action under a single, internally consistent and universal principle, the categorical imperative: "Act only on that maxim whereby you can at the same time will that it should become a universal law." From here, Kant goes on to argue that in order to follow this principle through consistently, we must assume (though we cannot prove) freedom of the will, immortality and the existence of God.

But within this context Kant is forced to make a distinction between the demands autonomous reason makes on itself and those which it can make on others. From the internal, subjective vantage point of conscience, we can consistently will only those actions which treat rational beings as ends rather than as means, for the simple reason that we reject our own instrumentalization. But society itself—or at least capitalist society—is quite impossible apart from such instrumentalization. Imposing such a morality as law would precipitate brutal repression and civilizational collapse. And so law, for Kant, must allow the maximum freedom which is consistent with similar freedom for others, essentially the norm of what Marx would later call bourgeois right, the norms of the market order.

There is an ongoing debate regarding Kant's position on race, with some scholars arguing that his position is organically racist and others arguing that, in effect, he does his best to avoid the worst forms of racism by attributing what he sees as defects of rational autonomy to culture and culture to climate (Zorn 2020). But why make this move? Why even ask if there are some human beings who *can* be legitimately instrumentalized, rather than arguing that those who we believe to be most developed should work to cultivate the virtue of all, as Confucius recognized? Why not treat them as ends in themselves? Aristotle and Kant answer this criticism differently. For Aristotle slavery is a material necessity, the condition of the very possibility of leisure and thus of effective liberty.

> If each instrument could do its own work, at the word of command or by intelligent anticipation, like the statues of Daedalus or the tripods made by Hephaestus, of which the poet relates that "Of their own motion they entered the conclave of Gods on Olympus." A shuttle would then weave of itself, and a plectrum would do its own harp playing. In this situation managers would not need subordinates and masters would not need slaves. (Aristotle 350 BCE/1946, 1253b15–1254a10)

But without what amount to robots, unless some are exploited none will be free. Even so, Aristotle is quite explicit that those who are enslaved are often in that condition unjustly, being in full possession of their rational faculties while their masters, enslaved to their own passions, actually *deserve* to be enslaved. Kant, on the other hand, seems to take for granted that there are some—who just happen to be in the lands colonized by Europeans—who unfortunately lack the capacity for rationally autonomy and are thus incapable of having rationally autonomous ends. Because of this they are in no more of a position to advance moral claims than a donkey—or a tree or a rock—and may be instrumentalized in good conscience.

To put the issue in the terms we used in our earlier work (Mansueto 2016), humanism is fundamentally an attempt to transcend contingency by creating a political subject which makes us masters of our own destiny. For the liberal form of the humanistic ideal this political subject is the property owning or rationally autonomous individual. But the self-determination of the property owning individual depends on the instrumentalization and even the enslavement of others. And those who are deprived of full rational autonomy, for whatever reason, are simply there to be exploited.

It might seem unsurprising, given these problems, that liberalism has become suspect. First we had very credible argument advanced by communitarian thinkers such as Roberto Magnabeira Unger and

Alasdair MacIntyre in the 1970s and 1980s that liberal theory is vacuous, lacking a substantive doctrine of the good (Unger 1975; MacIntyre 1981). More recently, it has been criticized by decolonial thinkers (Dussel 1992; Grosfoguel 2013; Burkhart 2019) as grounded in the act of conquest—*ego conquiro*—as the real basis of the *cogito* and thus of the form of subjectivity which the ideal of rational autonomy presupposes.

We will argue that this easy rejection of the liberal ideal is a dangerous move. First, it is historically inaccurate, with numerous schools throughout Asia in particular arguing for something like rational autonomy. Second, and more important, it leads to alternative ways of theorizing liberation which end up looking a great deal like the identarian and alterimperialist doctrines we criticized in the last chapter. Liberal theory may be vacuous and liberal politics radically inadequate, but this does not mean, however, that the *liberal ideal* is without merit. On the contrary, it is only by defending the value of rational autonomy that we can draw a hard line against fascism, which is quite capable of hegemonizing democratic and socialist images and concepts in service of its authoritarian agenda. Finally, as we have already seen, the emergence of the *Dark Enlightenment* has already shown that the defense of racism and patriarchy requires going behind historic liberal ethics and demanding not only as much freedom as is consistent with the comparable freedom of others but—for those with the Capital or monopoly rents on skill to demand it—the freedom to do precisely as one pleases.

The Democratic Imperative

The Historical Context

Democracy is something entirely different from liberalism. While it shares with liberalism roots in the broader humanistic project, it at once reaches back behind liberalism to the older ideals of civic humanism which found in civic life an authentic spiritual discipline, a means of cultivating human excellence, it also points radically beyond it in attempting to make the self-determination *effective* by making it *collective*. In the process it often comes into conflict with liberalism because effective, collective self-determination is possible only by imposing limits on individual rights.

There is no better way to illustrate this than by way of the comparison undertaken by Barrington Moore (Moore 1966) between the English and French Revolutions. In England, capitalist development came first, and the Revolution followed, along a path which established liberal rights first and only very gradually yielded to democratic demands—centuries later. Capitalist development in England, while certainly subsidized by colonial conquests, was driven by the enclosure of common lands and the displacement of the peasantry, as members of the gentry realized that they could make more money grazing sheep to supply wool for the emerging textie industry than by growing grain. England was the first strong monarchy in Europe, product of the Norman Conquest, which set about rationalizing and systematizing the patchwork authorities which had grown up under feudalism and which contributed mightily to primitive accumulation by the destruction of the monasteries and the distribution of their lands to rationalizing capitalist farmers. When revolution came, it was largely because the monarchy had been so successful that it had created a mass base for further and more rapid capitalist rationalization—especially more vigorous and consistent support for the enclosure of common lands—and then because the new revolutionary state which was created by Cromwell itself became overweening and undercut the freedom of the emerging bourgeoisie to do as it pleased with the fruits of its predations. It was the Glorious Revolution of 1688, of which John Locke was a key theoretician, which defined the future trajectory of English—and indeed, to a large extent, of American, civilization. In this context, democracy exists (and only exists) in order to hold the state accountable for the exercise of its principal task which is to protect the rights (which as we have seen are fundamentally property rights) of individuals.

In France, on the other hand, capitalism developed on top of intact feudal relationships as landowners leveraged France's unique comparative advantage in wine production to enter the world market—and leveraged feudal rights to extract more and more surplus from peasants. The French monarchy, meanwhile, was unable to rationalize itself, and transform itself into an effective force for industrialization. Moore describes the problem in these terms:

> In preindustrial societies it was practically impossible to generate and extract enough of an economic surplus to pay the members of the bureaucracy a salary that would ensure their real dependence on the crown. . . . The French monarchy tried to solve this problem by selling positions in the bureaucracy. (Moore 1966, pp. 57–58)

The result of this practice was, of course, to undermine the formation of a rational legal framework and the bureaucratic apparatus to enforce which could catalyze capitalist development. Indeed, while at first this measure may have won the monarchy allies within the bourgeoisie, eventually it tended to feudalize the bourgeoisie itself (Moore 1966, p. 60). At the same time, the increasing weight of feudal burdens radicalized the peasantry

> though limited capitalist penetration failed during the eighteenth century to revolutionize agriculture or eliminate the peasantry, it came in such a way as to increase very sharply peasant hostility to the *ancien regime*. Peasants resented the increase in feudal dues and revival of old ones by clever lawyers. (Moore 1966, p. 65)

There were, however, sharp divisions within the peasantry. The poorer peasants seem to have been interested primarily in gaining access to a plot of land, and to preserving those customs of the village community, such as gleaning rights, and the right to let their animals graze on harvested fields (Moore 1966, pp. 71–72). Since they produced little or no surplus above what they needed for their own consumption, the poorer peasants had little interest in high grain prices. In short, the poorer peasants vacillated between a struggle for partition and a struggle to restore the traditional rights of the village community, free from the burdens imposed by the nobility, and from the influence of the rich peasants.

The richer peasants, on the other hand, looked forward primarily to the abolition of feudal burdens and the creation of a free market in grain, which would allow them to make the most of the surpluses which they produced. For the most part they rejected attempts to divide up land among the poorer peasants, whether this land was part of the commons, or land seized from emigres after the Revolution (Moore 1966, pp. 71–73).

The urban masses were similarly divided (Sewell 1980). The great mass of journeymen, organized in the *compagnonages* were deeply committed to an anticapitalist and collectivist vision. They looked to the state, on the one hand, to provide employment and serve as a stimulus to economic growth, and, on the other hand, to regulate wages and prices just as their own organizations had done for centuries on a smaller scale. A minority of wealthier masters, however, together with the middle layers of shopkeepers, lawyers, etc., were seeking primarily to be free of feudal burdens and to seek their fortune in the marketplace.

The resulting upheaval can hardly be called a "bourgeois revolution." On the contrary, it reflected a complex and contradictory complex of bourgeois and socialist elements, with the moderate leaders of the Gironde seeking to abolish feudal privilege and restrictions, and put in place a liberal economic policy, while the poor peasants and the *sans cullotes* demanded the establishment of communal granaries, and strict regulations on the price of food. That the revolution failed to take on a fully socialist character was due primarily to weight of rich peasants who resisted these measures, which hurt their incomes and made them a strategic reserve for the bourgeoisie (Moore 1966, pp. 89–91). As a result the radical democratic revolution collapsed, and the bourgeoisie regained the upper hand.

The "capitalism" which emerged from the Revolution was, however, very different from that of England or the United States. Napoleon leveraged the wealthier peasants against the radicalized urban intelligentsia, providing unusually strong protections for the peasantry, so that as feudal restrictions were swept away, and capitalist relations gradually penetrated the countryside, large sections of the peasantry were able to survive and even prosper. This insured a home market for manufactured goods, just as the settlement of the Midwest and Great Plains by grain farmers had in the US. At the same time, he worked to integrate the intelligentsia into the state apparatus, at once granting privileges which softened its revolutionary fervor and effectively creating a reformed humanistic secular clergy. The French state supported a complex of schools and universities which created and inculcated a rational, secular, humanistic civic culture to balance the historic strength of the Church among the aristocracy and peasantry. In short, it was the organized, at least partially conscious, action of the masses, and not the spontaneous workings of the marketplace, which created the conditions for the industrialization of France.

Principal Theoretical Formulations

This midpoint between liberalism and socialism might well be called the "Rousseauean moment" of the revolution. And like the democratic revolution, Rousseau himself was the product of a complex of distinct and contradictory influences.

Rousseau understood himself as writing in the tradition of civic humanism and was clearly influenced by thinkers like Montesquieu and possibly even Spinoza. More specifically he took from civic humanism generally and from Montesquieu in particular, the idea that republican government depended on virtue as its principle as well as the broader idea that participation in civic life not only required but helped cultivate virtue (Montesquieu 1748/2018). But it must be remembered that both Montesquieu and Rousseau had strong ties to Geneva, where Montesquieu published his *Spirit of Law* and where Rousseau himself was actually born. There the early stages of the democratic struggle were closely intertwined with the Protestant Reformation and where the proclamation of a republic in 1536 was followed hard on by the appointment of John Calvin as spiritual leader of the city. And while Calvin himself certainly had roots in the humanistic tradition, there can be no doubt that he introduced a theology which was humanistic only in its reduction theological method to the hermeneutic disciplines.

It is, therefore, certainly possible to read Rousseau's account for the social contract as a theorization of the democratic revolutionary experience. Unlike Locke and most of the English theorists, Rousseau recognized no "natural rights" to life or liberty, much less to property, which the state was obliged to respect. On the contrary, prior to the establishment of the state, there was no right or morality. It was participation in the political process itself (one might even be tempted to say "participation in the revolution") which lifted human beings out of their animal state and made them fully social human beings. In becoming part of society, human beings alienated all of their rights to the state. Still, at the end of the process, the state establishes a "right" to property, or, rather, bestows property on the individual to be managed in such a way as to best serve the common good. But this is also a secularized Calvinism. There is no morality prior to the social contract, just as prior to conversion human beings are radically depraved. In the social contract they alienate everything and receive back a new identity as citizens, just as in the converted Christian it is not the old human being but rather Christ who lives.

This in turn introduces into the democratic ideal and into democratic theory an authoritarian and even totalitarian element which persists to this day, which we see not just in the manipulation of plebiscites to legitimate dictatorship, but also in the derivation of political authority, on both the Right and the Left, from revolutionary violence. Democracy, furthermore, is closely associated with nationalism. Both seek to create a political subject which makes humanity the master of its own destiny. For democracy this subject is the people as *demos*; for nationalism it is the people as an imagined cultural community, as *ethos*. But in the long run, in order to legitimate itself, the democratic state creates a shared identity in the form of a national language and culture and an at least partially mythological national history.

This does not, to be sure, mean that democracy excludes the ideal of rational autonomy. But that autonomy no longer belongs to the individual. Indeed, we have already seen that for Locke it is not the individual in general whose freedom is guaranteed by the state: some are enslaved. Nor is it even the property owning individual, who is himself free only because he is the property of God. It is only God, reflex of emerging Capital, who creates but does not consume, that is authentically free. Similarly, with Kant, the individual is only free as an occult "good will." The empirical individual cannot have, or even seek effective freedom except by instrumentalizing others. For Rousseau the General Will is free and citizens are free only to the extent that they identify with it.

* * *

If Hegel is not generally studied as a democratic theorist it is, in large part, because our own understanding of democracy has been dominated by the Anglo-American experience. But Hegel spent his youth deeply devoted to Rousseau, celebrated the French Revolution (though not the Terror) and welcomed the arrival of Napoleon, who he called a "world soul" in Jena, where he lived at the time, as a catalyst for the democratic transformation of his native Germany, where the democratic revolutions lagged behind. Indeed, what we see in Hegel, is precisely the completion of the process which Rousseau began. The drive towards rationally autonomous self-determination, which for Hegel was the driving force in human history and indeed the driving force of reality itself, could not be contained in or realized by the individual. Self-determination was possible only in and through the state, which crystallizes the collective action of the people into a rational system, in effect embodying the divine on earth.

> The divine spirit must interpenetrate the entire secular life: whereby wisdom is concrete within it, and carries the terms of its own justification. But that concrete indwelling is only . . . ethical organization. (Hegel 1830/1971, p. 3:552)

Hegel's credentials as a democratic theorist are also tarnished by the fact that he Hegel eventually made his peace with the Prussian State, accepting the Order of the Red Eagle from Fredrich Wilhelm III. But it was in this same final period that Hegel produced a scathing critique of Karl Ludwig von Haller's *Restauration,* which rejected not only democracy but also rule of law and effectively reduced political authority to property ownership. While his *Philosophy of Right* integrates liberal, democratic, feudal, and monarchic elements (with the church, since the divine has fully interpenetrated the secular, now an arm of the state) his real innovation is the presence of a hidden architectonic cadre in the "universal class" of civil servants of which the university based sapiential intelligentsia is the core. In this, we will see, he anticipates not only Marx but also Lenin.

Solutions to the Riddle of History

It is in this context that we must understand Marx's contribution—and its limitations. There are, in fact, many constraints on making effective the rational autonomy and self-determination which is the principal ideal of the humanistic tradition, but the principal *social* constraint is the need to sell our labor power in order to survive, which renders what we *do* subject to the will of another. This is why, after Marx, it becomes necessary for Capital to retheorize itself independent of any arguments for freedom understood as the exercise of rational autonomy. And it is why it is quite impossible to speak seriously of freedom today without addressing the question of how we are going to transcend the commodification of labor power.

This said, his self-proclaimed materialism and atheism notwithstanding, Marx stands very much in the tradition of Radical Aristotelianism, and is concerned with the metaphysical as well as the sociological dimensions of freedom. Indeed, we will see that Marx claims for revolutionary politics generally and for communism in particular, the capacity to transcend not only the social but also the metaphysical constraints on our freedom.

While for Hegel it is enough for "the divine spirit to interpenetrate the entire secular world, wherein it becomes conscious of itself," in the state, for Marx,

> The task of history is thus to establish the truth about this world once the otherworld has proved illusory. The immediate task

of philosophy, which is in the service of history, is to unmask human self-alienation in its secular forms now that it has been unmasked in its sacred forms. Thus the critique of heaven is transformed into a critique of earth, the critique of religion into the critique of law, and the critique of theology into the critique of politics. (Marx 1843/2009)

More specifically, for Marx, it is necessary to transcend the alienation of the specific capacity which links the human essence to the divine, i.e., to Being as such: our labor power. And this alienation is a result of the commodification of creative capacity, or the wage relation.

> This fact expresses merely that the object which labor produces—labor's product—confronts it as something alien, as a power independent of the producer. The product of labor is labor which has been embodied in an object, which has become material: it is the objectification of labor. Labor's realization is its objectification. Under these economic conditions this realization of labor appears as loss of realization for the workers; objectification as loss of the object and bondage to it; appropriation as estrangement, as alienation. (Marx 1844/2009)

Transcending this alienation results in nothing less than the effective deification of humanity.

> Communism as the positive transcendence of private property as human self-estrangement, and therefore as the real appropriation of the human essence by and for man; communism therefore as the complete return of man to himself as a social (i.e., human) being—a return accomplished consciously and embracing the entire wealth of previous development. This communism, as fully developed naturalism, equals humanism, and as fully developed humanism equals naturalism; it is the genuine resolution of the conflict between man and nature and between man and man—the true resolution of the strife between existence and essence, between objectification and self-confirmation, between freedom and necessity, between the individual and the species. Communism is the riddle of history solved, and it knows itself to be this solution. (Marx 1844/2009)

Humanity's essence is, in other words, nothing less than existence, or Being as Such: what the dialectical tradition has understood historically to be God. Religion seeks the realization of this essence beyond history, in a mystical union with the divine. Philosophy, by which Marx means the tradition of Radical Aristotelianism which reaches from the Latin Averroists through Spinoza and Hegel, up to his own work, teaches us to seek realization of this divine potential in this world. Liberal philosophy sought deification in the rationally autonomous individual. Democratic philosophy sought deification in the democratic state. Communism seeks it in human creativity itself, liberated from the chains of commodification.

We will consider socialism proper and the communist movement in the next chapter. For now we need to see how the attempts to work a compromise between the various forms of the humanistic ideal and the realities of capitalist development unfolded.

Principal Trends

History may not be *just* the history of class struggle, but neither is it *just* the history of unfolding civilizational ideals. Civilizational ideals, on the contrary, represent competing ways of *seeking being* which emerge under definite material conditions and using definite social structures, and contradictions between these three factors in turn lead to struggles between social classes and other political actors. If we are, therefore, to understand the legacy of the developing humanistic ideal in the present period we need to situate its development in this context and in particular in the context of:

- the ongoing process of capitalist development and its
- the hybridization of the various forms of this ideal with others as it is leveraged as a form of legitimation in struggles for hegemony.

We have already seen this process as we have traced out the origins and emergence of the ideal from the High Middle Ages through the first centuries of capitalist development. We will consider socialism as a distinct project in the next chapter, but for how we need to analyze how the liberal and democratic variants of the humanistic project developed over the course of the past century. Broadly speaking we can distinguish three broad core trends:

- Liberal Conservatives accept the liberal variant of the humanistic ideal and a restricted form of the democratic variant: that public officials hold their authority from the people and are entrusted with defending liberal freedoms and the rule of law. Democratic institutions are primarily a way of holding them accountable to this charge, not of broad popular sovereignty.

- Commuitarians accept the liberal and democratic forms of the humanistic ideal, as well as elements of the socialist critique of capitalism, but argue that humanism must be set in a broader spiritual context and/or that the amelioration of the contradictions of capitalism should be entrusted in so far as possible to intermediate institutions between the market and the state.

- Social Liberals, like the Communitarian Center, accept the liberal and democratic forms of the humanistic ideal, as well as elements of the socialist critique of capitalism, but argue for vigorous state action to ameliorate the contradictions of capitalism and to ensure that everyone has the resources they need in order for liberal freedoms to be meaningful to them.

While quite distinct at a theoretical level, in practice these trends shade into and syncretize with each other and with both Fascism on the Right and Socialism on the Left. Thus there are—or at least have been—liberal conservatives who understand property rights to extend to property in human beings and liberal conservatives who understand the right to life and liberty to include a social safety net and social supports which makes them look like moderate social liberals. There are also liberal conservatives—now generally called National Conservatives—who have adopted shifted from natural rights to contractarian legal theories and who have developed such strong nationalist legitimation strategies as to compromise their liberalism. There are communitarians whose respect for the autonomy of intermediate institutions amounts to a strong social conservatism which strictly limits their support for state intervention to defend the rights of women, historically oppressed peoples, and especially gender nonconformists (Religious Social Conservatives) and there are communitarians who, for similar reasons, favor restrictions on Capital which represent a much stronger departure from pure capitalism than that advocated by most social liberals (much of the Religious Left). There are, finally, social liberals (especially the core group of globalist, technocratic neoliberals in the tradition of Clinton, Blair, and Macron) who are focused primarily on creating economic growth as a condition for providing the social supports which make liberal freedoms meaningful for the whole population, and who are therefore reluctant to significantly restrict Capital, which they see it as an engine of growth. Many of these same moderate neoliberals are also committed to extending to historically excluded groups the rights which European men have enjoyed for some two hundred years, though in France, for example, this commitment is complicated by the politics around secularism and immigration. Finally, on the Left, social liberalism shades off into social democracy and even democratic socialism, which has become less and less about collective ownership of the means of production and more and more about public investments and income transfers. But as we will see, at a certain point, such transfers undercut the pressure on people to sell their labor in order to survive, creating a new and different road to transcending capitalism.

From Liberal Conservatism to National Conservatism

It no doubt seems strange, at least to those whose perspective is limited to the present period, to suggest that there was ever anything which might legitimately be called a "liberal conservatism," i.e., a conservatism which was skeptical about the more radical democratic and socialist variants of the humanistic project precisely because they threatened the freedom which was the principal value of its liberal variant. The way in which the principal political party within this trend in the United States has evolved has taught us to be suspicious about expressions of concern about "freedom" by representatives of Capital. As we have seen, the "freedom" being demanded by Capital and by the emerging strata of capitalist magnates and their associated technogentry and *Dark Enlightenment* intellectuals is not the liberal freedom of the rationally autonomous individual, limited by respect for the comparable freedom of others, but rather the unconscionable freedom for those with vast power to act without check or accountability, regardless of the impact their action has on others. This "freedom" has nothing to do with the liberal tradition. Nor do the claims advanced by social and religious conservatives against the extension of liberal freedoms to historically excluded communities. On the other hand, if the current position of Capital and of capitalist magnates—aspiring to something between feudal lordship and global imperium over a population of AI slaves—is something new, the historic arguments of liberals against democracy and socialism are not, and they too have certainly been colored by the class position of those who have made them.

This said, there *are* very powerful arguments to be made that freedom and democracy are not always compatible. While many in this trend look back to John Locke for their theoretical foundations, the trend was largely a product of the American and French Revolutions. *The Federalist* (1787) articulated, among other things, a concern that the tyranny of the British and their Monarch might give way to a tyranny of the majority, while Edmund Burke (Burke 1790) just a few years later argued that the French Revolution had already made this danger a reality. And Alexis de Tocqueville integrated this defining liberal conservative concern with his argument for the primacy of the intermediate institutions of civil society in making democracy compatible with freedom.

The argument here is simple. There is very little which prevents a unified and stable majority from imposing its will on a minority or on individuals who dissent from dominant beliefs and values. And while the dissenters might, of course, be feudal or capitalist exploiters who want to be "free" to continue their exploitation, or bigots who want to be free not to serve Blacks or members of the LGBTQ community, they may also be atheists or religious dissidents, revolutionaries looking to change the debate around capitalism, or Blacks or members of the LGBTQ community struggling to simply be who they are.

Ideologically, liberal conservatives have drawn on a range of different philosophical trends. In the Anglo-American world, as we noted above, the influence of Locke has been paramount. On the Continent Kant is more important, and grounds rights in human rationality, though again in a way which does not always effectively exclude racism. Ordoliberalism, influential in postwar German, draws on Weber among others and acknowledges the tension between the quasi-substantive rationality of the categorical imperative and the instrumental rationality of the marketplace, leaving room for very significant state intervention. More specifically, Ordoliberalism argues that the state must create a broader social context in which markets remain competitive and produce something like the optimum results which classical economics says they will. Often this is accompanied by a recognition of the importance of nonmarket, nonstate institutions and of spirituality and religion.

In practice liberal conservatism has tended to function as a defensive posture assumed by elements within the liberal bourgeoisie anxious to protect their privilege, generally by while conceding extensions of liberal freedoms which did not threaten their most vital interests and by at once supporting and trying to moderate state intervention designed to manage economic crises and to provide (limited) social supports to the working classes. This was the position of the Republican Party in the United States and of a range of both secular and Christian Democratic parties in Europe during the postwar period.

This authentically liberal, relatively humane, Center Right has now collapsed. This collapse needs to be considered at both the ideological and the political level. For liberal conservatives it was above all the increasingly inescapable contradiction between capitalism and the liberal ideal which led to schism. As proletarianization advances any meaningful freedom depends on significant state action to modify the operation of market forces and, in some areas, at least, significant limits on property rights. Here the developing ecological crisis, which led to limitations on property rights in land that affected especially extractive and agricultural interests, was an early catalyst for schism, followed by the aggressive implementation of the neoliberal project aimed at constructing a unified global market. When the free operation of the marketplace leads to universal proletarianization and the convergence of wages on a world market level that does not support any significant opportunity for individual human development, one must, in the end, choose between capitalism and freedom.

At the political level, the liberal conservative position simply became increasingly difficult to sell. Why would an electorate constituted by more or less universal suffrage support policies which protect the freedoms of those richer than they are *at their own expense*? As a result formerly liberal conservative parties either began to adopt an increasingly social conservative and ethnonationalist position, or else face competition from new parties which appealed to their old constituencies on precisely these bases. Thus, while in Europe, where proportional representation made small parties viable, liberal conservative groups have persisted, but have faced competition from new "populist" or "national conservative" (read fascist or protofascist) formations, in the US as far back as the late 1960s the Republican Party began using racist, patriarchal, and nationalistic rhetoric, drawing on these sentiments to win elections they would have lost on economic or internal policy, and actually helping to create ethnonationalism.

This rightward turn found mass constituency because of the alienation of labor. To an extent which the communist and socialist left has never fully acknowledged, the alienation generated by full proletarianization effectively undercuts the aspiration for rational autonomy and creative self-expression which communism, like liberalism and democracy, serves. Universal proletarianization and the global convergence of wages below the level necessary to support significant self-cultivation effectively undercut support for the liberal ideal. Indeed, it is precisely the extent to which people depend on wages which fall below the level necessary for self-cultivation, generally because of the inability to access or maintain social or cultural capital, which today marks popular definitions of the "working class" as those without a full university education. This is an incorrect definition of "working class" from an historical materialist perspective, and for good reason, as we will argue later. But the line of demarcation which it identifies is politically relevant. And it affects tendencies across all positions on the political spectrum which retain some commitment to the liberal ideal, not just those on the socialist and communist left. It is impossible to advocate a liberating future which one cannot even imagine, because one lacks any basis in experience of the freedom it would expand and enrich. Indeed, it is the fact that wages were below the level which made self cultivation possible which created a mass base for the authoritarian deformations of actually existing socialism, which promised the people not so much the free development of their creative potential as simply a clean apartment and a three square meals per day.

Meanwhile, under the leadership of elite think tanks such as the Mount Pelerin Society, the backward, extractive and agrarian sectors of the ruling class migrated from liberal conservatism to libertarianism and, as they realized that a libertarian agenda would never prevail in a democracy, towards the Dark Enlightenment. In order to understand this trend we must, however, look at what happened to pro-capitalist thinking after Marx. Whatever pro-capitalist scholars may have said, Marx's argument that capitalism undercut the humanistic ideal was compelling and definitive and even those who rejected his claim that the contradictions of capitalism could not be resolved and that a socialist transition was the only road forward felt the need to show *how* capitalism could be modified in order to support the humanistic ideal—or, to find a way to legitimate capitalism apart from that ideal. Social liberalism and the communitarian center represent the first alternative; neoliberalism in the narrow sense represents the second.

This dynamic is most apparent in the work of the Austrian School which, while retaining the *language* of liberalism and touting the threat of "socialist" tyranny actually legitimates capitalism first and foremost on the basis of its contribution to human *survival*. Thus F. A. Hayek—the theoretician of the neoliberal revolution—explicitly rejected the idea that we can rise rationally to a first principle which can explain the universe and order human action. Rather, we know facts and events and patterns of facts and events—essentially what we need for survival. Rational ideas about the Good and about Justice may be attractive, but they are ultimately dangerous. Nor, similarly, is there any such thing as human "society" but only individuals struggling to survive and thrive under conditions of scarcity. These individuals develop various *practices*, technological, economic, political, and cultural. Some work and others don't. Those that work become part of an established tradition. The others are eventually discarded.

Three points are in order here. First, whatever Hayek and his associates may say about their dedication to the cause of freedom, this is *not* a liberal theory, but rather an evolutionary theory which prioritizes survival value. The only freedom which is important here is that of the market, and that only because if promotes economic growth and thus has survival value. And the legitimate constraint on freedom historically acknowledged by all liberals—that my freedom must be compatible with the freedom of others—has been entirely discarded.

Second, this is the theoretical configuration which made it possible to create and ideological bridge between free market economics and social conservatism, as the market is merely one of the forms of spontaneous organization which promote human survival. The others: language, the family, and religion, for example, are at the center of national and sociocultural conservative ideology.

Third, while Hayek's evolutionary theory appears to make human survival value the criterion of his social theory, what actually survives and thrives is not human beings but rather Capital which, in the context of the global market becomes an emergent autonomous intelligence independent of the historic bourgeoisie. This is not the only power at work on the planet, but it is new and different and we must understand it.

Ultimately, of course, the national conservative and libertarian/neoliberal turns are incompatible with each other. Thus, the self-destruction of the Republican Party in the US as it has discovered that popular support for the deregulation and tax and budget cuts its bourgeois core desires are dependent now not only on a *base* which is fundamentally racist and misogynist in its outlook, but also on the demagogues who are able to mobilize this base, and who have no consistent commitment to the freedom of anyone but themselves.

Communitarian Liberalism

We class as Communitarian Liberalisms any theory which affirms liberal and democratic rights, but which rejects the methodological and normative individualism of most liberal theory, as well as its agnosticism regarding the nature of the Good as such which situates the aspiration for self-determination in a broader spiritual context. Under the heading of Communitarian Liberalism we include two distinct movements. The first is the tradition of Catholic Social Teaching, very broadly understood to include the full range of Catholic responses to capitalism and to humanistic secularism. This is largely a grafting of the liberal and democratic ideals, with some socialist elements, onto first Traditionalism and later onto the Neo-Thomism which eventually defeated Traditionalism and ultimately drove the Church's response to the liberal, democratic, and socialist revolutions. The second is the movement of postliberal social thought which emerged beginning in the 1970s and 1980s in the work of Roberto Mangabeira Unger and Alisdair MacIntyre which, while sharply critical of liberal *theory* affirms liberal *rights* while rejecting both methodological and normative individualism. This trend is actually quite close on substantive questions to Catholic Social Teaching, but Unger in particular is able to go further in freeing his doctrine from the social conservatism of Catholic teaching on gender.

It might be asked at this point why we do not treat in this context the various Protestant and Orthodox attempts to come to terms with the humanistic ideal, or with comparable efforts in other traditions. First, as we have already argued, Protestantism, rooting itself in a very high doctrine of divine sovereignty and thus in a univocal metaphysics makes it extremely difficult to sustain the ideal of self-determination. Indeed, even a thinker as sympathetic to liberal, democratic, and socialist politics as Paul Tillich had to substitute *theonomy* for *autonomy* as his ethical ideal. In order to go beyond this point to actually valuing self-determination, it is necessary to radically secularize the whole concept of conversion, justification, and sanctification, as we have already seen in Rousseau and Hegel, treating them as, in effect, *identical* with the liberal, democratic, and/or socialist revolutions. This is not really an attempt to offer a distinct way of grounding the humanistic ideal, but rather a claim that that ideal is, the end product of Christianity as such. This is very different, as we will see, from Catholic Social Teaching, which grounds liberal and democratic rights in a fundamentally Aristotelian and Thomistic concept of the human person as a rational and social being. It is also why liberal Protestantism has tended to simply evaporate as a distinct religious movement.

The situation with other religious traditions is very different. Our derivation of the humanistic secular idea from Radical Aristotelianism and in particular from the Jewish lineage of Radical Aristotelianism which leads from Moshe ben Maimon, through Gersonides, to Spinoza already identifies a fairly secularized Judaism as itself the root and core of the humanistic secular project, with the ideas of Locke and Kant, Rousseau and Hegel as bourgeois deformations of this project. When we consider the socialist project we will show how Marx represents an attempt to bring this original Jewish humanistic tradition into the present, and why that attempt was ultimately incompletely successful. Many, though not all, forms of Zionism similarly find the realization of the Jewish tradition in a liberal, democratic, or socialist state.

Other traditions have a much more complex and ambivalent with the concept of autonomy and self-determination. Traditions which have as their ideal *commanding right and forbidding wrong, achieving moksha or enlightenment,* or *restoring harmony within society and between human beings and the cosmos* may well come to value rational autonomy as a capacity in service to these ideals, and lead to relatively liberal, democratic, or socialist variants of historical traditions. But they do not regard rational autonomy as an end in itself, a way of achieving or approaching *theosis.* It is, furthermore, actually easier to derive rationales for socialism from traditional Islamic, Hindu, Buddhist, Confucian, or Taoist premises than it is for liberalism or democracy. While Catholic Social Teaching is *also* a syncretism, it is between more closely associated traditions than say an Islamic, Hindu, Buddhist, Confucian, or Taoist liberalism or democracy. We will thus have more to be said about syncretisms between humanism and these traditions in the chapter on socialism.

Catholic Social Teaching

We have argued in a preceding chapter that whatever its messianic roots and however it was modified by its engagement with other traditions, historical Christianity is at its core an imperial ideology. This is because at the very center of the tradition is a doctrine of absolute divine sovereignty, a demand for unconditional submission, and a theology of substitutionary atonement. We have shown that these doctrines are at least a reflex of Empire and possibly a conscious construction which, in any case, served to legitimate the Empire under the Dominate. While residual Hellenic and Jewish elements and syncretism with Celtic, Slavic, and to a lesser extent Germanic tradition brought into being a complex religion—Catholicism—which wasn't *just* a legitimation of Empire, the European Conquests and the Reformation largely purged Christianity of its non-imperial and anti-imperial elements.

At this point, however, the objection might be raised that there are a wide range of contemporary Christian tendencies which *are* anti-imperialist and anti-capitalist—liberation theology, for example, or Radical Orthodoxy. Particularly since this is a position which we ourselves once upheld (Mansueto 1988), albeit with some critical reservations (Mansueto 2002a), we need to provide an answer to the objection. We will do this by looking at the trajectory of Catholic theology beginning with the decision for Neo-Thomism in the nineteenth century, then exploring the tendencies which flowed into the Second Vatican Council and the movements which flowed out of it, especially the theology of liberation and the *Communio* trend. We will analyze Radical Orthodox as the culmination of this process.

* * *

In order to understand contemporary Catholic theology, we need to situate it in the context of the theological debates which flowed into the Second Vatican Council, and more broadly to understand the political-theological significance of the Council itself.

The Second Vatican Council must be seen as part of the long process of adaptation the part of Catholicism generally and the papacy in particular to the industrial revolution and capitalist development, the formation of the sovereign nation state (actually, as we have argued above, a system of regional competing or aspiring empires) and to the liberal, democratic, and socialist revolutions. And this is part of the larger history of the relationship between Church and Empire. Historically, the Catholic Church had carved out for itself both sociologically and theologically a position superior to but distinct from the political sphere represented by the

Roman Empire and its successor states. This settlement, expressed in and embraced by the Church in the political theology of Thomas Aquinas, respected the autonomy of the political sphere and entrusted secular lords with the task of governing in accord with natural law and specifically with guiding humanity towards the realization of its natural end—the full development of its natural capacities, intellectual and moral. The Church was responsible for leading humanity to full *theosis*, which we desire but cannot achieve except by grace, but also for holding the secular lords accountable for governing in accord with natural law. The Church had the right to dissolve the bonds between a people and their government, though not to usurp secular rule itself.

This political theology, even as it legitimated Empire, limited it in multiple ways. On the one hand, it retained for the Church the role of ultimate vicar of the divine sovereign, while denying the church the right to rule directly, except perhaps in certain limited regions where some prelate, whether a local abbot, a bishop, or the Pope himself, was *also and on an independent basis* sovereign. This in turn forced the Empire to legitimate itself in a hybrid manner, supporting the revival of civic humanism like that advocated by Dante and functioning as the secular arm of the Church.

This position was never popular with the emerging absolutist states in Europe that developed with the Norman Conquests, the Crusades, the Reconquista, and the Conquests of Africa, the Americas, and Asia and these monarchies tended to support Augustinian theologies, such as that of Anonymous of York (Goerner 1965) which modeled royal authority on an absolute divine sovereignty which Thomas rejected and which elevated Jesus' royal above his priestly office. Some of these theologies fed into Protestantism and others into Gallicanism and other nationalistic tendencies and, in spite of a resurgence, based in large part on support from monarchies which rejected the Reformation primarily for geopolitical reasons, Thomism tended to lose influence or else to be reconstructed in a way more compatible with absolutism over the period leading up to the middle or end of the nineteenth century. It was only with the defeat of the *ancien regimes,* with which it had been allied against the liberal, democratic, and socialist revolutions, that the Church turned decisively back to Thomas and resumed its role as guarantor of natural law, mounting a critique of capitalist exploitation and advocating for the right of workers to organize, a living wage, and public support for education, health care, and social insurance (Thibault 1971). This led to the emergence of Christian Democratic parties which exercised a kind of joint rule in Europe with Social Democrats throughout the postwar period, but it did little to reinvigorate the Church's influence on the spiritual life of Europe. Among other things, the Second and Third Thomisms which dominated Catholic theology, by making such a sharp distinction between nature and grace, were seen as denying any ultimate spiritual significance to this world and to human history. Appeals to mitigate capitalist exploitation might win votes from peasants and workers who still experienced this world as a "vale of tears" and remained embedded in traditional communities and oriented toward otherworldly beatitude towards their final good. But it was not going to draw support from the bourgeoisie and middle strata who, if they voted for the Christian Democrats, did so as a bulwark against socialism and who found the meaning of their lives in inner worldly activity, be it the accumulation of capital or the exercise of a liberal profession.

* * *

The *nouvelle theologie* (Milbank 2005) which fed into the Council was an attempt to address this problem by softening the distinction between nature and grace and making more explicit the sense in which human history—including the changes shaping the modern world—is itself a participation in the life of God. It is worth citing the Council's *Pastoral Constitution on the Church and the World,* which affirms this new theology, at some length.

> The joys and the hopes, the griefs and the anxieties of the men of this age, especially those who are poor or in any way afflicted, these are the joys and hopes, the griefs and anxieties of the followers of Christ . . .
>
> God did not create man for life in isolation, but for the formation of social unity. So also it has pleased God to make men whole and save them not merely as individuals, without any mutual bonds, but by making them into a single people . . .
>
> This communitarian character is developed and consummated in the work of Jesus Christ. . . . In His preaching He clearly taught the sons of God to treat one another as brothers. . . .
>
> He founded after his death and resurrection a new brotherly community composed of all those who receive Him in faith and in love.

> This solidarity must be constantly increased until that day on which it will be brought to perfection. Then, saved by grace, men will offer flawless glory to God as a family beloved of God and of Christ their Brother. (Paul VI 1965, 32)

The vision here is one of a humanity which, created in the image of a triune God, is essentially social in nature, developing its capacity for solidarity throughout the course of one single history, a solidarity which is consummated in the work of Christ, and brought to perfection in the Kingdom of God. In the place of the old dualistic theology with its sharp distinction between the finite human, secular, lay, realm on the one hand, and the divine, sacred, clerical, sacramental realm on the other, we see a unified process of divine-human activity pointing towards a τελοσ which transcends history only in the sense of being beyond our finite human comprehension. Everything we do, however, which authentically builds up solidarity, is a real contribution to the building of the Kingdom, and not merely a finite, nonsalvific participation in building what Christian Democratic thinkers like Jacques Maritain called "the true city of human laws."

At the same time, the conciliar documents are theologically and philosophically ambiguous and softening the distinction between nature and grace can lead in two very different directions. On the one hand, by stressing the sense in which "natural" humanity is already participating in the life of God and the sense in which "grace" is structured into the very nature of reality, the new theology can be read as endowing secular activity with ultimate spiritual significance, *quite apart from the authority of the Church or participation in the sacraments.* On the other hand, if everything good is already "grace" and if by grace we insist on understanding the free gift of a personal God mediated through the sacraments by the hierarchical priesthood and subject to the authority of the Church, then *everything good is radically dependent on divine action in a way which, frankly, would make most Calvinists blush.*

These two possibilities soon developed into two competing theological trends, associated with two different pastoral strategies. The first argued for what amounted to a strengthening of the Church's support for the broadly progressive civilizational aspirations of the popular classes, and situating these aspirations in the broader spiritual context of the Catholic narrative. This group included both those who argued for an alliance with the poor and the working classes—the so-called preferential option for the poor—even if this meant collaboration or alliance with the Communist Left and those who focused on the aspirations of the aspirations off the professional middle class or new petty bourgeoisie of the "North Atlantic" region.

Participation in popular struggles tended to produce a "leftist" or "liberationist" interpretation of the conciliar theology. Partly this resulted from the application of historical materialist sociology in the social-analytic stage of the "see/judge/act" process. Increasingly, leaders and participants in the base communities alike began to understand that realization of the historic aims of Social Catholicism were impossible within the context of a market driven global economy. The political aims of Catholic organizers began to drift leftward until they were indistinguishable from those of secular socialists and the distinction between these secular aims and the ultimate spiritual ends of humanity tended to disappear.

> God makes history. Why? Because by becoming one with the lot that every person has in history (*Gaudium et Spes* 22) he converts history, seemingly profane history . . . into the road by which the individual has access to transcendence and therefore salvation (*Gaudium et Spes* 22). . . . The historical work of all people will lead, by the grace of God to eschatological metahistory. (Segundo 1985, p. 69)

We have already explained in other contexts why we believe this approach to be inadequate (Mansueto 2002a). First, by pitting a revolutionary Jesus against collaborationist (Sadducean) and reformist (Pharisaic) Jews, liberation theology reinstates in a new form the historic anti-Semitism of the Christian tradition. This pattern is reinforced by the reaffirmation of Jesus as the Jewish messiah and by a failure to explicitly reject texts, such as Galatians and Romans which argue that justification is outside the Law, by faith alone, effectively rendering the Jewish *way* invalid. And by affirming the divinity of Jesus as unique and essential, liberation theology violates the principle that while revelation can extend what we know by reason, it cannot contradict what we know by reason. Nothing can be both Necessary and Contingent, finite and infinite at the same time. And if the divinity of Jesus is not essential and substantial but only accidental, then it is no different than the limited *theosis* which other human beings can achieve by means of the supernaturally just act, i.e., by fulfilling the Law. Thus, while much liberation theology certainly honestly understood itself as anti-capitalist, it was objectively a sort of

Neo-Ghibelline tendency, which aligned itself with Soviet socialist alterimperialism rather than the papacy.

Another way to put this is to say that liberation theology ultimately pointed beyond historical Christianity to a fundamentally new vision. But getting there involved rejecting core Christian dogmas, such as divine sovereignty, original sin, the idea that "Jesus died for our sins," and the claim that Jesus was either *moshiach* or divine. But when the hierarchy began to push back, as it inevitably had to, given that liberation theology would ultimately undermine the hierarchical priesthood centered on participation in an atoning sacrifice, the liberationists retrenched. Segundo's response to the two "Instructions" on liberation theology, while insightful and in many ways correct, failed to address the core questions. And it is no accident that the most capable defender of liberation theology was a Jesuit. The majority were Augustinian and Franciscan in theology if not by membership, and however "left" their politics, their theology bore the marks of the Augustianian Reaction, and was governed by a univocal metaphysics and Christocentric spirituality.

* * *

As liberation theology gradually gained influence in the Catholic Church during the 1960s and 1970s, a right opposition emerged which argued that communism remained the Church's principal adversary, and that while building or rebuilding a base among the poor of the Third World generally, and Latin America in particular, was vitally important, this work must be carried out within the context of a geopolitical alliance with the bourgeois states of the West, and an intense ideological struggle against dialectical materialism, feminism, and other forms of secularism. This is the course preferred by Woytila, Ratzinger, and by the international theological movement organized around the journal *Communio*.

The theological key to *Communio*-theology can be found in *Love Alone*, a small book by one of the trend's most creative theologians, Hans Urs von Balthasar (Balthasar 1968). Von Balthasar distinguishes between three approaches to theological reflection: the cosmological, the anthropological and the "aesthetic." The cosmological approach is the method of traditional Catholic theology, which used the concepts of Greek philosophy, Platonic or Aristotelian, as a criterion for the interpretation of the scriptures and the teachings of the church. Thus, in cosmological theology, the doctrine of God or the Trinity is explained in terms of philosophical categories of being, essence, person, etc. The anthropological approach is the method of most modern theology, which takes its categories from modern philosophy, or, by extension, from the social sciences, and interprets the tradition in terms of these categories. According to this perspective God is the perfectly good will of the liberals, the "ground of authentic being" of the existentialists,—or the liberator of the oppressed.

The difficulty of both of these approaches, von Balthasar argues, is that they reduce God, and thus divine love, to a postulate of human reason, something understandable, and in a sense necessary in human terms—something other than the fully free and unmerited love through which God reveals himself to us in the scriptures.

> Christianity is destroyed if it lets itself be reduced to a transcendental presupposition of man's selfunderstanding, whether in thought or in life, in knowledge or in action. . . . The moment I think that I have understood the love of another person for me—for instance on the basis of laws of human nature, or because of something in me—then this love is radically misused and inadequate, and there is no possibility of a response. True love is always incomprehensible, and only so is it gratuitous. (Balthasar 1968, pp. 43–44)

This is a critical point. What von Balthasar is suggesting is that any attempt to understand revelation in terms of rational, human criteria, be they Platonic, Aristotelian, Thomist, Kantian, Existentialist, or Marxist, has the result of reducing the love which is revelation to merely a necessary, and in some sense merited, reflection of our own human nature, or of the structure of being in general. To put this in another way, the *communio* created by divine love becomes simply a community of mutual interdependence, in which cooperation is rationally comprehensible on the basis of definite natural or social laws, and the ultimate purpose of which is the satisfaction of individual desires—rather than a communion based on selfsacrificial love which is spontaneous, gratuitous, and incomprehensible in terms of anything which we know about human nature. Such a rational harmony does not really overcome the egoism of the individual, and thus is not genuinely or fully redeeming in character. It is this danger which makes von Balthasar and Ratzinger so cautious about any rationalistic hermeneutic. Dialectical and historical materialism is simply the most radical variant of the rationalism they seek to combat.

Their strictures would apply as fully to Rahner as they do to Segundo or the Boffs, and, perhaps, more fully than they do to Guttierez.

Communio-theologians, furthermore, understand love first and foremost as self-sacrifice, modeled on the substitutionary work of Jesus on the cross.

> The sign of Christ can only be deciphered if His human love and surrender "even unto death" is read as the manifestation of absolute love.... His task, in love is to allow the sins of the world to enter into Him who is "dispossessed" out of love of God—to become the "lamb of God who bears the guilt of the world" (1 John 1:29) and my sins.... This is the dogma—the dogma of vicarious suffering, of bearing the guilt of others which in the last analysis determines whether a theology is anthropological or christocentric.... For it is precisely with this act that really unaccountable, inconceivable love begins and ends; a love moreover which qua love is self evidently divine. (Balthasar 1968, p. 182)

What is happening here is an attempt to purge from the Catholic tradition its syncretism with Hellenism and humanism and to advance a "purely Christian" theology. And of course "purely Christian" in fact means "purely Pauline" and purely imperial. It is thus not surprising the result looks a great deal like a sacramentalized and clericalized Lutheranism. The difference is that where Lutheran theology legitimated the emergence of the imperial successor states we call nations from papal authority, the *Communio* doctrine is an attempt to re-position the Church as a defender of European civilization in relationship to the threat of Soviet socialist alterimperialism. Indeed, through the efforts of Karol Woytila, *Communio* played a critical role in providing organizational and ideological support to the anticommunist opposition in Central and Eastern Europe—particularly in Poland. While there were clearly other significant factors in play, *Communio* also helped insure that the crisis of the Soviet bloc issued not in a more democratic socialism or even a social liberalism with Christian Democratic features like that which prevailed in Western Europe, but rather in protofascism.

This said, while the *Communio* trend played a critical role in the Right's strategy to defeat the Soviet Union, it was always a subaltern partner and has had limited success as a pastoral strategy for Church itself. Specifically, the percentage of the European population identifying as Catholic (in both Europe and North America) has continued to decline and has continued to express increasing independence from a hierarchy which increasingly rejects its aspirations quite explicitly. And those that *have* embraced the Church's right turn have, furthermore, generally turned even further right, opting for a full-blown traditionalism or even fascism and rejecting *Communio*'s centrist position on, for example, the climate, immigration, and economic justice questions. Indeed, much of the European New Right and White Nationalist movement has abandoned Christianity entirely for various forms of Neopaganism.

* * *

Radical Orthodoxy must be understood as emerging out of the contradictions between and limitations of liberation theology and the *Communio* trend. Against liberation theology, Radical Orthodoxy rejects what it sees as fatal concessions to humanistic secularism embedded in historical materialism and indeed all forms of social theory *and* the *ontotheology* with which it implicitly charges most traditional Catholic theology. In this sense it aligns itself theologically with the *Communio* trend. At the same time, Radical Orthodoxy wants to take seriously the sense in which everything participates in the life of God in proportion to its nature, which it regards as the foundation of Catholic sacramentality, and thus to affirm the struggle for social justice and indeed for socialism as a constitutive dimension, if not the fullness, of human salvation. It does this, we will see, by making a distinctive political-theological move, making the Church and not the State the architectonic human society. Politically, this is a partial rejection of the *Communio* trend, rejecting its alliance with Capital and trying to give political content to the idea of the Church as something which exists not above or below or alongside the State, but rather as an alternative to it.

In his early work, Milbank largely accepts the Heideggerian critique of ontotheology and argues, in effect, that the whole dialectical tradition is ultimately grounded in an ontology of violence in which will is pitted against will. This is illustrated for him not only in modern social theory, but also in the older dialectical ethics of Socrates, Plato, and Aristotle. Even Plato's ideal state, he claims, is an "armed camp," and Aristotle's whole concept of virtue is really just transformation of a fundamentally military ethic of heroism. Indeed, he points out Aristotle counsels his students to be haughty to those beneath them in station and to make sure that others depend on them (Milbank 1990).

Against this ontology of violence, Milbank proposes an ontology of peace, the carrier of which is the Christian Church which, following Augustine, he calls the "Other City," founded on different loves. Milbank argues that when we recognize Being as difference, we learn a nonpossessive love which at once cancels and preserves the distance between persons. This is the creative love of God, who brings into Being creatures different from Himself and authentically free, and who calls us to love each other in the same way. There is, Milbank argues, no way to ground this ontology dialectically; indeed, to try to do so is to yield to the very ontology of violence which seeks truth through struggle and contradiction.

Gradually, Milbank has clarified his position, and granted greater space for metaphysics. Even in *Theology and Social Theory* we find the seeds of an alternative critique of ontotheology, one which locates its point of origin not in Plato and Aristotle, or even in the Latin middle ages generally, but rather in John Duns Scotus, whose doctrine of the univocity of Being laid the groundwork for both the Reformation and secular modernity. What this doctrine does (and here I am clarifying and extending Milbank a bit) is to make the difference between God and human beings quantitative rather than qualitative. On the one hand this approach grounds divine authority in power rather than love; on the other hand it opens up the possibility, which defines humanity—that human beings, by building power (through, for example, scientific and technological progress) might be able to transcend finitude and achieve divinity. And another paper (Milbank 2009) Milbank further develops this thesis, dating the "ontotheological lapse" clearly to around 1300 and, following Benedict XVI, attributes this ontotheological lapse to the growing influence of Islam which, together with Judaism, because of the primacy which they both give to the law over the image as disclosing the divine, he deems resistant to an analogical metaphysics of participation. Only Thomas, along with Nicholas Cusanus and a few others, escaped this lapse and conserved an analogical metaphysics of participation.

The change in historical analysis has not, however, altered the basic character of Milbank's position. He argues, in effect, for a reflection on being and on society in the light of faith—in effect an organic neo-Augustinianism. Methodologically, this means the primacy of theology; substantively it means an ontology of difference and an ethic of nonpossessive love which is grounded, ultimately, only in revelation and specifically in Christ. Indeed, Milbank rejects any effort on the part of theology to draw on secular social theory. More specifically, he argues that this theory is not simply "agnostic" with respect to theological questions but that it represents a secularization of historically Christian positions, a secularization which follows necessarily from the univocal metaphysics which defines all modern thought.

This sounds, in many respects, like Caputo's weak theology (Caputo 2006). Where it differs is in Milbank's distinctive understanding of Christianity. The doctrine of the incarnation for Milbank uniquely grounds a metaphysics of participation in the divine. This, in turn gives his ethic of nonpossessive love a distinctly Catholic flavor. Where the weak theologians have found in Christianity an iconoclastic critique of all structures of domination, Milbank finds the image of a divine economy which includes and transforms social structures, creating a new ecclesial order based on the gift relationship. But I anticipate . . .

In order to understand the real significance of Milbank's position, we need to examine his social and historical analysis. In an unpublished paper (Milbank 2009) Milbank begins by arguing for a mode of analysis which takes from Marxism its broader concern with systemic and structural analysis, but which avoids economic determinism, situating the economic within a broader field which not only includes by which is ultimately defined by the religious. Following (but rather substantially revising) Bataille, he calls this perspective a "general economy."

> The advantage of Marxism, as opposed to "postmodern" analyses, would seem to be the way it offers a grasp of the overall logic of societies and a single diagnosis of oppression which thereby allows a concerted resistance to this in the name of greater justice. But the disadvantage would appear to be the surrender to an economic determinism which only fits the facts through an obvious forcing. . . . Yet suppose that there is a third option here . . . following Bataille (yet without his death cult), we try to fuse Marx with Mauss in order to diagnose for the various historical phases the operation of a "general economy"—or in other words the entire logic of both production and exchange in *every* sphere—economic, political, religious, reproductive, erotic, imaginary, and so forth (although the distinction of spheres is itself a historical upshot and will only sometimes apply).

Milbank suggests that the precapitalist economy

> was *not* an economy in the restricted sense, but a mode of general economy which held the material and the symbolic together. It

is rather capitalism which invents a distinct "economic" realm, indifferent to the political standards of the just wage and the just price, to the content of what is produced and to the mode of government which secures the freedom of the market.

Indeed, capitalism, for Milbank, is *founded* on the enclosure of the sacred.

> As Karl Polanyi long ago acknowledged in *The Great Transformation*, what capitalism initially accumulates or "encloses" is not simply that which serves people's "real" needs. Beyond the most basic level of subsistence the latter is indefinable. What capitalism really encloses . . . is "the sacred," taken in the very broadest sense. That is to say, it seizes both land and people who previously have been considered to occupy positions, arrangements and roles of social, political, cosmic and religious as well as merely "economic" significance.

This enclosure does not, however, create purely secular social order. On the contrary, it is the product of what Milbank calls a "Christian heresy." This heresy is nothing other than Protestantism itself, which is founded on the same univocal metaphysics which lies behind the modern project generally and which, by its very nature, divests the material of its participation in the divine, and thus of its symbolic significance. The intimate link between Capitalism and Protestantism is apparent in the English Reformation which, for Milbank (extending the insights of Weber 1958; Moore 1966), becomes the unique constitutive act of capitalism itself.

> Nevertheless, the emergence of fully-fledged capitalism first in an England and then a Scotland permeated by Calvinist influence, now appears newly significant. In England the aristocracy and gentry and even their tenant farmers connected their new capitalist agrarian power with the memory of the secularization of sacred land in the seizure of the monasteries (so setting in train the "gothic haunting of the whigs" in their houses built of ecclesiastical rubble).

And the role of the English Reformation in capitalist development was not only economic.

> It is *not* simply the case that Protestantism ideologically supported the de-sacramentalisation of terrain, it is also true that the emergent capitalist economy was itself part and parcel of a new less sacramental mode of religious practice. Thus in the

old "religious economy," a material surplus was generally converted into sacred buildings and liturgy combined with a store of public charitable resources all managed by lay fraternities whose practice approximated to that of the celibate clergy. But in the new "religious economy" the surplus was re-cycled for the expansion of material production and the growth of profit, and the poor were now subject to a disciplinary management in a re-definition of the very nature of "charity." The entire realm of material production and exchange, instead of being seen as a participation in the divine-human *commercium* itself, was now rather seen as the realm of proof of divine arbitrary benefit for the body alone, a field of testing for the reality of inward faith and finally as one of oblique and unreliable proof of election.

The capitalist economy in the narrower sense, and the modern sovereign nation state function *within* the context of this heretical theology, as expressions of humanity's unrestricted, vice-regental dominion over a desacralized earth. The current situation is, for Milbank, first and foremost simply a radical extension of this process of enclosure, to the point that there is, in fact, almost nothing left to enclose. For contemporary capitalism, in other words, nothing is sacred.

Because of this, any resistance to capitalism in the present period will inevitably be a *religious* resistance, and will, in fact, take a very specific form:

> Refusal now is likewise is liable to take on a more absolute and global political form: as David Harvey notes, contemporary struggles are less over relative wage and working conditions as over attempts to resist further enclosures of whole ways of life. Hence they tend to occur in areas still "on the margins" of the globalizing process (South America and India: resistance to crop-patenting, ending of Coca production, dam projects etc) but can nonetheless enlist to some degree the solidarity of concerned consumers in the richer parts of the world—thus globalization also permits the possibility of world-networks linking worker with consumer co-operatives. . . . Today the only persisting struggles against capital are in some measure struggles to protect sacrality and often include specifically religious dimensions.

Indeed, Milbank argues that

> successful socialism has *always* been "conservative" in that it has *necessarily* only been able to build upon inherited "sacred" values, since these alone symbolically fuse matter and the ideal, thereby

posing the only possible alternative to mere exchange value, whose other phase (as Baudrillard divulged) was pure use-value seen as production for its own sake. This means that the "route to socialism" lies not only not necessarily through capitalism, but rather *not at all* through capitalism. Instead it lies through the bending of inherited sacral orders in more egalitarian directions, augmenting certain more democratic, participatory elements which are usually already there to some degree.

This said, Milbank does not believe that just *any* religion provides an adequate basis for resistance to global Capital. Indeed, he argues, non-monotheistic cultures, such as "Japan, China, and most of India . . . lack the counter-globalizing force and reach such as is most certainly provided by Judaism, Islam, and Christianity" (Milbank 2007). In another essay Milbank lumps together all non-Christian metaphysical systems under the heading of "impersonal religions which celebrate fate or the void" and identifies them with the nihilism of modernity (Milbank 1999).

But most monotheisms also fail to live up to Milbank's standards. Judaism, he argues, has largely allied itself with an evangelical Christianity for which the establishment of the state of Israel is a sign of the end times, while reducing its own religious content to a "wooden legalism." Protestantism, on the other hand, cannot catalyze resistance to capitalism because it is itself the very root of capitalism, and survives as a "religious supplement" only to explain the brutality of the market, to contain the damage which capitalism does to the social fabric, and because it can itself function as a type of capitalist enterprise (Milbank 2007).

Milbank, interestingly enough, has little to say about Islam in his "Geopolitical Theology." On the one hand, he acknowledges that some manifestations of contemporary Islam, such as the Iranian revolution, represent real resistance to the enclosure of the sacred and thus to global Capital, though he seems to attribute this largely to the influence of European Marxism and conservative romanticism, and only partly to the greater influence of mystical traditions and philosophy. On the other hand, he argues that the *sharia* lacks the specificity to ground any real resistance to capitalism, and seems to suggest that Sunni Islam in particular tends to a rational legal ethical universalism which is ultimately compatible with the capitalist world order. Indeed, as we noted above, Milbank attributes the modern turn towards a univocal metaphysics to the influence of Islam itself (Milbank 2009).

It is, ultimately, only Catholic Christianity which offers for Milbank the resources necessary to mount an effective resistance to global Capital. This is because, in the Incarnation, Christianity posits the participation of the human in the divine and thus the *reversal* of the capitalist enclosure of the sacred.

> Christianity is also Christendom precisely because it is the religion of the Incarnation. Were its universalizing tendency only a spiritualizing one, as is ultimately more the case for Judaism and Islam, then it would conceive of salvation more simply as our raising ourselves above the local and specific in response to the call of God. . . . It would generously be able to imagine modes of this raising being able to be conveyed in other images and other words: it would be able to be "multi-cultural." But because it is founded on the scandalous and dangerous idea that the infinite was in some sense born from a finite womb, in fulfillment of a particular local tradition, it is committed to the idea that the only way to the spiritually universal is through the gradual conjoining of all times and all spaces in an open-ended continuum of meaning. The project of individual salvation is then inseparable from the project of the pacification of the earth announced by the angels to the shepherds in Luke, which Paul tried to set in motion by establishing a kind of new polity, the *ecclesia*, that was also an international gift-exchange network. (Milbank 2007)

The Incarnation, in other words, implies a radical transformation of the economy and of the state.

> Within the "general economy" of antiquity, the "economic" in the narrower, special sense was confined to the area of household management or its more large-scale equivalent, such as the provisioning of troops. The "economic" existed ultimately to sustain the possibility of a more elevated "political life" of negotiated friendship in debated agreement amongst adult males. But as Mondzain points out, Christian theology now spoke of a "divine economy" that was at the very heart of "divine government" and no subordinate aspect. This "economy" was at once a proportionate distribution of being to the finite creation in various modes and degrees, and at the same time an "exceptional" extra-legal kenotic and dispensatory adaptation of the "theological" inner-divine Trinitarian life to the creation and especially the human creation, through processes of "provision" that included the "economy of salvation." (Milbank 2007)

The Incarnation also has political implications:

> If the Father only exercises his omnipotence through a sharing of himself in the image, that monarchic authority is here re-defined.... The Trinity is a "monarchy" Gregory averred, but only in the sense of a supreme unified *arche* whose principle of order already exists as a set of reciprocal relations or *scheses*. The divinely economic "rule by image" is therefore not a deceiving bedazzlement by a reserved and manipulating paternal will, but rather the always-already begun emergence of paternity *only* in filial expression, which is then open to interpretative and loving reception by the Holy Spirit, the third person of the Trinity. (Milbank 2007)

This points, ultimately towards

> the primacy of an ecclesial rule which surpasses the mere imposition of law and the upholding of regulation, but rather reaches economically to people's detailed needs and the endeavour to reconcile all creatures to all other ones, while permitting the people themselves to participate in this economizing transmission. This is not, as Mondzain implies, an ideological sanctification of a rule which the iconoclasts were trying to secularize, but just the opposite: an attempt, equivalent to that of Augustine in the west, relatively to secularize the imperial power and to insist on the primacy of trans-political social purposes. (Milbank 2007)

This "primacy of ecclesial rule" lies, ultimately, at the heart of Milbank's project.

> A truly orthodox Catholic position would demand radical resistance to the American empire, capitalism, and conservative evangelicalism.... The only hope for the future substantive peace of global inter-related harmonious consensus lies in re-inventing in some fashion a Catholic mode of terrestrial occupation, both sacramental and political.... Secular authorities should remain independently occupied with the things of time, but the ultimate measure of justice here is the degree to which this occupation opens already the way to human deification under grace. To sustain this measure, the Church should now encourage the social growth of a far more egalitarian mode of economic gift-exchange, beyond anything so far known in Christendom, yet in consistency with its even as yet still unenclosed sacral commonalities. (Milbank 2007)

Practically, *Radical Orthodoxy* has been associated with *Blue Labor* and, to a lesser extent, with the *Red Tories*. *Blue Labor* attempts to reground the socialist project in an ethics of virtue and to reframe Labour policy in a way which emphasizes localism and subsidiarity, as well as social institutions which cultivate virtue. It has tended towards soft Euroskepticism and some hesitation with regard to open immigration. The *Red Tories* on the other hand tend to blend a more organic traditionalism at the theological level with a commitment to paternalistic policies which protect but do not empower the working classes.

* * *

There is much to commend in Milbank's work. Milbank's analysis of the univocal metaphysics which at once expresses and legitimates the secular project is profoundly insightful and has deepened and enriched my own work. And his use of Bataille's theory of "general economy" allows him to analyze the Reformation and Primitive Accumulation as part of a single, global process, so that there is not merely an "affinity" between the Protestant Ethic and the Spirit of Capitalism, as Weber argued, nor is Calvinism merely the "ideological superstructure" of a process of primitive accumulation which was, at the "real" level, entirely economic; the Reformation—along with some similar developments in Baroque and Enlightenment Catholicism—and Primitive Accumulation constitute, on the contrary, a single, inseparable whole. Milbank is correct that capitalism is, at root, an enclosure of the sacred and that resistance to Capital requires resistance to further enclosures and the rebuilding of community beyond the state.

It is precisely because of the depth and complexity of Milbank's analysis that it points us to the very heart of why even most the profoundly Catholic modifications of Christianity are inadequate. This issue can be addressed at either the philosophical or the theological level. At the philosophical level Milbank is an articulate defender of an analogical metaphysics which centers around our participation in the creative life of God. But he does not consider the third alternative in the debate around the predication of Being: that of an equivocal metaphysics, and whether or not it might offer a more credible account of the human condition. This is the metaphysics is which advocated by Moshe ben Maimon and which is, in many ways, definitive of Judaism. In an equivocal metaphysics it is understood that God exists in an utterly different way than we do—or perhaps better, that God does not *ex-ist* at all. This does not exclude participation. God, as the power of Being as such, is the Being in and through whom we exist. But as contingent beings we are not can never become this Being. Existence is *being outside*. And what we are outside of is God, not in the sense of have a separate source of being but in the sense of being fundamentally something other than the Being we crave.

Humanity, in this sense, as the *desire to be God*, is fundamentally trapped in a contingency hell from which we cannot escape. Even for Catholicism, grace does not overcome our contingency and *theosis* is only accidental (in the Aristotelian sense of being a quality superadded to our nature). But Christianity does not comprehend—or rather chooses, for political reasons, to ignore—the implications of a correct understanding of the human condition for its doctrine of original sin. Sin is not an arbitrary turning of the will away from God. It arises, rather, because we are aware of a good we cannot have and inevitably pursue it with means which end up harming ourselves and others. Being rational, we know that the highest Good is Being as such or God, but being finite and contingent we pursue this necessary and infinite end with contingent and finite means. Desiring the pure generativity which is God we end up seeking immortality and dominion over the resources which would permit it. And even if we hold ourselves back from conquest and exploitation, we still have to eat. Even if we refrain from eating animals we eat plants. We live by killing other living things . . .

While Christian theology has always held back from drawing this issue so starkly, this is the real logic behind its doctrine of original sin. We can't escape sin for the simple reason that we must engage in some degree of violence just to live. And once you realize this, and join that realization to belief in a divine sovereign who commands us to engage in an absolutely unselfish love—well we look pretty bad. And the demand that we at least submit and obey not only seems reasonable. We crave it. Thus, the theology—but also the psychology—of Empire and ultimately of fascism.

But there is another way to look at our situation. Our problem is not moral but metaphysical. We are drawn into being by the incredible beauty of God, by the lure of Being as such. But there can be no Being as Such outside of God, who is One. Even if, contrary to the Mahayana, we allow that there *is* something with inherent existence, the Buddhists are still right about contingent being: we are empty. And our failures and our involvement with evil—which is, of course, just non-Being—are inevitable. But we can also do things that God cannot. We can mend the torn fabric of the universe, the very awareness of which, because the only possible response to such suffering is infinite pain, is contrary to the divine nature. We don't participate in the life of God by enjoying a taste of eternity. We participate by redeeming space and time—always and only in part to be sure. The result is not *theosis*. Nor is it the Kingdom of God, on earth or anywhere else. It is something radically other than God, but something which is better than it otherwise would be because we finite and contingent beings are aware of God and act with care and generativity, however imperfect.

This all becomes very important when we consider the terrible history of messianism, of which both Christianity and socialism are prime examples. If we believe that anything other than divine perfection is mortal sin then we have only two alternatives: a regime which takes it for granted that human beings are inherently sinful and aims only to maintain order—while allowing those who pursue their rapacity in an orderly and disciplined way to prey on and instrumentalize everyone else (the Augustinian alternative), or else one that demands perfection of everyone and tries to discipline or simply eliminate anyone who falls short (a degree of "commanding right and forbidding wrong" which even most Islam would reject as demonic, but which gives us a good description of a socialism—e.g., Maoism—which has not utterly abandoned the communist ideal). In this sense Jiang is absolutely correct that it is necessary to rescue the communist ideal from Christian political theology (though it is it not at all clear that this means we need also to rescue it from liberalism, or resign ourselves to it being no more than *xinxue*, no more than a "learning of the heart").

Theologically, Milbank's problem comes, very simply, from the core dogma of Christianity: that Jesus was both divine and human and that therefore something like that is possible for us, which in turn means both that it is legitimate to levy on human beings moral demands which are incompatible with our finite and contingent nature and also that if we somehow fulfill these demands (presumably through the assistance of divine grace) we will somehow actually transcend our finitude and contingency. And as much insight as Milbank has shown regarding the dangers of a univocal metaphysics, such a grace is possible only for an absolute divine sovereign who can act contrary not only to the laws of nature but also to those of logic. The doctrine of the Trinity, which the divinity of Jesus requires, is an impossible attempt to reconcile absolute divine monarchy with a form and degree of human participation in the life of God which is logically impossible.

It is in this light that we must understand Milbank's defense of monarchy. However much he and other monarchists may insist that the king reigns but does not rule, the events surround the recent death of Elizabeth II and the ascent of Charles III have illustrated clearly that the very essence of monarchy is the ability and the *right* to command, even contrary to law, positive and natural, as Charles has in his orders suspending basic services, including medical care and his brutal and dismissive treatment of his staff, during the royal funeral. The king is indeed a sacred figure, the image of God, but the divine he reveals is, even in this petty exercise of royal prerogative, an image not of grace but of terror.

This, then is the problem with Milbank's proposal of the Church rather than the State as the architectonic institution of human civilization. *We do need something other than the State, an institution which does not aspire to become or to control the State, to lead the human civilizational project.* And we will show that the priority placed by the Communist Party on State Power rather than decommodification is at the center of the transformation of socialism into an alterimperialism. But this institution cannot be founded on an imperial *mythos*, on the story of an absolutely sovereign God who requires the sacrifice of his Son as the condition of forgiving the disobedience of his creatures (or indeed of any *mythos* which makes the need for forgiveness the principle problem of the human condition), even if this Son was also a revolutionary messianic leader. And the option for an analogical rather than an equivocal metaphysics, while it softens this problem and prevents theocratic dictatorship, is not sufficient to overcome this problem. Both the *mythos* and the *metaphysics* of Christianity must be rejected in favor a story and a theory which, while taking seriously the reality of evil, understand it to be the inevitable result of our finite and contingent condition and which is inspired to mend the broken fabric of the world by the incredible beauty of God who exists in an entirely different sense than we do, and who lures us forward, repenting and learning from our many failures to be sure but always growing towards a Being we know we will never achieve.

"Postliberal" Communitarianism

Developing alongside Catholic Social Teaching, and significantly overlapping with it, there are a range of communitarian doctrine which emerged beginning in the 1970s and which took as their point of departure a critique of liberal theory, focusing most especially on the failure of liberal theory to provide a substantive doctrine of the Good. Here we will look at two variants of this theory, the "narrative" Aristotelianism of Alisdair MacIntyre and the eclectic but highly innovative synthesis of Roberto Mangabeira Unger.

MacIntyre (MacIntyre 1981, 1988) locates the source of all understandings of the Good in culturally specific narratives which present distinctive, compelling visions of human excellence and social justice. These narratives develop by means of a dialectical process catalyzed both by debates within traditions and encounters between them. This dialectic draws out the implications and limitations of existing views and drives towards increasingly more adequate formulations. Narratives compete with each other in an ongoing dialogue. Those which are able to incorporate the insights of other narratives without compromising their own integrity tend to win out; those which are incorporated or which cannot find adherents lose. He makes no attempt, however, to ground his ethics in a rational metaphysics, the impossibility of which he seems to accept, even as he embraces "narratives" developed by thinkers who, like Augustine and Thomas, were nothing if not metaphysicians.

MacIntyre sees his theory as an extension of Socratic, Platonic, and Aristotelian dialectics. Indeed, he claims to represent the vanguard of a Thomistic revival. Nothing, in fact, could be further from the truth. What we have here, rather, is a return to the moderate sophism of a Protagoras against the extremism of a Gorgias or a Callicles—a moderate, "constructive" postmodernism pitted against the deconstructive radicalism of Derrida and his allies. In the final analysis the ground, such as it is, remains the same: tradition and social convention. Indeed, in the light of MacIntyre's attempt to join Thomistic philosophy with Augustinian theology on the basis of an epistemology and (absent) metaphysics which both would have rejected, it is probably most accurate to it regard him as an intellectual heir of the French traditionalist Joseph de Maistre, who in the wake of the French Revolution gave a rightist spin to the same conventionalist morality which, in the works of Rousseau, had been one of the touchstones of the Revolution.

This is, no doubt, why in spite of his continued criticism of capitalism MacIntyre has conciliated conservative Catholicism and has been reluctant to criticize the Church's departure from its historic commitment to Thomism. In the end, he is not a Thomist but rather a left traditionalist like Milbank.

This is, in fact, the danger of essentially all post-liberal communitarianisms which are not informed by the dialectical tradition and immunized against fascism. Indeed, it is due to the fact that Unger and MacIntyre have at least some roots in that tradition that they avoid conciliating the Right to the extent that they do. It is more difficult to say the same for thinkers like Patrick Deneen. Deneen, to be sure, criticizes liberalism for legitimating massive inequalities and has criticized aspects of National Conservatism. But he has also participated in National Conservative meetings and met with authoritarian leaders such as Victor Orban. Adrian Vermeule, similarly, has argued openly for Catholic integralism and for what he calls "common good constitutionalism,"

> based on the principles that government helps direct persons, associations, and society generally toward the common good, and that strong rule in the interest of attaining the common good is entirely legitimate. . . . This approach should take as its starting point substantive moral principles that conduce to the common good, principles that officials (including, but by no means limited to, judges) should read into the majestic generalities and ambiguities of the written Constitution. These principles include respect for the authority of rule and of rulers; respect for the hierarchies needed for society to function; solidarity within and among families, social groups, and workers' unions, trade associations, and professions; appropriate subsidiarity, or respect for the legitimate roles of public bodies and associations at all levels of government and society; and a candid willingness to "legislate morality"—indeed, a recognition that all legislation is necessarily founded on some substantive conception of morality, and that the promotion of morality is a core and legitimate function of authority. Such principles promote the common good and make for a just and well-ordered society.
>
> [The main aim of common-good constitutionalism] is certainly not to maximize individual autonomy or to minimize the abuse of power (an incoherent goal in any event), but instead to ensure that the ruler has the power needed to rule well. . . . Just authority in rulers can be exercised for the good of subjects, if necessary even against the subjects' own perceptions of what is

best for them—perceptions that may change over time anyway, as the law teaches, habituates, and re-forms them. Subjects will come to thank the ruler whose legal strictures, possibly experienced at first as coercive, encourage subjects to form more authentic desires for the individual and common goods, better habits, and beliefs that better track and promote communal well-being. (Vermeule 2020)

* * *

Roberto Magnabeira Unger's *Knowledge and Politics* (Unger 1975) points the way to a communitarianism which is less vulnerable to co-optation by the Right.[1] Unger argues that liberal theory provides a fundamentally inaccurate picture of human nature and human society, in which individuals are motivated by arbitrary desires and the principal role of human society is to restrain the inevitable war of all against all which results by means of rule of law. Unger proposes instead that we share a common human nature rooted in reason, with desires which flow from that shared nature which are ultimately ordered to the good, and which we realize through what he calls organic social groups. Any danger that these groups might themselves undercut individual freedom was to be addressed through protections for the rights of free expression, free association, and free work. *Part of what is distinctive here is that Unger regards liberal theory as an inadequate ground for liberal rights.*

This and other early works by Unger helped shape the Critical Legal Studies movement and opened up a discussion around liberal theory which had long been taken for granted, but it was regarded as insufficiently developed, leaving too many unanswered questions regarding what it might lead to in practice (Richards 1976). In his later work Unger puts more emphasis on what he calls the plasticity of the social, arguing against Marx that not only do human beings make their history, but they make it in an entirely open ended way, without any limits imposed by underlying structures which unfold in accord with an inevitable logic (Unger 1987).

---

1. In the US postliberalism and, especially, communitarianism is often associated in particular with the work of Amitai Etzioni (Etzioni 1993). Etzioni was certainly an important public advocate for communitiarn views. But his work operates at a lower level of abstraction and does not address the fundamental questions which would need to be answered in order to treat it as a political theology. Thus our focus on other thinkers.

Unger has also written an extended criticism of *many worlds* cosmologies and a defense of the unity of the universe and the reality of time (Unger and Smolin 2014) and situates his larger social theory and political project in the context of a philosophy of religion which affirms both the priority of humanity's spiritual interests and the critique of religion mounted by the great masters of the hermeneutic of suspicion, such as Marx, Nietzsche, and Freud.

Religion, he argues, is fundamental, because our search for meaning is fundamental—as is the uniquely contradictory reality of human existence. We are capable of asking what it all means, but unable to arrive at a definitive answer to this question. We have the idea of immortality, and yet know we will die. No matter how much we have, we always want more, or at least something better. And we are constantly reminded of these limitations through the petty routines imposed by material existence, which amount to constant small deaths. The problem with historic religions, he argues is that they have claimed to resolve or at least soften these problems by transcending the world or transforming it partially or totally. This, he argues is a false promise. Religion must accept the contradictions of human existence as insuperable while engaging people in a transformation of the world in a way which rejects the compromises made by historic religious institutions—and by historic socialism. "The goal," he says, "is not to humanize society but to divinize humanity . . . to raise ordinary life to a higher level of intensity and capability" (Unger 2014).

Unger really has accomplished something very significant. His early works were one of my principal inspirations and I find myself turning to his later work again and again in spite of some significant differences. Specifically, he articulates quite effectively both the enduring value of the liberal ideal and the vacuity of liberal theory, arguing that rational autonomy in fact depends on strong communities of meaning and value. He affirms the priority of the spiritual while fully integrating the hermeneutic of suspicion and the critique of religion associated with it and he affirms the priority of philosophy over mathematical physics as the architectonic discipline, reigning in the unwarranted speculations of many worlds theory. And he does this all in a way which shows an understanding of the contradictions of capitalism and of politics itself as a spiritual discipline. He situates the humanistic project in a broader spiritual context without giving ground to dogmatic orthodoxies.

This said, I do have some concerns about Ungers system. First, while I affirm Unger's moderate realism in mathematics and his affirmation of the unity of the universe, it is not clear that he fully understands the diversity of many worlds claims. In particular we will, in a later work, argue for the *possibility* of a hierarchy of "worlds" or *cosmoi* which approach the reality of Being by different degrees, allowing us to make sense of religious language about "heavens" and "hells" and other sorts of *bardo*. This is, in turn based in a new moderate realist interpretation of quantum theory which argues that the quantum wave function allows matter to be in multiple states because material existence, being pure potential, is in fact fuzzy by nature. Neither the co-existence of multiple possible state nor the "reduction" of wave-function potentiality to existential act has anything to do with subjectivity or observation. Rather, as we ascend what is often called the Great Chain of Being from fundamental forces through mineral, plant, animal, and rational beings, towards God, things become more fully real and determinate, their potential being reduced to act as historic Thomism suggests. The extent of this reduction creates an ontological hierarchy which *could* result in a hierarchy of "worlds."

Second, I fund find Unger's rejection of "deep structure" theories (including dialectical and historical materialism) as deterministic fundamentally flawed. These theories depend on a sharp distinction between underlying structure and phenomenal reality and it is these underlying structures which operate in a law like manner. Phenomenal reality is the result of multiple combined and contradictory structures which are ordered to diverse civilizational ideals and which operate on diverse material substrates, so that the course of events, while never arbitrary, is too complex to support a doctrine of linear progress like that advocated by more simplistic forms of liberalism and socialism. Understanding underlying structures, however, is critical to specifying the nature of social contradictions, which are different than surface conflicts. As a result, I have significant concern that Unger, in coming to the correct realization that communism is not the "resolution of the contradiction between essence and existence" is not fully clear that the persistence of generalized commodity production (the requirement that people sell their labor power in order to survive) generates mass alienation and must be transcended, not only to advance the full development of human capacities but also to prevent the persistent reassertion of authoritarianism and fascism.

Finally, while I fully embrace Unger's rejection of the claim of historic religions (including secular religions such as humanistic or technocratic secularism) to offer a "definitive solution to the riddle of history" his understanding of these religious traditions seems limited and in particular he seems unaware of the extent to which "high" mystical theologies across multiple traditions *require* us to overcome the idea that the purpose of religion is to realize *our* aims, but instead require that we grow beyond those aims to actually seek God for God's sake, quite apart from what that means for us—or, as in the case of Buddhism, to realize and find joy in the realization that the self-existence we crave is impossible, dedicate ourselves to (and find our highest joy in) helping others achieve this realization. The result is a spiritually literate classical humanism rather than the high spirituality which his underlying insights would otherwise support.

* * *

Ultimately, we will argue, it is impossible to articulate a communitarian theory with a critical appropriation of dialectical and historical materialism and without engaging more directly the question of political theology. Communitarianism, even when strongly democratic, explicitly committed to liberal values, and sharply critical of capitalism, like that of Unger is fundamentally a species of left traditionalism which, partially reversing the Durkheimian and Comtean inversion, locates the ground of ethical principles and thus of the political order in human society and the human search for meaning, effectively endow human society with divine prerogatives. This is problematic whether these prerogatives are exercised by organic groups and mass democratic parties as Unger argues, or by judges who set themselves above the written constitution.

Thus the critical importance of the dialectical tradition which provides a way of grounding ethics utterly independent of will—divine or human—in the underlying structure of reality. And dialectical materialism, whatever its problems, is an integral part of this tradition and can help us separate politics from will once and for all. In order to do that, however, we will need to understand the internal contradictions of socialism and what historic socialism failed to fulfill its promise. First, we need to consider a final variant of the liberal tradition.

From Social Liberalism to Neoliberalism

Social Liberalism as an Ideal

Marx identified contradictions within capitalism which, he believed, would lead inevitable to economic crisis, class struggle, and ultimately to social revolution. These contradictions included:

- A tendency for Capital, in an effort to maximize accumulation, to invest in technological progress which increases productivity and thus drives down the value of labor power, because it takes less living labor for workers to reproduce themselves, with the result that workers can no longer purchase the products they product. This leads to recurrent crises of "overproduction" or "underconsumption" which ultimately make capitalism itself untenable.

- A tendency for this technological progress to lead to a decline in the rate of profit and the redeployment of Capital to low technology, low wage activities in the colonies, which delivered a higher rate of return, but reinforced the first contradiction, the tendency towards underconsumption.

In reality, these contradictions proved to be very far from fatal, at least in at least in the imperial metropoles which could export them in some measure to their colonies and which had sufficient wealth to redistribute in order to stabilize their economies during times of crisis, and at least in the medium *durée* of a century or two. And by addressing the economic contradictions which it needed to address for its own reasons, the liberal bourgeoisie was able to address, at least in part, the criticisms of capitalism advanced by radical democrats, socialists, and communists.

The reforms to which the bourgeoisie acceded in order to address the contradictions of capitalism had two distinct sources. On the one hand, elements within the bourgeoisie became increasingly sensitive to the ways in which the development of actually existing capitalism limited the realization of the liberal ideal. *Social liberalism* argued that while capitalism has demonstrated its superiority as a catalyst for economic growth, without significant state intervention the vast majority of people will not be able to reap the benefits of this growth and make use of the freedom afforded by the liberal order. While social liberals reject the historical materialist claim that there are inevitable internal contradictions within capitalism that lead eventually to a revolutionary crisis requiring that capitalism be superseded, many do acknowledge the existence of irrationalities which only state intervention can rectify. The trend has diverse roots, including the English New Liberals, such as Thomas Hill Green, Leonard Hobhouse, and John Hobson (Green 2006; Hobhouse 1994; Hobson 2000), who argued that individual liberty was meaningful only if prosperity was shared in a way that allowed people to use it, and early "centrist" sociologists such as Lester Ward (Commanger 1950) in the United States, Emile Durkheim in France, and Max Weber in Germany, who attempted to chart a path between the Social Darwinism of Herbert Spencer and William Graham Sumner on the one hand and historical materialism on the other, arguing that capitalism brought enormous progress but also had enormous human costs which, however, they argued could be ameliorated. These contributions were layered over with the economic contributions of John Maynard Keynes (Keynes 1936), who argued that capitalism had profound tendencies towards underconsumption which could only be overcome by intervention to support demand by means of regulated collective bargaining, public investments, and income transfers, and of the German Ordoliberalism (Fevre 2921), who focused on the need to maintain the conditions for authentic competition and warned that growing economic power could lead to growing political power which undermined the liberal order.

At the same time, as we noted above, many of Marx's followers argued, following Engels, that the gradual progress of industrialization would lead to the expansion of the proletariat until, with universal suffrage, the social democratic parties could come to power by means of electoral struggle alone, and begin a socialist transformation. In practice, however, because the alienation engendered by the commodification of labor power tended to gradually erode the workers consciousness of themselves as *creative*, and instead formed them merely as consumers, the policies implemented these parties tended to stop short and of fundamental structural change and gradually converged with those of social liberals.

Social liberal policies centered around:

- regulated collective bargaining which linked increases in wages to increases in productivity, with raises for unionized workers serving as a kind of benchmark for nonunion workers,
- social security, unemployment, and income transfers for those who could not work, and

- public investments in both the military and in research, education, and infrastructure.

All of these tended to support effective demand and to overcome the tendency of the rate of profit to decline high skill, high technology, high wage sectors. This is precisely the "Fordist" regime (Aglietta 2001) which the most advanced capitalist countries implemented in part just before the First World War and then more fully in the wake of the Great Depression, as the liberal bourgeoisie and working classes organized at the "trade union" and "social democratic" levels came together in a popular front to resist fascism. By transferring surplus from the wealthiest strata to the working class and to forced investment in progressive sectors of the economy, they were able to squeeze another 30–50 years of meaningful civilizational progress out of capitalist societies.

The correct assessment of the legacy of social liberalism or the welfare state is one of the principal lines of demarcation between social liberals and social democrats on the one hand and maximalist "democratic socialists" and most communists on the other. The first argue that the postwar period represented a real step towards resolving the contradictions of capitalism and making the freedoms promised by the liberal order real and effective for the people as a whole. The project is simply incomplete. Maximalist "democratic socialists" on the other hand, along with most communists, see the period as one of technocratic management of the contradictions of capitalism—for communists made possible by the superprofits from imperialism—and ultimately unsustainable as a form of transition in the long run.

In our view neither analysis is accurate. On the one hand, the gains of the postwar period both for the working class as a whole and for women and oppressed minorities in particular were very real, and in fact represent much, if not all that an authentically communist government would be able to do for its citizens in the early decades of a transition. On the other hand, the room to make this progress with the support of a section of the bourgeoisie and thus less intense class struggle *was* due in part to imperialist superprofits, though higher levels of productivity must also be taken into account. And the model does not seem to have been sustainable, though we will argue that this for political and ideological rather than economic reasons. In order to test this thesis, we need to consider the crisis of social liberalism.

The Crisis of Social Liberalism

The dominant historical narrative at both the popular and scholarly levels takes for granted that the period following the New Deal and World War II was one of sustained economic growth and widespread prosperity—a period that lasted until the end of the 1960s or the beginning of the 1970s when, suddenly, the entire model suddenly went into crisis. Growth ground to a halt while prices soared, putting an end to a long period during which it might have seemed reasonable to believe that the contradictions of capitalism could in fact be resolved within the system. And there is a surprisingly broad consensus as well, across the entire political spectrum, that this crisis was the result of wage increases exceeding growth in productivity, which led to declining profits and a crisis in capital formation. Where the Left differed from the Right in its analysis (Weisskopf 1979; Brenner 1998, 2016; Mosley 2016) was in pointing out the role of globalization, as Capital was able to work around "nation-state" level economic regulation, redeploying capital to the periphery while not reinvesting in heavy industry at home. Imperialism, not excessive income transfers and over-reaching by labor in the collective bargaining process was the cause of "stagflation."

In reality, neither the picture of the postwar period as one of sustained growth and low inflation nor the picture of the 1970s as a period of "stagflation" is really accurate (Amadeo 2022). Growth in real GDP averaged 0.1 percent annually from 1946 to 1950, 3.63 percent during the 1950s, 4.3 percent during the 1960s, and 3.2 percent during the 1970s. Inflation averaged 6.74 percent per year from 1946 to 1950, 1.8 percent during the 1950s, 2.96 percent during the 1960s, and 8 percent during the 1970s. Unemployment averaged 4.43 percent from 1946 to 1950, 4.28 percent during the 1950s, 4.66 during the 1960s, and 6.49 percent in the 1970s. The 1970s did, in other words represent a bit of a stall, probably driven in large part by oil prices, but by no means a catastrophic collapse.

More important from the vantage point of our argument, however, is the fact *that there is no evidence that wage growth exceeded growth in productivity at any point in the postwar period*. On the contrary, the two tracked each other closely from 1950 until roughly 1970, and sharply diverged, with *productivity continuing to grow while wages stagnated*, resulting in a sharp decline in labor's share of the valued added (Roper 2020). What we do know is that corporate profits as a percentage of GDP, after a peak just short of 10 percent in the early 1950s remained between roughly 5 percent and 7 percent through the next two decades, before plummeting in 1970, rising sharply to about 8 percent in the late 1970s, plummeting again to around 3.5 percent in the mid-1980s, and then rising sharply to between 10 percent and 12 percent, where it still sits today (Kavadas 2022). Wages as a share of GDP, on the other hand, after remaining relatively stable around 48 percent to 52 percent during the 1950s and 1960s, fell sharply to 42 percent in 2011, with a brief partial recovery to around 45 percent in the late 1990s and again during the pandemic (BEA 2021).

So what actually happened? We know now that whatever support the New Deal and the Great Society enjoyed within the liberal bourgeoisie—and it was no doubt significant—there were always dissent (Denton 2012). And the economic heyday of Fordism—the 1950s and early 1960s—witnessed the rise of a mass far right under the cover of anticommunism, while groups like the Mount Pelerin Society (Mirkowski and Plehwe 2009; Burgin 2012; Jones 2012; Slobodian 2018) tutored the bourgeoisie in Austrian School economics and *National Review* forged a fusion between libertarian economics and social conservatism which laid the groundwork for a fascist resurgence.

If the New Deal and the Great Society were very far from being a *revolution*, what followed had all the hallmarks of a *counter-revolution*. On the one hand, Austrian School and monetarist economists persuaded the liberal bourgeoisie that they had been excessively "generous" with the working classes, which were beginning to feel "entitled," and that "the country" could no longer afford such largesse. Meanwhile, fascist ideologues and operatives led by Kevin Phillips leveraged the racism and misogyny in both the South and in Northern industrial centers to build a base for reaction. Carefully executed special operations—the election of Woytila in 1978 and the intervention of Reagan operatives to delay the release of the US hostages from Iran in 1980—coupled with what has likely been decades of election fraud brought the Right to power in 1980, when it began to systematically dismantle the gains the working classes had made since the 1930s, oppressed minorities since the 1950s, and women since the 1960s. When the Soviet Union dissolved in 1991, the Right was able to claim that it had "won the Cold War" when it would, in fact, be more accurate to say, that the Russian Empire simply entered a period of retrenchment and abandoned socialist alterimperialism for full blown fascism.

It is in this context that Marx's most egregious error comes to the fore. While the economic contradictions of capitalism may not be unmanageable, the alienation it creates *does* in fact alienate human beings form their essential nature, transforming creative participants in the self-organizing process which is matter in to consumers and creating, as Erich Fromm (Fromm 1941, 1943) authoritarian personality structures which provide an enduring mass base for fascism. *The crisis of social liberalism was, in other words, a product of a long planned, carefully prepared counteroffensive from the Right, and especially from those sectors of the bourgeoisie in lower technology, lower wage industries less dependent on rising real wages and cultural pluralism. This counteroffensive found a ready constituency in the fully proletarianized and thus maximally alienated working classes of the advanced capitalist countries.* And let us be clear. The working classes responded to the fascist offensive *not because of any economic insecurity*. On the contrary, the economic dislocation experienced by the working classes after 1978 came . . . well . . . *after 1978, as a result of the fascist offensive*. The working classes responded to fascist overtures because of the alienation and the authoritarian formations—patriarchal and racist—it engendered.

This rightward turn in the US, with analogues in Europe and to some extent globally, led to the global defeat of the international workers movement, whether it was operating in alliance with national bourgeois, petty bourgeois, and peasant elements in the old "Third World," or in alliance with the liberal bourgeoisie and petty bourgeoisie as in the US, Europe, and Japan. This in turn facilitated the creation of a unified global market not just in goods and services, but in Capital, completing the process of capitalist development. A weaker working class in the old imperial metropoles, coupled with accelerated deployment of Capital globally has led to a convergence in global productive and real wages, undercutting anticapitalist resistance in the old Third World, where it has given way to something more like a social democratic reformism (though with less investment in liberal and democratic norms) while leaving the proletariat of the old imperial metropoles to contemplate a long term stagnation which it experiences as (relative) decline.

Eventually, of course, the underlying contradictions of capitalism, which social liberalism had softened, began to reassert themselves, leading ultimately to the Great Recession of 2008. This took the form of a financial crisis because, as underconsumption tendencies reasserted themselves, the bourgeoisie responded by supporting demand not through income transfers or public investment but rather by extending more and more credit to an already overextended population, resulting in real estate and other speculative bubbles which, predictably, eventually burst.

5

What Was and Is Socialism?

Historic Socialism

Fundamental Contradictions

It remains for us to consider the current position of the Left, situating that position in the historical context of the socialist project. This requires us to return to Marx and to analyze how his project—with the contradictions we identified above—was appropriated by various constituencies and various interpreters, and how their decisions led us to the current conjuncture.

There are two fundamental contradictions in the communist project. The first is metaphysical, the second social-psychological. Marx makes it clear that the fundamental aim of communism is, we have seen, nothing less than *theosis*. "Communism is the . . . resolution of the contradiction between existence and essence." But is such a thing possible? Can we cross the boundary between contingent and necessary being or, to use the language Marx prefers, the threshold between necessity and freedom, by political means—or indeed by any means whatsoever? The answer to this question should not be controversial. Struggling for and even achieving justice, living in a society governed by rule of law, by just laws made with the consent of the people in accord with natural law, and free to act in accord with the dictates of an informed conscience, without being subject to any master or "employer," represents a tremendous advance for humanity. But it does not make us God. Indeed, there is *no* spiritual rather the "bourgeois ideologists," i.e., what we have called the humanistic intelligentsia, which ultimately comes to understand "the line of march, conditions, and ultimate general result" of the historical process and which therefore leads to working class to state power, on the basis of which it begins the transition from capitalism to socialism (Marx and Engels 1848/2000).

This analysis in turn provides the principal point of reference in relationship to with the various schisms within the international workers' movement are generally marked. *Utopian Socialists* reject Marx's focus on the political in favor of building intentional socialist communities or communes. *Anarchists and Libertarian Socialists* reject Marx's emphasis on state power as the key strategic goal, and in particular the idea that the state is a privileged instrument of social transformation. Among those who accept Marx's emphasis on political struggle and agree that state power is the first step in socialist construction, there is a further division between *Social Democrats* and *Communists*. Social Democrats argued originally that the process of industrialization itself would lead to the gradual, spontaneous growth of the proletariat and thus of the ranks of the socialist parties, which would eventually achieve state power by means of electoral struggle, and then gradually build socialism and eventually communism by means of incremental reforms (Engels 1880/1978). Later they regrounded their gradualism on an expectation of the moral progress made possible by civic engagement and education, which cultivated rational autonomy and thus a good will (Bernstein 1899/1909). Communists (Lenin 1902/1929) argued that the alienation engendered by the commodification of labor power makes spontaneous class consciousness impossible, and instead saw the need for a conscious revolutionary leadership drawn from the humanistic intelligentsia to lead a revolution which conquers state power by means of insurrection or popular war, building mass support by promising land reform, the defeat of fascism, national liberation, etc. This last schism more or less overlapped with the schism between those who saw socialism as requiring a developed industrial base and who therefore did not see revolutionary potential in colonized, agrarian regions, and those who believed that it was precisely the "weak links" in the imperialist chain which would break first, and thus prioritized the struggle against imperialism.

Social democracy gradually evolved over the course of the last century in an increasingly reformist direction, losing sight of any attempt to actually transcend capitalism and instead becoming a means of managing its contradictions, so that in practice it has become indistinguishable from a more left leaning social liberalism. More recently, however, we have seen the resurgence of "democratic socialist" currents which propose to return to the original social democratic vision, often shifted towards an extremist maximalism which is to the left of historic communism on everything except the question of conscious leadership and anti-imperialism.

The communist movement, meanwhile, is generally understood as having divided around:

- how to undertake the process of socialist construction (the transition from capitalism to communism),
- the strategic implications of fascism, decolonization and the national liberation movements, and the postwar period of capitalist stabilization in the imperial metropoles.

With respect to the process of socialist construction, Trotsky and his followers, while accepting the need for a vanguard party and the possibility of revolution in underdeveloped countries, tended to be skeptical about the political potential of the peasantry, argue for vigorous "primitive socialist accumulation" based on forced collectivization, rejected the possibility of socialism in one country, and came to see historic socialist societies as bureaucratically deformed workers states or even as a new form of class society which they called "bureaucratic collectivism" or "state capitalism." Stalin, on the other hand, accepted the centrality of the worker peasant alliance and the possibility of socialism in one country, but also came to embrace primitive socialist accumulation through forced collectivization, essentially breaking the worker-peasant alliance early in the process of socialist construction. The Right Opposition or International Communist Opposition, led by Bukharin, accepted the worker peasant alliance and the possibility of socialism in one country but rejected primitive socialist accumulation (Bettelhiem 1976, 1978).

From here the divisions become much more complex. Stalin and the Comintern, which he effectively controlled, responded to the rise of fascism and the Great Depression by claiming that capitalism was in its death throws and that social democrats, because they had in the past supported their own bourgeoisies in interimperialist struggles, were essentially "social fascists" and should be treated no different from the emerging fascist regimes of Italy, Portugal, Spain, and Germany. This was the so-called "Third Period Line." It was only in 1935 that he conceded the need to form a broad popular front with everyone opposing fascism, a commitment he then abandoned in 1939 when he announced what amounted to an alliance with Hitler. This in turn only lasted until Hitler broke the pact and invaded the Soviet Union. This, coupled with the millions of deaths resulting from forced collectivization and the effective liquidation of the entire membership of the original Bolshevik party during the purges of the late 1930s made it apparent that the Soviet Union had ceased to be a revolutionary society and was itself drawing on the socialist ideal to legitimate the militarization of the population—yes, to resist the German invasion and ultimately contribute to the defeat of fascism, but also to defend and strengthen the Russian Empire.

The rise of fascism drew increasing attention to the impact of the alienation resulting from the commodification of labor power on the development of class consciousness, with the Frankfurt School arguing increasingly that capitalism really was an iron cage from which escape was impossible. Gramsci, on the other hand, who shared the Right Opposition's critique of Stalin's break with the peasantry and his wavering on the need for a broad popular front against fascism, argued that communists needed not merely to control the state but also and perhaps more importantly to establish a cultural hegemony which allowed them to form people intellectually and morally to resist fascism and to become capable of communism.

Decolonization and the national liberation struggles added a further layer of complexity to the political terrain. The decision of the right wing of the Kuomintang under Chiang Kai-shek to break their popular front with the Communist Party of China in 1927 and massacre Communist leaders in Shanghai gave a measure of credibility to the otherwise transparently absurd Third Period Line. As Mao gradually came to power he veered far away from Stalin in both theory and practice, affirming the centrality and permanence of the worker peasant alliance and rejecting the idea of primitive socialist accumulation—though there was what amounted to forced collectivization. Then, when the Twentieth Congress of the Communist Party of the Soviet Union revealed Stalin's crimes and cult of personality, Mao defended him and took a sharp left turn, attempting a rapid industrialization almost overnight with the Great Leap Forward and, arguing that the persistence of petty commodity projection led to a danger that capitalism might be restored (and had in fact been restored in the Soviet Union) undertook a Cultural Revolution designed, ostensibly, to save China from the same fate.

Elsewhere decolonization and the national liberation struggles led to a radical rethinking of the relationship between imperialism and capitalism. Lenin (Lenin 1916/1963) focused on imperialism as a distinct stage in the development of capitalism. As economies become more technology intensive the rate of profit drops and the bourgeoisie redeploys its resources to low technology, low wage venues, leading to a new wave of colonization distinct from the conquests of the sixteenth and seventeenth century which contributed to primitive accumulation. Dependency and World Systems theorists (Amin 1978/1980), on the other hand, regard capitalism as fundamentally imperialist from the beginning, and the working classes of the imperial metropoles as sharing in the surplus extracted from what came to be called the Third World (which is what made social democracy possible), and therefore as no longer really a revolutionary force. Some dependency theorists embraced Maoism; others supported the new wave of communist led "national liberationist fronts" aligned with the Soviet Union but well to the left of the post-Twentieth Congress CPSU, which continued to counsel most Third World communists to form a popular front with their national bourgeoisies and avoid armed struggle.

The new social movements of the 1960s and beyond challenged the primacy of the socialist and communist movements as the principal forces for liberation without, however, really leading to an alternative strategy for systematically addressing the aspirations of all historically oppressed communities.

The national liberation struggles found echoes in the imperial metropoles, especially in countries such as the United States with large internal colonized populations and so even in the imperial metropole *par excellence*, at least from the vantage point of the Left, there was a growing section of the socialist and communist movements which tended to so prioritize the struggle against imperialism as to reduce the struggle against capitalism to one for national liberation. Indeed, this trend has continued all the way into the present period, and while "communities of color" are less likely to theorize their struggle in terms of the national question, often criticizing the very concept of the nation state as itself colonial, there continues to be a significant part of the Left which regards the relatively privileged populations of the imperial metropoles as lacking revolutionary potential, with those of European descent invited to join the struggle as "allies" or "co-conspirators" without any revolutionary trajectory of their own.

The struggles for women's liberation and LGBTQ rights introduced fundamentally new approaches to understanding the nature of oppression and certainly influenced the socialist and communist Left, but never really created a new strategy for fundamental social transformation, whether radical feminist and independent of historic socialism or in conjunction with it. The change that has happened on this front, and it is very significant, has either happened at an almost molecular level, through struggles within relationships unfold, or through targeted policy changes, such as the rapid and dramatic establishment of the right to same sex marriage in the last decade.

Many student radicals, motivated by their own struggle to resist proletarianization, were drawn to socialism and communism by the work of the Frankfurt School, transmitted by way of Herbert Marcuse, who hailed them as a new revolutionary force. But this group was never able to develop its own organic forms of thought and organization, nor did it form enduring and productive strategic relationships *as a social category* with either the historic proletariat or the new social movements. Some simply abandoned their concern for rational autonomy as petty bourgeoisie and joined Trotskyist or Maoist sects which were mere caricatures of their historic antecedents. Others plunged into the mass movements, doing good work there but without any long range strategic perspective. Many more contracted the Heideggerian virus and descended into poststructuralist nihilism and academic isolation.

The only real effort to theorize a new revolutionary unity during this period was represented by the populism of Ernesto Laclau and Chantal Mouffe (Laclau and Mouffe 1985). Coming from an Althusserian background, Laclau rejected any underlying teleological ordering of social classes or other political actors to given political ends and instead regarded both ruling and popular, hegemonic and counterhegemonic blocs as *constructed*. This might have led to an extension of the concept of the popular front to include not just the *classes* which historically composed it, but also women (and later the LGBTQ movement), colonized peoples and oppressed nationalities, and environmentalists, generally), but instead it favored construction of an amorphous "people" united around what he acknowledged were "empty signifiers" such as "social justice" rather than around staged objectives and a negotiated compromises which recognized and attempted to mitigate the inevitable contradictions within any such alliance (Laclau 2005). One might see Laclau and Mouffe, in this regard, as theorists of the so-called *Socialism of the Twenty-First Century*, the Left Populist formations of Southern Europe, and the Democratic Socialism of the Millennial Left in the United States. While the first achieved some significant electoral victories, they came at the cost of significant compromise with authoritarianism, while the latter conserved the sectarianism and infantile behavior of the European and North American Trotskyist and New Communist movements while shedding even the pretense of political discipline or strategic focus which the Leninist tradition provided.

The Complex Social Basis and Political Valence of Historic Socialism

This way of telling the story of historic socialism, however, presupposes that all these diverse trends actually had or have the same aim and simply disagreed over how to get there or perhaps on the degree to which it was even possible. But this is rather like believing that all Christians really have been single mindedly devoted to building the Kingdom of God without any interest in the destiny of earthly kingdoms or empires or that all liberals care exclusively about rational autonomy and not at all about the wealth that the liberal order allows some to accumulate. It is politically unconscious theology.

What we need to do instead is to understand the complex ways in which the communist ideal has, like the various axial ideals and the liberal and democratic ideals before it, become entangled with other interests and how this has affected the fate of the communist ideal. We have stressed in the past that there were many different interests at stake in the emerging socialist and communist movements (Mansueto 2010, 2016). These included:

- the humanistic intelligentsia, which provided the core constituency for communism understood in the strict sense as transcending the alienation engendered by the commodification of labor power,
- elements in the technical intelligentsia, which understood socialism as a way to unlock the development of productive forces held back by the internal contradictions of capitalism,

- the artisan class, especially as it was being subjected to proletarianization, which shared many of the concerns of and frequently overlapped with the lower echelons of the humanistic intelligentsia,
- the fully proletarianized working class in industry and outside it, which was already so alienated that the development of their class consciousness tended to be limited to the trade union or political (social democratic) level, seeking better wages and working conditions, including an increase in the social wage (free or subsidized social insurance, education, health, housing, food, etc.) or else, after the seizure of state power by the Communist Party, to prioritize consumption over investment,
- the peasantry, especially the middle and lower peasantry and proletarianized agricultural workers, who understood socialism as a way to resist enclosure, clearances, and proletarianization, and to restore traditional communitarian forms of land tenure, and who supported socialist revolution largely on the basis of the promise of land reform,
- marginalized workers unable to even sell their labor power and forced to live from charity, crime, or odd jobs, what Marx called the *lumpenproletariat*, for whom socialism represents a survival strategy which might either open up opportunities for social participation or at least separate income from labor.

Based on this analysis, we have argued (Mansueto 1988, 1995, 2010) that there were, in effect, two different socialisms:

- a revolutionary and humanistic socialism based in the humanistic intelligentsia, the artisanate, the peasantry, and the most exploited sectors of the proletariat and lumpenproletariat, which aimed at reducing and/or eliminating capitalist *exploitation* and at the decommodification of labor power and the restoration of creative control to direct producers, and
- a productivist socialism based in the national bourgeoisie, the technical intelligentsia and the more privileged sectors of the working classes focused on leveraging state power to unleash the development of productive forces held back by the internal contradictions of capitalism and to thereby increase standards of living.

Social democratic and communist parties integrating different, competing, and often utterly incompatible inflections of the socialist project sought state power by means of electoral struggle, insurrection, or popular war and created regimes which were then hegemonized by technocrats who transformed it into a means for the primitive accumulation of capital in colonized regions and for the management of the internal contradictions of capitalism in the imperial metropoles.

This analysis is in accord with histories of socialism (Bettleheim 1974, 1977, 1982), which have made a sharp distinction between a productivist tradition which extends from Engels, through Kautsky and which includes both Trotsky and Stalin and a tradition focused on the primacy of the class struggle which has its roots in French Socialism and the Russian *Narodniki* with their focus on the peasantry and their voluntaristic strategy and tactics, and which then flows into Leninism, the Right Opposition, and in different ways Maoism, dependency/world systems theory, and the Gramscian tradition.

This analysis remains, in so far as it goes, at least partly valid. But it ignores a vital dimension disclosed by our analysis in this work of Empire as a distinct way of being and as the critical link between humanistic and productive readings of the socialist project. Here we would like to suggest an alternative approach based in part on the scholarship of Jie-Hyun Lim (Lin 2019) and in part on our own efforts to understand the nature and likely trajectory of the planet's largest socialist country: China.

Of critical importance here is understanding correctly the nature of the Russian *Narodnik* movement. The *Narodniki*, because they were agrarian socialists and put the peasantry at the center of the struggle for socialism, are often considered to be critics of Marxist productivism. In reality, however, they simply had a different economic analysis. Specifically, they rejected the idea that Russia or any other relatively poor country could follow a capitalist path to development. This is because they could never develop a domestic market for manufactured goods. Their insistence on land reform was driven, first and foremost, by the idea that only land reform could create such a domestic market and make industrialization possible (Lin 2019).

Lenin's *The Development of Capitalism in Russia* (Lenin 1899) is generally seen as rejection of this analysis and thus as a rejection of *Narodnism*. But this may not be entirely accurate. There was already a sharp distinction within the *Narodniki* between "doctrinaires" who insisted that capitalist development was utterly impossible in Russia and the "critical"

Narodniks who took a more nuanced position. We know, furthermore, that the Russian Social Democratic Party evolved directly out of Plekhanov's *Black Partition*, which argued within a *Narodnik* context for long term organizing and education among the peasantry, and that Lenin's concept of a vanguard revolutionary party was developed out of the populist Chernyshevsky's work and that he ultimately opted, in the 1920s, for a rural demand led approach to industrialization not at all unlike that advocated by the *Narodniki*. While Stalin abandoned this strategy in the face of the rising danger of fascism in the late 1920s, it continued to be upheld by the Right Opposition and it is very much the strategy undertaken by Mao in China, where criticisms of the "theory of the productive forces" targeted not so much the goal of rapid industrialization (witness the Great Leap Forward) as the idea that industrialization had to follow a given, law-like pattern and could not be "rushed." If the Communist Party of China has not entirely rejected Mao but rather insists that he was right 70 percent of the time, it is because *they understand the core of Maoism to be the liberation of China from imperialism on the basis of a prolonged popular war, followed by the leveraging of mass movements to industrialize the country and restore China to its rightful place in the world.*

There was a tendency in the 1970s and early 1980s for some Western Maoists to conclude from the rural demand led character of China's industrialization (Bettelheim 1976, 1978; Amin 1980/1982) that there was, in fact, more continuity between Mao and the Right Opposition than there was with Stalin. While Bettelheim was correct to highlight China's very different and more successful agrarian policy, though, we need to remember that this is not how Mao or the Chinese party saw things. On the contrary they defended Stalin's legacy after the XX Congress of the CPSU. Where they differed on revolutionary strategy it was in rejecting the claim, which the Mensheviks had also made of Russia, that China was insufficiently developed for a socialist revolution and that the Communists should remain in alliance with the Kuomintang. Stalin himself had supported the rural demand led industrialization strategy favored by Lenin and Bukharin against Trotsky's doctrine of primitive socialist accumulation, and changed direction only when the refusal of peasants to produce enough to feed the cities and the rising threat of fascism convinced him that the Soviet Union faced an existential threat. And it is Stalin's work on language and the national question which provided the broader context in which antimperialist national liberation struggles were given socialist content during the second half of the twentieth century.

The Russian Case

At this point we must confront a very difficult fact. *It turns out that there is a very strong parallel between the development of historic socialism in the Soviet Union and China and to a lesser extent in the old "Third World" generally and historic fascism as analyzed by historical materialist theory.* Communist theory has historically understood fascism in the context of imperialism. Imperialism in the narrower Leninist sense is an attempt to compensate for the declining rate of profit in high technology, high skill, high wage sectors by taking colonies to which capital can be exported into lower technology, lower skill, lower wage, and thus higher profit activities. In this context, fascism is understood as an attempt on the part of failed or declining imperial powers to build or defend colonial empires by militarizing their societies and preparing for war. This is the pattern of all of the historic fascist powers. German, Italy, and Japan were rising powers that had, as yet, largely failed at securing a colonial empire; Spain and Portugal were old imperial powers that were in decline (Poulantzas 1974).

The problem is that Russia and China in the early and middle twentieth century can *also* be considered failing or declining imperial powers. Indeed, there is simply no other way to characterize them. And the fact that the regimes which attempted to restore their fortunes came to power by way of a social revolution led by a communist party does not by itself mean a great deal. Italian fascism clearly emerged out of the socialist movement, and there were well defined "leftist" tendencies within German National Socialism. The Russian Socialist Revolutionary Party drew its concept of the "people" (*narod*) from the font of the same of nineteenth century romantic nationalism as did the Nazis (*volk*). And Jie Hyun Lim has, furthermore, shown that there was widespread interest in fascism on the part of early Third World revolutionaries from around the world.

> The interesting encounter between a colonial Korean Marxist and Italian Fascism challenges the intellectual dichotomy of right-wing fascism and left-wing socialism. From the viewpoint of the transnational formation of modernity, the convergence of fascism and socialism as radical anti Western modernization projects was not that improbable. The Italian futurist Filippo Marinetti, who became an inadvertent progenitor of fascist art, was deeply respected by Russian Futurists, who in turn supported the Bolshevik Revolution. Left-wing Fascists such as Berto Ricci, and Ugo Spirito, were also pleased when the Soviet Union

began to incline toward fascism in the 1930s. Left-wing Fascists in Italy could see the shift of emphasis from revolutionary internationalism to nationalist strength and development in the Soviet Union. Mussolini himself made it explicit that he would prefer "Italy as a Soviet republic" to "Italy as a British colony." The cliché that the two extremes always meet does not explain this awkward convergence of intellectual ideas in the interwar period. (Lim 2019)

Finally, we should note that the upshot of the two most significant socialist revolutions has, in fact, been the preservation and revival of two very large historic empires: Russia and China. In spite of their current *de facto* alliance, we need to consider these cases separately. Up through the 1920s the Soviet Union followed the rural demand led strategy for industrialization which the worker-peasant alliance and the identity of the party as a sort of quasi-fusion between socialism and agrarian populism dictated. Stalin supported this strategy and leveraged his support to crush Trotsky who wanted to engage in "primitive socialist accumulation" in order to jump start industrialization and create the level of prosperity he believed was necessary in order to realize the communist ideal—and to satisfy the more immediate aspirations of his urban middle class constituency. Ultimately, however, this strategy ran into two difficulties. First, the rise of Nazism presented the Soviet Union and the communist project generally with an existential threat which required more rapid industrialization that even optimistic advocates of rural demand led industrialization expected. Second, the peasants were, as always, disappointing their *narodnik* advocates and, in the absence of anything on which to spend the money they might earn from selling surplus grain, refused to produce more than they needed to consume, effectively starving the cities.

The schism which emerged around agrarian policy was accompanied by a parallel split regarding the best response to fascism, with the Right Opposition, led by Bukharin, who favored continuing rural demand led industrialization, stressing the importance of a broad popular front with social democrats and liberals, while Stalin attacked social democrats as "social fascists." If Trotsky regarded world revolution as the precondition for realizing the communist project, the right opposition saw the communist project as in continuity with the liberal and democratic projects and indeed with the history of human civilization as a whole and wanted to leverage a struggle against a common enemy to make that point, while drawing on the support of liberal and democratic allies to give rural demand led industrialization more time. Stalin, finally, was concerned primarily to build a strong, independent Soviet Union which could defend itself effectively. After he crushed the right opposition, he abandoned his attacks on liberals and social democrats and adopted a popular front policy from which, however, he did not hesitate to deviate internationally (e.g., his 1939 pact with Hitler), and which had essentially no reality internally.

What Stalin did succeed in doing was to make the Soviet Union a global power which was able not only to defend itself but to contribute significantly to the struggle against fascism. After the war it took the lead civilizationally in a range of fields from mathematics and materials science to languages and philosophy and from espionage (an historic strength for Russia probably rooted in the complex, highly inflected character of the Russian language, which made mastering other Indo-European languages easy) to space exploration. And even Stalin did not entirely abandon the higher aims of the communist project. On the contrary, his *Economic Problems of the Soviet Union* (Stalin 1953) argues that the next steps for the Soviet Union involve reducing the workday and expanding opportunities for ordinary workers to participate in the artistic and scientific apparatus that the party had built.

At the same time Stalin *did all these things in a way* which meant that the Soviet Union took on significant fascist characteristics, militarizing or at least regimenting a population united around a national-popular ideal in order to salvage a failing empire. And if he did not entirely abandon the higher ideals of communism, he did effectively liquidate the bearers of that ideal, the communists who had actually fought for the revolution. At the end of the purges, aside from Stalin, there was only one Old Bolshevik left standing: Kalinin, the nominal head of the Soviet State until shortly before his death in 1946. And even he was unable to protect his own wife from Stalin.

The effect of this process was profoundly demoralizing for Soviet society. As workers were still forced to sell their labor power in order to survive, the Soviet population remained alienated and was more interested in increased consumption than in building a socialist spiritual civilization. The party never really even theorized this problem, much less develop a strategy to address it. And murdering everyone who lived for that ideal hardly helped.

The Soviet Union was able to continue to grow until the mid-1970s, based on the strength of its scientific/cultural apparatus and was able to continue to project power globally for several years after this based on its ability to leverage the national liberation movements as a strategic reserve. But the Stalinist emphasis on heavy industry and military investment ultimately produced the same result as the rural demand led industrialization favored by Lenin and Bukharin: a "scissors crisis" in which absenteeism and alcoholism soared as workers who had secure food and housing and massive ruble bank accounts but nothing to spend the money on simply checked out. The humanistic intelligentsia, meanwhile, had largely lost faith in socialism, it being entirely unclear how a regime which centralized effective control over economic resources could ever be compatible with free expression and rational autonomy, while the technocratic intelligentsia largely took at face value the West's claim that rigorous market discipline was a necessary precondition for economic growth and development. When Gorbachev's attempt at a managed transition towards an as yet undefined mixed economy and democratized socialism failed to produce instant results, the system collapsed.

That, at least, is how the transition appeared. But other interpretations are possible. We know that Russian support for the Right in the United States dates back to well before the collapse of the Soviet Union. Even if Stalin ought not to be simply branded a "fascist" he certainly created a system with enough fascistic features to cultivate a generation of fascists. Perhaps sudden the "collapse" of a system which was finally taking seriously both accumulating contradictions of its economic strategy and the requirement that any authentic communism build on respect for liberal rights and democratic accountability was simply a strategic retreat engineered by the part of the growing Russian Right to avoid Russian integration into Europe and to keep intact as much of the old Soviet repressive apparatus as possible pending a later attempt to restore the Russian Empire on a fully fascist basis—an attempt we see in the Russian invasions of Georgia in 2012 and of Ukraine in 2014 and 2022.

The Chinese Case

China is a far more complex case. While China has shown itself capable of some profoundly serious errors, such as the current repression of the Uyghurs, the party continues not only to affirm its socialist character but to make real and significant investments in addressing climate change, improving the living conditions of those still excluded from the prosperity which is increasingly common along the East Coast, and more broadly linking its imperial authority to real civilizational responsibility.

We have discussed the history of socialism in China in detail elsewhere (Mansueto 2010). Here we merely summarize and situate our earlier analysis in our revised and enlarged theoretical context. First, while China remained faithful the strategy of land reform and rural demand led industrialization far longer than the Soviet Union, and rejected in principle the "theory of the productive forces," at least as long as Mao lived, this did not mean a rejection of rapid industrialization, as the catastrophe of the Great Leap Forward demonstrates. And this was not unrelated to the imperial character of the Chinese state, as the fact that it followed hard on the break with the Soviet Union suggests. On the contrary, given the long-term development of Maoism, including the attack on Liu Shaoqi for "self-cultivation," and the Cultural Revolution, which was, among other things, an attack on the Confucian tradition which had legitimated the Chinese state, but also held it accountable, it seems likely that Mao's "agrarianism" was at least in part a way of countering the influence of the urban intelligentsia, humanistic as much as technocratic, within the party, even if many of those mobilized to attack scholars during the Cultural Revolution were themselves young intellectuals.

Second, in this regard the period of "reform and opening" which followed Mao's death should be understood as an option to pursue the rapid growth necessary for the restoration of China to global leadership and to contain the influence of the humanistic intelligentsia in a more thoughtful and sustainable way. Thus, the willingness first to tolerate rapidly increasing inequality in the name of growth and then, under Hu Jintao, to temper that with an emphasis on sharing the wealth with and spreading development to areas other than the East Coast. Thus, the absolute NO to demands for liberal rights and a liberal understanding of the rule of law, and the even more absolute NO to demands for democratization. When the party says that Mao was right 70 percent of the time, they mean it. The party upholds Mao's "original intention" (rather, the original intention of Maoism) while rejecting its methods.

Finally, it was inevitable that with a quarter of the planet's population and an economy which can support it while generating a substantial surplus, China would seek to reclaim its leading role on the planet. This does not mean that China is dangerously expansionist or aggressive. But in a globally interconnected world effective participation by a major power *means* leadership—both advancing a particular civilizational ideal or vision of what it means to be human and defending the very broad sphere of influence in which that ideal has historically held sway.

Nowhere do we see this vision more clearly articulated than in the work of Jiang Shiqong, one of the leading theoreticians of Xi's wing of the Communist Party of China. Jiang makes a distinction between maritime empires and regional civilizational empires. He argues that regional civilizational empires, including Christendom prior to colonialism, linked imperial expansion with civilizational development, while after it began to expand globally Europe saw its colonies only as a means of enrichment. The nation state system and international law actually serve to conceal the imperial and exploitative nature of the system (Shigong 2020). For Jiang the Chinese revolution is both about communism *and* about imperial restoration. He does this by contrasting Christian and Chinese civilizational ideals.

> Western civilization is built on a philosophical-theological tradition of binary antagonisms, between phenomenon and existence, life on earth and life in heaven. In the Christian tradition, the ultimate goal and meaning of human existence comes from God in heaven, which is why the final goal of Western striving is to arrive at the realization of various versions of the "end of history." But in the tradition of Chinese civilization, the worldly and otherworldly realms are not strictly separated, and are both absorbed in a complete world where heaven and mankind are one. The goal and meaning of life for Chinese people was not how to get into heaven, but rather how to locate a universal, lasting meaning within the historically existing "family-state universe."

The specific meaning of the present period must be understood in the context of a correct periodization of the Chinese Revolution. Jiang identifies several stages.

- The democratic revolution, from 1921, when the CCP was founded, through 1949, when New China was established and the CCP completed the nation-building mission of the democratic revolution, "realizing the great leap from thousands of years of feudal autocratic politics to popular democracy."
- The socialist revolution, from 1949 and the founding of New China, through 1978,
- The period of "Reform and Opening," from 1978 through the opening of the Nineteenth Party Congress, when our Party "followed the

tide of the times, responded to the wishes of the people, and had the courage to reform and open up . . ." This is also the period of "getting rich."

- The present period, beginning with the Nineteenth Congress of the Chinese Communist Party, which is the "period of becoming strong."

Central to this past period, is a firm rejection of liberalism and of a one-sided emphasis on the rule of law, and especially a rejection of the Western concept democracy.

> The rule of law and the rule of man are not completely opposed to one another but are complementary. A society governed by the rule of law cannot ignore the need to provide people with ideals and beliefs and a moral education. It cannot ignore the positive role played by moral values and a healthy social climate in governance, nor can it ignore the key historical function of leaders and great people, political parties and the masses. In the annals of human history, what has always played a determining role in the unfolding of history is people, because the history of mankind was itself created by people, and good institutions require people to administer them. One important reason that Western thinkers are continually examining the flaws in the Western democratic system is that these democratic institutions are corrupting human nature. This is especially true in competitive elections controlled by money and the mass media, which have reduced "democracy" to mere "elections." This kind of system will find it difficult to produce politicians who can genuinely represent the people. It will instead easily produce glorified lobbyists at the beck and call of various interest groups.

At the same time, Jiang rejects a traditionalism which would simply abandon the past one hundred years as a mistake and return to feudalism.

> At the same time, a group of cultural conservatives has also emerged with the launching of the slogan of the great revival of the Chinese nation. They have developed into a kind of "revive antiquity group" and advocate the "Confucianization of the Party," denying the historical accomplishments of the nationalist revolution led by the CCP in terms of equality, and going so far as to negate the May Fourth Movement and the Republican Revolution. In this context, the dregs of feudal restorationist thought have floated to the top, joining together with

commercial capital and cultural capital, hoping that these feudal relationships and interests will penetrate the Party.

Restoring China's status as a leading regional civilizational empire, in other words, means re-affirming the principles that give Chinese civilization meaning. And that means re-affirming China's commitment to Communism.

Communism now confronts the challenge of being transformed from a philosophical concept to a "communist society" with concrete institutions and structures. Whether in the case of Lenin's fantasy of "Soviet power plus electrification" or Mao Zedong's imagining of eating from the "community pot" in the period of the People's Communes, ideals, once they descend into the world, lose their original luster. It was precisely the inner tension between communism as a philosophical concept and the construction of a communist society in a genuinely scientific manner that led Mao Zedong to begin to wonder about basic philosophical questions such as whether communist society was a contradiction in terms. It is like the "pursuit of the millennium" in Christianity, in which God's return to earth can only be repeatedly pushed forward. If we really were to experience God's judgement here on earth, Christianity might also lose some of its luster. What we must pay particular attention to is the fact that when Xi Jinping emphasizes a return to Communist principles, he is not talking about the "communist society" that was of a piece with scientific socialism but is instead using the idea that "those who do not forget their original intention will prevail," drawn from traditional Chinese culture. In so doing, he removes communism from the specific social setting of the Western empirical scientific tradition, and astutely transforms it into the Learning of the Heart in Chinese traditional philosophy, which in turn elevates communism to a kind of ideal faith or a spiritual belief.

For this reason, communism will never again be like it was under Mao Zedong—something that was meant to take on a real social form in the here and now—but is instead the Party's highest ideal and faith. It has become part of Party education and Party cultivation, the "Learning of the Heart" of the CCP. Communism is not only a concrete society to be realized in the distant future but is also the highest ideal that will be absorbed into current political practice, a vibrant spiritual state. Communism is not only a beautiful future life, but is also, and more importantly, the spiritual state of Communist Party members in their practice of political life. In this way, communism merges with specific historical process and daily life as ideals and struggles. Precisely within the context of traditional Chinese culture, the understanding of this highest ideal is no longer that of Marx, who thought within the Western theoretical tradition; it is no longer in humanity's Garden of Eden, "unalienated" by the division of labor within society. Instead it is intimately linked to the ideal of "great unity under Heaven" (*tianxia*) from the Chinese cultural tradition. The last section of the report to the Nineteenth Party Congress begins with the phrase "when the Way prevails, the world is shared by all," an ultimate ideal that encourages the entire Party and the people of the entire nation. And in the specific contents of the report, we also find the passage, developed on the basis of the notion of "great unity under Heaven" from China's tradition, to the effect that "the young will have education, the students will have teachers, the workers will have remuneration, the sick will have doctors, the elderly will have care, those seeking housing will have housing, the weak will have support."

Within this context, China emerges as a global integrating, civilizational power—one which can create space for many different systems and models, so long as they are ultimately ordered to Communism understood as a broad moral idea. In this sense, Jiang is re-affirming China's role as not merely a regional civilizational empire, but as *the* leader of humanity.

In the report to the Nineteenth Party Congress, the word "contribution" appears eleven times, the most in any such Party report in history. And the reason that the CCP takes its "contribution" to humanity as its own guide to action is precisely to prove that the great revival of the Chinese people is not nationalistic, but cosmopolitan. One root of this cosmopolitan spirit is in the Confucian universalistic tradition, as we see when the report to the Nineteenth Party Congress invokes the notion of "when the Way prevails, the world is shared by all"; another root is the communist belief in the liberation of all of humanity. The report to the Nineteenth Party Congress especially points out that "the Communist Party of China strives for both the well being of the Chinese people and human progress. To make new and greater contributions for mankind is our Party's abiding mission."

While many scholars propose the "Chinese model" as being distinct from the "Western model," Xi Jinping in his July 1, 2016 talk commemorating the founding of the CCP chose instead "Chinese wisdom" and the "Chinese solution." The very choice of these concepts illustrated Chinese wisdom, because a truly universal theory can contain within it varied developmental models. In fact, the "five basic principles of peaceful coexistence" long upheld by the New China, and the traditional Chinese cultural notion that "the righteous king does not seek to rule people beyond the reach of law and civilization" are part of a shared vision.

This is, in many ways, a very compelling vision which, among other things at once affirms the communist ideal and is frank about the fact that, Marx to the contrary, we do not yet know how to realize it. It is also (mostly) honest about the reality of China as an imperial state while seeking to order its aspiration for global leadership to higher end.

This said, there are problems with Jiang's analysis. First, while he is more frank than most in acknowledging the imperial character of the Chinese state, *in spite of also continuing to regard it as socialist,* he prefers the more ambivalent term "civilizational state" which, as we have seen, is based on a claim that Western (Hellenistic-Roman and European-American) Empire is purely exploitative and instrumentalizing while other multiethnic territorial states based on conquest (Civilizational States such as China or *Dar-al-Islam*) are not. In order to be fully in accord with the evidence, Jiang would need to acknowledge that the Chinese Revolution was, *from the very beginning,* an attempt at imperial restoration, and that *this is as integral to nature of actually existing socialism as the desire to transcend capitalism.* Second, as we have seen, it is not at all clear to what extent the "communist ideal" can be separated from the liberal tradition. While communism clearly rejects individualism in many senses—both as an account of how human beings are and as an account of what they ought to become—communism was, for Marx, very specifically the condition of transcending the alienation of labor which derives from the wage relationship, an aim which makes sense only in the context of a humanistic doctrine of rational autonomy and thus the liberal tradition. It may be that Jiang envisions a world in which there are "many communisms" and China respects the right of the West to find its own path. But what of those closer to home? In what sense does China's policy towards the Uygurs and the Tibetans—or for that matter Hong Kong, which Jiang helped to shape—represent a willingness to accept authentically varied developmental models within its broad civilizational-imperial framework?

China cannot be dismissed as *just* an alterimperial formation which is leveraging Chinese civilizational traditions to mobilize its population for industrialization in order to reclaim its position of global leadership. It *is* this, but it is *also* a civilizational empire which is working out a retheorization of the communist ideal in the context of its Confucian, Taoist, and (for better or worse) Legalist heritages and acting on this emerging synthesis in ways that it clearly believes and which can be reasonably argued are in the interests of humanity as a whole, combatting climate change, checking the emergence of Capital as an autonomous intelligence and continuing to lift its people out of poverty. That it does these things imperfectly is not sufficient cause for condemnation. That it does them at all does not exempt it from criticism.

Dark Liberation

To anyone writing in the 1990s or early 2000s the idea that socialism would have made a comeback of any kind would have seemed unlikely at best and for most it seemed ridiculous. And yet one quarter of the way into the new century we see what in many ways is remarkable resurgence of anticapitalist movements which claim significant continuity with historic socialism. Many of these also embrace—and many cases prioritize—ecological struggles and the struggles of indigenous and colonized peoples as well as the struggle against patriarchy and gender oppression. But even among those who never *do* anything meaningfully anticapitalist there is a broad consensus among a wide range of social categories globally that capitalism, far from marking the end of history, is in fact a miserable failure.

Within the emerging Left we identify the following tendencies:

- the various Left Populisms and Democratic Socialisms which have emerged in Europe and the Americas in particular in the past two decades,
- the spectrum of ecological and identarian movements which to one degree or another *assume* anticapitalism, and
- the libertarian socialisms which have emerged out of elements in largely defeated national liberation movements in marginal locations such as Chiapas and Rojava.

And yet, as we noted above, we are still very far from seeing any of the numerous tendencies on the emerging Left advance a credible strategy for defeating Capital and transcending the commodification of labor power. Is this simply a failure of political maturity on the part of a new New Left which has had to rebuild after both the Old Left and the old New Left were either compromised by neoliberalism or alterimperialism or else utterly defeated? Or is it a reflection, as with historic socialism, of the actual class and other social interests of its proponents?

In order to answer this question we will need to take a deep dive into the what the emerging Left claims is a fundamentally new way of theorizing the struggle to transcend capitalism without succumbing to either reformist co-optation or the authoritarian deformations which characterized historic socialism.

* * *

To those who have followed the careful process by which the Right in the United States has cultivated a "bull-pen" of conservative and especially conservative Catholic intellectuals to help it map its road back to power since its defeat in 1932 and the failure of the "Business Plot" in 1933 to overthrow Roosevelt and install a fascist regime (Reimann 2017), figures such as Carl Schmitt and Martin Heidegger represent a familiar type. In the wake of Germany's defeat in the First World War and the democratic revolution of 1918, in which significant elements pressed for the transfer of power to workers councils on the Soviet model, the ruling classes began plotting their restoration. Then as now the conservative Catholic small and petty bourgeoisie provided the intellectual shock troops for that restoration. Little did they know that they would also shape the direction of the *Left* a century later.

The critical thinkers in this regard remains Heidegger and Schmitt. If Lenin wrote the history of the long twentieth century, then Heidegger and Schmitt seem to be writing the history of the twenty-first. We have already analyzed in some depth both Schmitt's basic claims: that all modern political concepts are simply secularizations of theological concepts (Schmitt 1922/2005) and that against historic natural law theories and more recent concepts of popular sovereignty, that "the sovereign is he who decides the exception" (Schmitt 1921/2014). The first is uncontroversially true. The second, we have shown, in so far as it is a claim based on Roman legal theory, fundamentally misreads that legal tradition.

What we need to do here is to show what Schmitt shares with Heidegger, and how both together have articulated a political theology which at once defines a major section of the far right and which has also, since the 1960s, come to hegemonize the Left, providing a theoretical basis for the covert *rapprochement* with fascism which has defined much of the Left since at least the time of Stalin, and extending that *rapprochement* well beyond those who continue to uphold Stalin.

Social Basis

Professionalism, Alterprofessionalism, and the Hotel Abyss

While there can be little doubt that the industrial proletariat did, in fact, provide much of the mass base of both the social democratic and communist movements, and while it has *always* been peasant movements which have brought communist parties to power, the *leadership* of the socialist and communist movements has historically been drawn from what Marx and Engels called "the bourgeois ideologists."

> Finally, in times when the class struggle nears the decisive hour, the progress of dissolution going on within the ruling class, in fact within the whole range of old society, assumes such a violent, glaring character, that a small section of the ruling class cuts itself adrift, and joins the revolutionary class, the class that holds the future in its hands. Just as, therefore, at an earlier period, a section of the nobility went over to the bourgeoisie, so now a portion of the bourgeoisie goes over to the proletariat, and in particular, a portion of the bourgeois ideologists, who have raised themselves to the level of comprehending theoretically the historical movement as a whole. (Marx and Engels 1848/2000)

This is the same group that Marx had earlier identified with Philosophy, which he called the "head of the revolution" (Marx 1843/2009). It is also Hegel's "universal class" of liberally educated civil servants. It is what we are here calling the "humanistic intelligentsia" (those trained in and attempting to live from or at least devote their lives to the practice of—the liberal arts and in particular the humanities and the humanistic social sciences). And while in the nineteenth century—and to a lesser extent even today—elements of the humanistic intelligentsia were and are derived from the bourgeoisie as such, this group (which is a social category and not a class), is predominantly *petty bourgeois* both in its origins and in its class position and, as capitalism develops, is subjected to increasing proletarianization. By this we mean that, on the one hand, unlike the proletariat as such, members of the humanistic intelligentsia enjoy significant creative control over their work, but like the proletariat they see this control gradually slipping away, by way of attacks on academic freedom and faculty governance in universities, the decline journalism as a liberal profession, etc.

Since this is the group which actually *does* social theory and philosophy, we do well to take into account its specific interests as we analyze its theoretical products and assess them as political strategies. And by the early twentieth century the humanistic intelligentsia had three well defined political options on the table. The first was what its proponents call "professionalism" and its critics "technocracy," i.e., a privileged, semi-autonomous role based on the exercise of one's specific discipline within the context of bourgeois society, on the condition that it remain "value neutral," i.e., that it provide advice regarding the *means* to *ends* which are determined by others: nominally "the people," acting through democratic structures, but in practice the bourgeoisie. This is the option represented by Weber in *Science as a Vocation* (Weber 1919/1968). This option generally involves an alliance with the liberal and advanced, technocratic bourgeoisie and, in practice, with the more fully proletarianized elements in the population by way of social liberal and social democratic parties. The second option was communism—a bid for all-sided global leadership based on an alliance with the proletariat and other exploited classes, especially the peasantry, aimed at ending for *everyone* the commodification of labor which was the principal form of capitalist oppression experienced by the humanistic intelligentsia. In the context of this option, the humanistic intelligentsia trades some of its autonomy for a global leadership role in the context of a Leninist vanguard or Gramscian counter-hegemonic party—again in alliance with the proletariat as such, the peasantry if there is one, and often in popular fronts with the liberal bourgeoisie. The third option was Romantic Reaction—an alliance first with absolutist monarchic and aristocratic and later with imperialist and colonizing bourgeois elements who, the intellectuals in question imagined, promised a return to a less instrumentalizing, preindustrial, precapitalist past. This is, of course, the option of the traditionalists de Maistre and de Bonald, of Nietzsche, and ultimately of Heidegger and

Schmitt who, however, introduce a new element to the strategy (Lukacs 1953/1980).

As King and Szelenyi (King and Szeleny 2004) have suggested, an integral part of *professionalism* as a class strategy is artificially maintaining the scarcity of professionals. This is something physicians, for example, have done very well, attorneys reasonably well, and academics very poorly. We are, after all, in the business of training our own competition. Pierre Bourdieu makes a compelling case (Bourdieu 1988/1991) that Heidegger's famous obscurantism, something which has since been mimicked by scholars throughout the humanities, was designed to confer on the philosopher an oracular *mana* which set him apart from ordinary humanity and, in effect, made doing philosophy inaccessible to the vast majority of people.

By the 1920s and 1930s the contradictions of historic socialism were becoming apparent. State ownership of the means of production turned out to be a means not to the decommodification of labor power but to the full proletarianization of the entire society, including the vast majority of the humanistic intelligentsia. And Stalin began systematically liquidating precisely those elements within the humanistic intelligentsia who actually insisted on exercising the critical rationality which had drawn them to the socialist project in the first place. But this was also the period, of course, during which fascism was ascendant, as a cluster of political formations around the world drew on the alienation and authoritarianism generated by the commodification of labor power to legitimate the destruction of not just the socialist but also the liberal and democratic projects, and to militarize their societies in pursuit of the colonial empires which Capital needed in order to survive. Intellectuals like Heidegger seemed to imagine that they could leverage their philosophical obscurantism into a privileged position within, or even hegemony over, the fascist regime. When this did not happen, the humanistic intelligentsia began its historic retreat.

George Lukacs—who is himself shares much of the class background and social concerns of this social stratum—is also its most insightful critic. He describes it in a 1933 essay on the *The Grand Hotel Abyss*:

> A part of the intelligentsia is detained and stopped in a state of chronic despair, on the edge of the abyss, so that it settles herein at home . . . on the edge of the abyss, and refuses to move forward. In other words, it makes a gesture of radical progress, and often sincerely imagines that it will radically move on.

> Objectively, however, it constantly goes in circles in this state of chronic despair, on the edge of the abyss . . .
>
> Grasping this strange cultural despair, on the surface deeply hostile to the present order and yet richly accommodated (and, as we'll see, patronized), is the principal riddle the Sphinx poses those who venture the rough ascent to the Grand Hotel Abyss—from the outside.

Castalian Stream (Castalian Stream 2022b) sets the context:

> The exciting aspect of taking out a room in the Hotel Abyss is the sense you get of daringly, radically rejecting everything that stands: "liberalism," "modernity," "capitalism," "biopower," "Western metaphysics," . . . the list goes on. It is a prospect which confers the intellectual a pleasing hint of omnipotence. We are soaring above the sociopolitical fray, at least in our minds.

Lukacs continues:

> The less flattering aspect (better not to raise it, to be honest) is that our criticisms of things become so "radical" as to effectively cancel themselves out. They confer a distance and elevation, a "pathos of distance," on their holders. They easily diminish others' concerns and criticisms as insufficiently "deep" to "get to the root of problems." But beyond that, they change very little and prescribe no action beyond our own disdain.

The Frankfurt School to which Lukacs was close ideologically if not personally, represented a final attempt to link the concerns of the humanistic intelligentsia around alienation with a continuing commitment to alliance with the working classes. On the one hand, the Frankfurt School represented "petty bourgeois socialism" or even an aristocratic socialism *par excellence.* Drawn from the bourgeoisie and petty bourgeoisie, many of its members had studied Weber and studied with Heidegger and they were profoundly sensitive to the fact that the critique of capitalist instrumentalization could easily be turned on actually existing socialism. And their organic connection to the proletariat was very limited at best. Nevertheless, despite some ideological problems—such as Benjamin's fascination with divine violence and Adorno's radical pessimism—they maintained their commitment to the socialist project. And Fromm's (Fromm 1941) analysis of the links between the alienation engendered by the commodification of labor power and the authoritarian personality structure on which fascism depended are critical to understanding not only historic fascism but what has followed.

After the defeat of fascism, the liberal bourgeoisie—increasingly, it seems likely, under pressure from occult networks on the far right—broke the popular front and imposed on the humanistic intelligentsia a return to professional "value neutrality" which increasingly included an implicit or explicit "anticommunism" clause. Many of those who submitted—especially those who came from places of privilege themselves—found positions of honor and responsibility in the social liberal order; those who did not were marginalized. Meanwhile, however, the rapid expansion of higher education created a new "mass intelligentsia," which could not really be accommodated within even the also expanding ranks of the professional middle class, at least not at the levels of that class which provided the professional autonomy which the student generation of the 1960s saw being exercised by "the best and the brightest," who were actually a small, privileged stratum. This was the social basis for the student movement of the 1960s (which actually extended well into the 1970s, and which had a significant "afterlife" in the 1980s). And it is not surprising that the Frankfurt School, with its focus on resistance to the alienating impact of the commodification of labor power and its distance from the rest of the working classes, was an inspiration to this movement.

But just as the mass student movement was edging towards socialism, it became apparent that historic socialism was irredeemable. Krushchev's reforms beginning 1956 represented a break with the worst of Stalinist repression, but if anything seemed to move the Soviet bloc further away from the communist ideal of the decommodification of labor power. The Maoist alternative catalyzed the excitement of many in the 1960s and 1970s, among other things precisely because it targeted the persistence of commodity production under socialism, and led to the formation of an entire Maoist "new communist movement." But it soon became apparent that Maoism was, if anything, vastly *more* repressive, *especially* for the intelligentsia, than Stalinism. Stalin murdered those he saw as a political threat. The Cultural Revolution targeted the entire intelligentsia, regardless of its political orientation or practical activity, even at the cost of nearly destroying Chinese Civilization. And while some of the later Third World national liberation movements, especially in Latin America, engaged a range of new constituencies, embracing, for example, a significant movement of radicalized Catholic clergy and laity, and *partly* avoided the creation of a monolithic single party-state, they too turned out to be mostly about creating a national state bourgeoisie and about a micro-alterimperialism rather than about liberating people from the need to sell their labor power in order to survive.

In the Soviet bloc the process was a bit different. The humanistic intelligentsia welcomed periods of reform—1956, for example, and in a more limited way 1968, but was inevitably pushed to the side as reforms were either crushed or the opening they created reserved for technocratic managers rather than humanistic advocates of decommodification. By the mid-1980s, when Gorbachev made it clear that real reform was coming, the humanistic intelligentsia in the Soviet bloc had largely given up the dream of "socialism with a human face" and facilitated the collapse of the system and a capitalist restoration.

This is the point at which the political valence of the poststructuralist appropriation of Schmitt (and Heidegger) becomes clear. Beginning in the 1960s a group of French intellectuals pioneered a new strategy for the humanistic intelligentsia: what we might call "critical professionalism." Critical professionalism allows the humanistic intelligentsia to criticize the increasing proletarianization of their own stratum, while refusing to engage Capital, and thus abandoning the rest of the proletariat and working classes. We see this illustrated most clearly in the work of Michel Foucault. Foucault (Foucault 2007) argues that while premodern states aimed only a control over territory, modern states exercise a detailed control over bodies which he calls *biopolitical*. Thus, ancient empires merely taxed their citizens; modern states (or rather the modern corporations which modern states protect) aim at total control of the production process. This thesis, which certainly points to something real but also misunderstands it, became the basis for the strange politics of an entire generation of the humanistic intelligentsia which aimed at resisting proletarianization without resisting Capital, or indeed without even mentioning its existence. Indeed, it is incontestable that historic socialism *also* represents a practice of biopolitics, so poststructuralism comes off seeming even handed and, even if it was not as enthusiastic about capitalism as the Right would like, this made it relatively unobjectionable. Heidegger's obscurantism was maintained as a way of promoting the artificial scarcity of professional deconstructionism, and we have the humanistic academy which took shape from the 1980s onward—perhaps earlier in Europe.

The strategy worked—for Capital. An entire generation of the humanistic intelligentsia (or more) was cut off from the struggles of the working classes and other oppressed communities, and focused on "deconstructive" activity which it understood as liberating but which was actually aimed at disarming the Left. But the strategy did not work for the humanistic intelligentsia itself. Graduate programs continued to churn out doctorates and universities cut tenure track lines and shifted responsibility for most of their teaching mission to adjunct faculty and a lower caste of largely unprotected "teaching faculty." And the handful who got tenure assisted their employers by denying it to anyone who questioned the poststructuralist orthodoxy. Seeking allies, poststructuralist academics offered their theories to the women's movement and to movements against imperialism and racism, which had the effect, in turn, of cutting *these* movements off from any possible alliance with the proletariat. It also promoted an "allergy to power" as itself instrumentalizing and oppressive, which condemned those who took this route to political impotence.

The result is an absurd situation in which very comfortable humanistic academics earning large salaries and still enjoying very significant autonomy (on condition that they not deploy it against Capital) talk about revolutionary violence and say other things which *sound* incredibly revolutionary—but *intend nothing*. Are they merely soothing their consciences by occasionally nipping at the hand that feeds them? Or are they up to something more sinister?

Alterimperial Elites

As the humanistic intelligentsias of Europe, North America, and Oceana retreated into refined despair, their counterparts in Asia, Africa, and Latin America found inspiration in many of the same sources which led to the development of fascism and hope in the process of decolonization and in the national liberation struggles which followed the Second World War. We have already noted above the work of Jie Hyun Lim (Lim 2019) regarding the interest of "Third World" intellectuals in the work of Italian Fascists. In the light of our rereading of the history Russian and Chinese socialism this was no mere intellectual dalliance. *On the contrary, we must understand historic socialism as an attempt to restore marginalized or colonized empires by making available to them the technological and economic capacity with which capitalism had endowed the United States, England, France, and Germany but seemed to be denying to the historically more advanced societies of Asia. And we need to recognize that this is a* dynamic which is actually quite close to that which led to the emergence of fascism in Spain and Portugal, Italy and Germany and Japan. Where socialism in Europe grew out of frustration with the limits which capitalism placed on the autonomy promised by liberal and democratic revolutions which were, nonetheless, very real, socialism in the imperial "weak links" and colonies grew out of frustration with the limits capitalism seemed to be imposing on technological and economic progress. And coupled with Lenin's explanation of this phenomenon, his theory of imperialism, and the resulting commitment of the communist movement to national liberation, it provided a way to frame socialism as a means of restoring ancient glories on the foundation of modern industrial technology and of reclaiming—or claiming for the first time—the place of venerable civilizations in the global halls of power.

A few qualifications and clarifications are in order here. First, it *does* make a difference *ethically* that the national liberation movements which emerged after the second world war were struggling against the principal imperial powers of their day and for the right of their people to self-determination. It was *right* to support these movements or at least their stated aims. Political choices must be made between real alternatives and there is a presumption in favor of a people or a state which has been conquered and exploited and is now struggling for relief. Such presumptions are over-ridden only in cases where those leading the struggle for "liberation" show themselves to be worse oppressors than those they displace, as was the case with the *Khmer Rouge*. But we should also not be surprised that cases like the *Khmer Rouge* emerge when the basic structural dynamics behind national liberation movements look so similar to those behind fascism and when we discover that these movements have common ideological sources.

A great deal of the confusion on this matter is the product of Lenin's doctrine of *revolutionary defeatism*. Watching as the social democratic parties of Europe lined up behind their own bourgeoisies during the inter-imperialist conflict of the First World War, Lenin counseled communists instead to struggle *against* their own bourgeoisies—advice he made concrete when he returned from exile in Germany in a sealed train to seize power in Russia and then make significant concessions to his German patrons, moves without which the Bolshevik Revolution would likely have been impossible. And to the extent that Lenin was responding to an abandonment of the longer term aims of socialism in favor of a reformism made possible by exporting the contradictions of capitalism to the colonies, his underlying insights were on the mark. But the communist movement took what was originally a confused mixture of profound analytic insight (the link between social democracy and imperialism) and correct a *tactical* judgement (that in *this* and *perhaps* many other circumstances communists should work for the defeat of their own countries) and turned it into an absolute principle which has, at the same time, been unevenly applied. Thankfully, for example, the Comintern eventually counseled communists to form popular fronts with their own bourgeoisies against fascism. But the rigid application of the principle of revolutionary defeatism with respect to struggles in the global South has led to demands that communists support Islamic fundamentalists in their struggle against the imperfect but entirely legitimate Jewish State of Israel, *itself* the product of a national liberation struggle.

Third, we should be clear that the presence of some fascist elements in a struggle does not mean that there may not also be authentically liberating elements also present. To use the present example *Hamas* and *Herut* both have fascistic roots. But both Zionism and the struggle for authentic self-determination for Palestinians are both authentically liberatory movements. The world is rarely a struggle between good guys and bad.

Finally, it may be asked how the characterization of national liberation movements as *alterimperial* and thus in danger of fascistic inflexion could ever be applied to the many small countries which have prosecuted national liberation struggles. The answer is that the modern sovereign state itself is a product of what we have called *Empire* as a civilizational ideal and that while scale can make a deformed liberation struggle more or less dangerous, all modern states are, to some degree, would be empires.

Theoretical Expressions

Hermeneutic Socialism

But what evidence do we have that the emerging Left is actually infected with the Heideggerian virus? Surely the heyday of poststructuralism is long past? And the principal theorists of the emerging Left—Žižek and Baidou in particular—*understand themselves* as breaking with the legacy of Heidegger and poststructuralism. But is this really true?

Žižek mounts a sharp critique of identity politics as a reflex of liberal globalism and argues that struggles around gender and race must be understood in a context in which the question of class remains fundamental and architectonic. Drawing on Lacan he reinstates an historical materialist theory of ideology which at once nuances Marx and his interpreters but breaks with poststructuralist relativism. But when we come to the question of political theology, Žižek remains resolutely Schmittian:

> As a culmination of the political theologies of Schmitt and Agamben, Žižek's handling of the political and the theological through the politico-theological—or the theologico-political—role of *the one who decides on the exception* presents sovereignty and the sovereign at the intersection of the thought of Hegel, Lacan, and Marx. To a certain extent, at that intersection, the historical, the psychological, and the political-ethical-economical contribute to what the sovereign is and what sovereignty does. For Žižek, Hegel, Lacan, and Marx bring a matrix of concerns to what it means to do political theology as a politicizing and theologizing that advance and complexifies Schmitt's and Agamben's respective meanings of what "exception" is and what happens to that which is relegated and regulated by a "state of exception". (Woodson 2021)

And however much Žižek's roots may lie in Hegel, Marx, and Lacan, the way in which he develops these thinkers is shaped by his political theology:

> What becomes all the more apparent with Kotsko is that, even when acknowledging the contributions of Hegel, Lacan, and Marx to Žižek's theologizing—if setting aside it as "materialist theology"—there is certainly more that can be said about the nature of "the political" in Žižek, and how Hegel, Lacan, and Marx politically speak to and are, in themselves, politically spoken to with Žižek's theologizing. For Žižek to arrive at a self-described materialist approach means to do so through political negotiations, which are predicated on Žižek's holding sovereignty over Hegel, Lacan, and Marx—how Žižek theologizes "the political" in the role of the sovereign is as *the one who decides on the exception*. (Woodson 2021)

And the concrete political significance of this theology is clear.

> The attempt to think politically, without religious categories, was a failure, Žižek argues, and contends that today's political thought has been turned into an ethics and a legal philosophy that promotes moral values and ethical policies. Seeking change in this way, Žižek argues, is a closed loop where every attempt

> to transgress the law, insofar as it is carried out within its framework, actually affirms it. (Koltaj 2019, p. 51)

We are, in other words, once again back to the left-fascist critique of the rule of law.

Much the same is true of Badiou. Here the similarity was noted early. Jean-François Lyotard was among the first to accuse Alain Badiou's evental philosophy of advocating a dangerous decisionism by labelling him "a sort of new Carl Schmitt" (Badiou 2004a, p. 172). Under the provocative subheading "Badiou Absolutiste?," Peter Hallward has pursued a related line of critique by gesturing towards formal overlaps between Badiou's notion of the subject of truth and absolutist theories of sovereignty (Hallward 2003, pp. 285–86). Nina Power has also explored common elements between Badiou's and Schmitt's critiques of Rousseau (Power in Ashton et al. 2006, pp. 309–38). It is clear, then, that the spectre of Schmitt has haunted Badiou's project since its starkest, and arguably most brilliant, exposition in *L'être et l'événement* (1988) (Wright 2008).

This particular author goes on to argue that the conflation of Badiou's event with Schmitt's exception is a misreading:

> In what follows, I attempt to exorcise this spectre by disentangling Badiou's notion of the event from Schmitt's logic of the exception. My aim is to dispel any *prima facie* similarities between the two concepts that might reduce what I will call Badiou's "politics of the void" to the reactionary tradition he sets himself against, and upon which Schmitt draws. I identify numerous apparent proximities between the event and the exception before separating the two concepts by contrasting their respective theories of naming.

This may well be sufficient to establish a *distinction* between the two concepts, but as we look deeper into Badiou's system we find, not surprisingly given his Maoist roots, a profound voluntarism and decisionism:

> There is, however, a second sense of law, the transgressive sense, which marks the rupture of the decisive event that gives birth to a new order, time and subject. Here, a new law comes upon an established regime in order to bring about a new order. Fidelity to the event and the transgressive law of that event allows for the event to persist through time. Badiou will often refer to revolutions to illustrate his ontology of the event. The Russian Revolutions, just like the French Revolution, displaced a Tsarist order or lawfulness with a revolutionary one. The event of the Russian

> Revolutions not only created a new epoch or time but also new subjects (the revolutionary socialist/communist subject) and a new order of law—a new lawfulness emerged with the Russian Revolutions. It should be remarked that the event itself never is present or appears in the way that its ordered elements appear. The event stands out of the set, though it structures the set: the event is the ultra-one of the set that constitutes the event itself. (Calcagno 2016)

We are, on other words, back to the idea, whose root was not Schmitt but Benjamin, that revolution is fundamentally an act of divine violence which shatters the existing moral and legal order and establishes a new one. There is no way, outside this arbitrary decision of the revolutionary/sovereign, to tell the difference between a good legal order and a bad one. And lest we assume that socialist revolutions always lead to good legal orders, we should remember what those legal orders look like after socialism ceases to be a revolutionary aspiration and becomes settled law. Jiang Shiqong is, after all, also a Schmittian.

> It is his Schmittian insight that the constitution itself depends on sovereignty that has led Jiang to articulate the theory of an unwritten Chinese constitution, expressed summarily in a 2009 article on "Written and Unwritten Constitutions." The modern Chinese state, he argues here, was founded by a popular revolution that established the sovereign dictatorship of the Communist Party. It is the unwritten historical fact of this dictatorship, not the written document known as the constitution of the state, which structures the whole of the Chinese constitution and has embodied the continuity of the Chinese state through three successive written constitutions—whether it is inscribed as an "absolute" dictatorship or a "constitutional" dictatorship subject to certain written limitations. When the relative position of the Party and the state is brought into question, as in the "unfortunate" conflict between Mao and the chairman of the state Liu Shaoqi in the 1960s, it is the Party, not the state, that has revealed itself to hold the crushing power of life and death. (Garton 2020)

And, of course, the revolutionary events that constitute a new sovereign are at the same time unveilings or disclosures of Being which reveal a new God. Both in power and out, in other words, this new wave of "socialists" and "communists" are constitutively decisionist in their political theology, and deeply and profoundly deformed by the fascist philosophy they have embraced.

What has happened, in effect, is that the humanistic intelligentsia has realized, in the wake of the neoliberal era and its crisis, and especially since the Great Recession, that it *must* resist Capital if it is to retain its autonomy, but it insists on doing this in a way which not only fails to appeal successfully to the rest of the petty bourgeoisie, the proletariat, and the peasantry, but which is grounded (consciously or unconsciously) in theory which actually excludes such an alliance. This is because a resistance to Capital grounded in a pure decision rather than in the teleological ordering of matter—*all matter*—to Being and the participation of humanity in the creative power of Being through its labor—*all its labor*—is essentially a resistance of the would-be dictator to the current dictator, and nothing more.

The Genealogical Turn and Biopower

There have, however, been new developments out of the hermeneutic tradition which explicitly understand themselves as a critique of the totalitarian power of *both* the fascist and the liberal types. This is definitive the "genealogical turn" which traces its roots to Nietzsche but which has been most fully developed by Foucault and Agamben.

Just what sets the genealogical turn apart from its purely hermeneutic predecessor? Let us see what Foucault himself has to say in his essay on Nietzsche, genealogy, and history:

> Genealogy . . . must record the singularity of events outside of any monotonous finality; it must seek them in the most unpromising places, in what we tend to feel is without history—in sentiments, love, conscience, instincts; it must be sensitive to their recurrence, not in order to trace the gradual curve of their evolution, but to isolate the different scenes where they engaged in different roles. . . .
>
> In short, genealogy demands relentless erudition. Genealogy does not oppose itself to history as the lofty and profound gaze of the philosopher might to the modest perspective of the scholar; on the contrary, it rejects the metahistorical deployment of ideal significations and indefinite teleologies. It opposes itself to the search for "origins." (Foucault 1971, p. 145)

Two points are in order here. First, it would seem as if genealogy is seeking out connections of some kind. After all, the various elements of a lineage must be connected in some way. But it does not specify just how these elements might be connected. This would be one thing if Foucault was proposing a more open-ended search for the nature of those connections than previously undertaken by "science" understood as the search for causal explanations. But this search is not open ended. It does not just allow for possibilities other than causality, but in fact excludes causality, and especially teleological causality. Second, understood in context, this can have only one meaning, because at the time this essay was produced there was only one theoretical system with any political significance which did, at least sometimes, propose teleological causation: dialectical and historical materialism. It is fine for Foucault to couch his essay in terms of a critique of Whig history which tells all stories as leading to lead to the single end of the liberal order, but at the time no one believed in Whig history. And except for a brief period after the collapse of the Soviet bloc when Francis Fukuyama revived this idea (Fukuyama 1989)—no one has believed it since. Foucault is mounting a covert attack on Marx.

It would appear, at times, that Foucault is simply arguing against teleology in the name of some sort of "value free" inquiry in the Weberian sense.

> An entire historical tradition (theological or rationalistic) aims at dissolving the singular event into an ideal continuity—as a teleological movement of a natural process. "Effective" history, however, deals with events in terms of their most unique characteristics, their most acute manifestations. (Foucault 1971, p. 169)

But this is not the case: "Genealogy . . . seeks to establish the various systems of subjection: not the anticipatory power of meaning, but the hazardous play of dominations" (Foucault 1971, p. 154).

Foucault, furthermore does have a special concern about a particular form of domination.

> There are . . . times when force contends against itself, and not only in the intoxication of an abundance, which allows it to divide itself, but at the moment when it weakens. Force reacts against its growing lassitude and gains strength; it imposes limits, inflicts torments and mortifications; it masks these actions as a higher morality and, in exchange, regains its strength. In this manner the ascetic ideal was born.

> Here asceticism—taken in it Weberian sense as disciplined work for the purpose of pure accumulation—is stripped of its obvious causal relationship with capitalism. (Foucault 1971, p. 154)

Foucault does the same thing for the rule of law. Rather than situating the rule of law in its actual social context and showing how, in protecting the right of the rationally autonomous individual, it sometimes also protects the rights of Capital, he rejects it entirely: "The law is a calculated and relentless pleasure, delight in the promised blood, which permits the perpetual institution of new dominations and the staging of meticulously repeated scenes of violence" (Foucault 1971, p. 155).

Ultimately, however, this rejection of univocal models of causality is shown to be mere pretense.

> In a sense, only a single drama is ever staged in this "nonplace," the endless repeated play of dominations. The domination of certain men over others leads to the differentiation of values; class domination generates the idea of liberty; and the forceful appropriation of things necessary to survival and the imposition of a duration not intrinsic to them account for the origin of logic. (Foucault 1971. p. 155)

Note the internal contradictions here. Not only has an attack on monocausal theory (teleological explanation) terminated in a monocausal theory (everything depends on the will to power) but the language itself encodes a reliance on the very causality that is being disavowed (leads to . . .). And the whole argument ends in a rejection of the very logic on which argument of any kind depends.

While claiming to reject causal explanation, Foucault in fact regards everything as a function of domination. We, on the other hand, situate relationships of domination in a much broader context which includes an underlying material base (the ecosystem and indeed the larger structure of the cosmos), structural factors, economic, political, and cultural, and, yes, a teleological ordering to Being which we have demonstrated (Mansueto 2012) is the condition of any possible explanatory theory. And looking at Foucault's genealogy in the light of our own perspective we see one thing: the interests of a social category which is concerned primarily with the effects of domination. And here we have two candidates. The first is that likely suspect: the humanistic intelligentsia which is suffering from proletarianization, but primarily in the form of a loss of autonomy rather than in the form of economic exploitation. And we can take as demonstrated at this point that Foucault's theory functions at one level as an attempt at resisting proletarianization without resisting—or even naming Capital—and if forced to do so, mentions the most powerful force on the planet as simply one historically contingent form of domination among others. *Poststructuralism, then, is an attempt on the part of the hermeneutic intelligentsia to "liberate" its struggles from those of the proletariat and peasantry and indeed from the rest of the petty bourgeoisie.*

Let me be clear. I have no problem with the humanistic intelligentsia acting on its own behalf. It should be clear that I am an advocate for the liberating potential of this, my own, social category. But such advocacy must be transparent. It cannot be presented as a systematic critique of all other social interests while at the same time concealing its own. It must be realistic: open to alliances which give it some real prospect of success. And it must advocate for *all of the oppressed*, not just for its own interests, no matter how legitimate. And Foucault fails on all these fronts.

Still, it would be tempting to see Foucault as representing a step up from Heidegger. There does not appear to be the same demand here that except for the few "gods" who reveal Being in a new way and give "voice" to an entire people simply act as interpreters of what the current advent of Being and its reigning god demand. Indeed, Foucault seems to insist that history (as a scholarly discipline) has a liberating function: "History . . . should become a differential knowledge of energies and failings, heights and degenerations, poisons and antidotes. Its task is to become a curative science" (Foucault 1971, p. 160).

But then we must look at what Foucault actually proposes—which is that the rule of law simply "permits the permits the perpetual institution of new dominations and the staging of meticulously repeated scenes of violence." This is not the point of view of a petty bourgeois intelligentsia which has not yet matured to the point of alliance with the other working classes or which has retreated from alliances which, for reasons good or bad, are perceived as having failed. This is the point of view a grand bourgeois, even super-bourgeois magnate who is confident enough in his power to dispense with even the rule of law, which the bourgeoisie as a whole has understood as the very condition of its existence. Or perhaps there is a still greater power which sees itself as the great disrupter of which Foucault and his followers are the unwitting agents?

Creating a New World—Literally

We need, finally, to consider the most radical extension of Heidegger's work, what has come to be called the *ontological turn*. For those who are not familiar with it this "turn," it originated in cultural anthropology and from the perspective of its advocates within that discipline represents simply a further extension the discipline's constitutive commitment to taking difference seriously. Specifically, advocates of the ontological turn argue that the idea that different societies approach a common reality by way of different cultural perspectives misses important aspects of "difference."

> Eduardo Viveiros de Castro . . . has described a range of Amazonian societies with the term "multinaturalist" (1998). By this he means that they understand "humans" (I use the label in inverted commas because as we will see it can refer to subjects that Europeans or Americans would typically understand to be of a different species—animals, for example) to share the same culture, soul, or perspective, but to differ across the bodies they possess and the worlds that they perceive. All subjects, in other words, share the same point of view: they see their appendages as hands and feet, their living quarters as houses, what they drink to be beer, and what they eat to be manioc rice. The difference lies in what they perceive to be these things: if I am in possession of a certain sort of body—one like yours—I will see the same things you see when you see manioc rice, and beer, and houses. However, if my body is different to yours—if it is that of a jaguar, for example—I will see beer where you see blood, a house where you see a den, and rice where you see animal remains. Furthermore, bodies can, with some effort, be exchanged, put on, and discarded like clothing, much as we think of ourselves as being able to exchange viewpoints, whether through religious conversion, for example, or indeed through the practice of anthropology. In this context, in other words, difference and similarity have shifted axes across nature and culture: Amerindians are not culturally relative, for to them all humans share the same culture and view on the world; they are naturally relative, for not all humans share the same body and the same world. (Heywood 2017, p. 475)

It should be clear from the beginning that there is a disturbing ambiguity about what is being advocated here. On the one hand we see a claim that *in some sense* different societies *actually constitute the worlds that they inhabit*. On the other hand, advocates of the ontological turn have, said that they are simply trying to take difference seriously and that their claims are methodological and not *ontological*, that they are not claiming that the societies they study inhabit a universe different from our own. But this position is not really tenable. Either we believe that the various entities in which a particular society worships, for example, exist—or we don't. And if they exist for them and not for us that marks a real difference in worlds, a difference which the ontological turn attributes to *worlding,* to the constitution of worlds by our respective societies, and not simply to differences in cultural perspective.

Now there can be no question that human societies *shape* the world they inhabit. But the claim that human beings *constitute* worlds represents a very dangerous semantic sleight of hand, for the simple reason that it negates entirely and by fiat the distinction between necessary and contingent Being and the role of material conditions in constraining and shaping the course of human development. We do not need to believe that contemporary "Western" science has the final world about the nature and structure of the world we inhabit or deny that hunter-gatherer or horticultural societies might have insights regarding that world to recognize that this world has certain inescapable features over which we have no control. It has at least three spatial and one temporal dimension. It characterized by at least four fundamental forces which are fine-tuned in a way which allows the emergence of complex organization. Matter and energy are conserved—never created or destroyed—but the latter tends to dissipate, so that complex structures require the input of energy in order to sustain themselves. And even so the most complex forms of which we are aware—living organisms and intelligences—die. And none of the societies studied by anthropologists who have taken the ontological turn would really deny any of this, even if they might put it rather differently, or assign a different meaning to it.

There are, furthermore, other ways to take difference seriously. I am inclined to agree with advocates of the ontological turn that the older sort of cultural relativism, which understands difference simply as one of perspective, and which treats all perspectives as equally (in)valid, is inconsistent and disrespectful, because if fails to take seriously the claim of many, or even most perspectives to actually capture something about the nature of reality. But it is possible to integrate a weak or moderate perspectivalism with a strong realism which acknowledges that the world is vastly more complex than any of our perspectives, some of which may, nonetheless, be more accurate than others. It is also possible that the world itself, while real and shared, is less determinate than we imagine—that it is *objective and independent of our observation, analysis, interpretation, or "worlding"* but actually ambiguous and in flux, an approach which we will apply in a later work to the interpretation of certain quantum formalisms.

Authentic cultural humility consists in acknowledging that other cultures might actually be closer to the truth than we are and that even if they aren't that does not give us a general right to impose our understanding of the world unless that is the only *way to prevent grave evil. But the only way to ground an entirely unconditional right on the part of colonized and indigenous peoples to believe and act as they wish is to grant a comparable right to colonizers.* And then we are back to Dugin.

Once again, therefore, we must ask whose interests are served by the ontological turn. Already many anthropologists have pointed out that the turn draws attention away from the critical challenges facing the "indigenous" communities the turn attempts to understand, many of which have to do with the material conditions of their existence (Bessire and Bond 2014). There is, however, one social stratum which has *consistently* generated ideologies which claim that human beings constitute or create the world in which they live: the *rentier* stratum of the bourgeoisie, which consumes without producing, even indirectly and whose wealth consists not in claims on *surplus* which allows them to accumulate, but rather in claims on *labor* the value of which rise with the price of shares and decline whenever wages increase (Lukacs 1953/1980).

With this in mind, it should be clear that the ontological turn merely completes the work undertaken by the hermeneutic and genealogical turns. It disconnects us from the material conditions under which humanity seeks Being and forces us to embrace the perspective of those who (imagine that) they have escaped materiality: the *rentiers* and, we will argue, Capital as an emergent intelligence independent of the historic bourgeoisie.

* * *

Laclau's vision of a decisively post-Marxist Left has clearly come to fruition. The struggle to transcend the commodification of labor power and to end capitalist exploitation, where they have not been silenced entirely, are drowned out in a cacophony of demands for liberation, all or nearly all legitimate in their *content*, but profoundly problematic in their form, as bare assertions of the will to power, ungrounded, and without any basis for unity with each other than besides that which is constructed by one aspiring revolutionary leadership or another.

It should be clear at this point why the emerging Left has made so little progress. At its best it makes no effort to frame the struggle against Capital in ways which might ground an alliance between the petty bourgeoisie, proletariat and peasantry. At worst it simply resumes the positions of Heidegger and Schmitt—i.e., of the fascism of the last century. To the extent that it attracts a mass base at all—e.g., in parts of Latin America—it simply repackages revolutionary nationalism (itself a close relative of fascism) for use in the context of nominal electoral democracies.

But what is the alternative? I have already argued elsewhere that the road forward for humanity involves understanding the struggle against Capital within the much broader context of the liberation struggles which began in the Axial Age, of which the liberal, democratic, and socialist revolutions were an extension. This means rooting our critique of capitalism in our understanding of what it means to be human, and ultimately in what it means *to Be,* and to understand our strategic aim as nothing less than a struggle for the full realization of our humanity.

We need now to look at what that might mean from the vantage point of political theology.

6

Communism as a Spiritual Project

Statement of the Problem

We have now reached the crux of our argument. We have shown, on the one hand, that the humanistic project with its emphasis on rational autonomy is at once continuous with the axial projects which locate the ends of human life in spiritual development and civilizational progress (most directly, to be sure, with Hellenism and in particular the dialectical tradition) and also that it adds something distinctive to those traditions, by advancing the idea that everyone has, at least *in potentia*, the ability to decide for themselves what it means to be human, to engage in work which is a creative expression of both what Marx called their *species being* and their distinctive individual capacities, to participate in deliberation regarding the common good, and to pursue their chosen spiritual paths at whatever level is appropriate to their degree of growth and development. We have also seen that the liberal and democratic variants of this project are too limited. As long as people are forced to sell their labor power in order to survive, they are forced to do not what an informed conscience commands but what their employers desire and are thus subject to total instrumentalization. From this point of view communism is a necessary condition for realizing not just the liberal and democratic projects but also the various axial projects as well. It is morally obligatory and Marx's contribution in demonstrating this places him among humanity's great prophets, pointing the way to a deeper understanding and realization of the human vocation.

This said, we have also seen that Marx's theorization of the communist project is not entirely adequate. Specifically, he failed to distinguish clearly between necessary and contingent Being and ended up arguing that purely political changes can carry humanity across the threshold from contingency to necessity, resolving, as he put it, the contradiction between existence and essence and, in effect, building God. And it is not really meaningful to argue that Marx eventually abandoned his youthful excess on this point or that the socialist and communist movements never really embraced it in the first place. On the contrary, it would be more adequate to say that this dynamic of godbuilding and messianism is integral to the logic of historic socialism and that socialist and communist parties have simply chosen not to talk about it and have disciplined or expelled those who do, whether to advocate it (Rowley 1978) or even to constrain it in a way which actually serves the interests of the party (Lukacs 1923/1971). It is precisely the logic of godbuilding which drives an effort to transcend finitude by means scientific, technological, and economic progress, as the economic precondition for true communism, legitimating the transformation of socialism from a form of transition to communism which aims at the decommodification of labor power into a strategy for primitive accumulation and imperial restoration.

Furthermore, even where Marx is *most* right, in his analysis of the alienation generated by the commodification of labor power, neither he nor most of his interpreters have understood the very dark implications of this analysis. The alienation generated by the commodification of labor power means that the proletariat, far from spontaneously developing into a conscious revolutionary class dedicated to transcending capitalism, is in fact profoundly susceptible—along with all other social classes—to authoritarian ideologies, patriarchal and racist, and has frequently been transformed into a mass base for fascism. And there are no other social categories, including the humanistic intelligentsia, which are exempt from this dynamic. Living under capitalism we are all pulled towards fascism by the inexorable logic of alienation, a logic which can resist only by means of intentional spiritual discipline, supported by communities committed to this resistance.

There have, to be sure, been any number of "integral humanisms" (Maritain 1936) which situate the communist and the humanistic projects in a broader spiritual context, complementing politics with spiritual practice. But as we have seen, this is not enough. Christian humanisms and Christian socialisms in particular, but to a lesser extent Muslim,

Hindu, Buddhist, and Chinese socialisms conserve the logic of empire which was inserted into these traditions either as they were hegemonized as legitimating ideologies (in the case of the various "Hinduisms" and "Buddhisms" and the Chinese schools) or at the moment of their foundation, as in the case of Christianity and Islam. In the case of the former, as we have seen, this was mostly a matter of claiming for the emperor virtues which he did not actually possess, creating a rationalized sacral monarchic form of legitimation in the postaxial age of *Empire*. This is unfortunate, but relatively straightforward to combat, and in fact tended to soften *Imperial* rule and as legitimation also involved accountability. For Christianity and Islam, on the other hand, the logic of empire is constitutive, embedded in the ideal of divine sovereignty, so that even rule which is in other respects relatively just produces and reproduces authoritarianism.

From this point of view the metaphysics of power and political theology are not arcane presuppositions of politics. On the contrary, they *define* political projects. It is thus vitally important that we get them right. Specifically, we must guard at the metaphysical level against any turn towards a univocal metaphysics. A univocal metaphysics creates a zero-sum game between God and humanity in which our effort to realize ourselves is itself sinful and the only way to honor God is through radical submission. And the only credible alternative to this submission is to reject and deny God, and seek to transcend finitude by means of scientific and technological progress, the first form of godbuilding. The result at the level of political theology is precisely the sovereign who decides the exception, who grounds the legal and moral order on the basis of an original act of violence which he claims to be divine.

We have also suggested why an analogical metaphysics, while preferable to the doctrine of univocity, is also inadequate. First of all, by allowing that mythological language which cannot help but depict God as *a* being, and which depicts God as acting in time, and more specifically as a sovereign ruler whose commands *constitute* ethics, even an analogical metaphysics can leave intact the whole dynamic of divine command, human sin and disobedience, and the need for redemption which, except for the tiny minority with the philosophical sophistication to grasp the analogy of Being, unfolds much as it does in the context of a univocal metaphysics. An analogical metaphysics also implies that *theosis* of *some kind* is possible, leading ultimately to the idea that a God-Man is possible, and along with it a Kingdom of Heaven in which evil has been defeated once and for all. Properly understood, to be sure, within a theology informed by an analogical metaphysics, God commands only in the sense that the act of divine Being as such *outside of space and time* is identical with the Eternal Law of the divine nature and *theosis* and the Kingdom of Heaven are pursued by cultivating virtue, including supernatural virtues which stretch us beyond our mere humanity, and by means of political action on behalf of justice. But ultimately the promise of beatitude is a false one. Contingency is not overcome, and cannot be, either on earth or "in heaven," for the simple reason that Necessary Being is by nature One and any multiplicity would destroy its necessity by making it dependent on its divine other. The beatific vision, precisely to the extent that it is a vision of God, is also a profound knowledge of our own limitation and of the injustice we have committed as a result of these limitations. Indeed, in order to make his *Paradiso* credible as a state of beatitude, a poet as great as Dante had to strip those who entered it of their memory of their sins, and deprive them of any knowledge that higher degrees of beatitude might have been possible, something which is tantamount to also stripping them of their individuality. An analogical metaphysics, furthermore, while it does not ground a sovereign who creates a legal and moral order by "deciding the exception" through divine/revolutionary violence, *does* imply the possibility of the God Man who brings into being a divided sovereignty in which the representative of His divine nature—the spiritual lord—teaches, sanctifies and governs in accord with the natural and divine law while the representative of his human nature—the temporal lord—while *obligated* to govern in accord with natural law, cannot be compelled to do so. The result to defer justice indefinitely to a beyond in which it is still impossible because our contingency and finitude, which are the occasion of choices which lead to injustice, remains intact.

It is in this context that we must return to Jiang's argument that it is necessary to extricate the communist project from Christian political theology, which begins by demanding *theosis*, and ends by deferring even much more modest change to the beyond. That said, it is also vitally important that we not allow the communist ideal to become a means of legitimation for what amount to restored civilizational empire which is, in effect, what Jiang is arguing for when he reduces communism to a *xinxue* or "learning of the heart" which softens but does not attempt to transcend the alienation of labor. While the Dharmic and Taoic traditions have much to teach us about living with and growing in and through finitude and contingency, the humanistic tradition is not wrong to value overcoming contingency *to the extent and in the way we actually can*, by achieving rational autonomy and collective self-determination, at least to the extent of creating mechanisms which hold leaders accountable for their actions and undercut unwarranted claims to *auctoritas*. Our task in this chapter will be to show how it is possible to define a metaphysics and a political theology which walks this line—and then to translate it into a strategy for transcending the commodification of labor power and of the instrumentalization of humanity.

Metaphysics and Political Theology

An Equivocal Metaphysics of *Esse*

The Dialectical Tradition

How does one make a positive argument for the equivocity of Being? There is, to be sure, a long tradition going back to Aristotle which holds that the term "being" is used in many different ways, as for example in reference to *substances*, which he says exist in themselves and to *accidents* which exist only in other things. And while arguments from the analysis of ordinary language are not fully demonstrative, they do carry some weight—enough, for example, for us to ask why anyone would ever have thought that the term "being" was used univocally when it is obviously not. And so a *univocal* metaphysics should be self-evidently ridiculous. It should, in other words, be *obvious* that God does not "exist" in the same way we do. That said, understanding that the term "being" is used in many different ways still allows that these ways are similar enough to permit analogical predication, or what the scholastics called "priority and posteriority." Fire is not just hot; it makes things hot, and so it hot in higher degree than say the food it is used to cook . . . so we need to explain why we reject this alternative, beyond warning against its political and spiritual consequences.

God *is* in a qualitatively different sense than *things*. When we say that a donkey exists, we are saying that something which has a specific nature or essence that of a donkey is an object of possible experience, the subject/object of cause and effect, a possible object of attraction or aversion, etc. When we say that the donkey is particularly wise and loving, we are saying that we can additionally observe a quality that goes beyond its donkeyhood. And the same is true of things which are beyond ordinary human experience the existence of which we infer by way of a combination of observation, mathematical formalization, and perhaps experiment, such as quarks. But God has no essence other than Her Being, and no superadded qualities which are not convertible that Being.

This becomes even more clear if we consider what it really means to say that something has a given essence or nature. As we have argued elsewhere (Mansueto 2005, 2010a), the essence of something is ultimately simply its structure. In the case of possible beings, we can define this structure precisely using mathematical formalisms. As beings move from potency to act this becomes less and less possible. Thus, physical systems can still be described quite well by mathematical formalisms, but since they actually exist there is always some distance between mathematical formalism and physical interpretation, as the ongoing debate regarding what the relativistic and quantum formalisms which describe matter actually mean. Mathematical formalisms are helpful in understanding the operation of biological systems, but there is no formalism describing a dog or a donkey, and indeed, with biological systems, even taxonomy becomes difficult as the debate between phenetics, cladistics and evolutionary taxonomy (Mayr 1988) demonstrates. And what is true of biology is even more true of the social sciences and the hermeneutic disciplines. This is because as things move from potency to act they are increasingly ordered to something beyond themselves—their *telos* or meaning, which they pursue in a multitude of complex and unpredictable ways.

Now we know what it is to which all contingent beings are ordered. It is Being as Such, which they seek by exploiting various laws which allow them to persist and even grow in Being. Thus, minerals leverage the Boltzman Order principle to maintain their form. Living things seek Being by not only maintaining their form but through the process of nutrition, growth, reproduction, and evolution—and in the case of animals, through sensation and locomotion. Rational beings are conscious of their aim and develop ever new ways to pursue it. But no matter how complex and organized a system becomes, there is always something "left over" besides its being. Indeed, the more complex a system's "strategy" for seeking Being, the more complex the structure that is "left over."

Rising dialectically to the idea of God, is thus not in *any* sense a matter of degree. God is not a still more complex system seeking Being by means that, since they are in advance of our own, we cannot fully understand. Such a being would be either a significantly more advanced rational animal or something beyond animality entirely—what many civilizations have called angels and demons. God is, rather, the end which everything else seeks, the Power of Being as Such. God is related to things as end to means.

Now the relationship between means and end is neither univocal nor analogical, but equivocal. Means *exist*. Ends, by their very nature, to the extent that they are still ends and not something already realized (logically or chronologically), do not. And we never realize the Power of Being as Such. And yet ends, which do not exist, are more powerful than means, which do. It is the end which calls the means into Being and not vice versa. It is only the fact that we seek Being by, among other things, preserving our existence that makes us think that existence is more important than an end which does not exist.

Put in another way, God acts and *only* acts as Final Cause. This is evident from the cosmological argument from motion, as first set forth by Aristotle's *Metaphysics* (Aristotle 350 BCE/1952, 12.7), which we can loosely paraphrase as follows:

> Things move.
>
> Everything that moves must have a mover.
>
> There can be no infinite regress of movers (because then there would be no first mover and thus no motion).
>
> Therefore there must be a first mover which is itself unmoved.
>
> But how does something move things without itself moving? The Unmoved Mover moves by teleological attraction, relating to the things it moves as Beloved to Lover.

Thus, when we say that God *is*, we acknowledge that God is the subject of causality. But God cannot be the object of causality, or change, because that would entail a loss of the perfection which makes God attractive in the first place. Similarly, God cannot act as formal cause, because to do so would confer on things God's own form or essence, which is to Be, and would do so perfectly, so that nothing would exist and there would only *be* God, which is clearly not true. Finally, God cannot act as material cause because that would mean that God was subject to change and growth which is contrary to divine simplicity and perfection.

This has profound implications for the way in which we consider theism and atheism. On the one hand, the concept of God properly understood as the power of Being as Such excludes all theisms which retain any trace of the notion that God is *a* being or the Supreme Being ruling over a universe of other beings. It also, however, excludes any possible atheism since we can infer from empirical observation that things seek Being and that God is, at the very least, an *ideal* for rational beings. Thus when Sartre, the great archatheist, argued that "humanity is the desire to be God" (Sartre 1943), he was actually demonstrating that he was no atheist at all. *A mature understanding of God presupposes a renunciation of any claim that God does anything at all for us other than the one thing which She is always and already doing: drawing us into Being.*

We will consider shortly the political implications of such a theology. First, however, we need to answer some objections. The first of these comes from Scotus: i.e., the claim that nothing other than a univocal metaphysics makes natural theology possible. This is easily answered, as it was by way of natural theology that we arrived at our equivocal metaphysics in the first place. Beginning with contingent beings, we need to explain why there is something rather than nothing and we arrive at the Power of Being as Such which, however, is not really "something," but rather the power by means of which things exist.

We can also answer the (hypothetical) Radical Orthodox objection that an equivocal metaphysics renders sacramentality and participation in the life of God impossible. The question here turns on what we mean by sacramentality. If by a sacrament we mean and outward sign of inward grace, then the concept of sacrament is derivative from that of grace which then depends on a God who exists and exists in some degree as we do—i.e., on a univocal or an analogical metaphysics. But if we mean by sacramentality a participation in the generativity which is Being, then sacramentality is entirely possible with the context of an equivocal metaphysics. Indeed, God is already present in everything, as the power by which they exist, even if She cannot be identified with them.

While Milbank and the other Radical Orthodox theologians do not address the question of equivocity directly, and seem (incorrectly, I think) to regard Judaism and Islam as implying a univocal metaphysics, his critique of these religions accuses them of "wooden legalism" which identifies spirituality with ethics and ethics [at least in the case of Judaism] with the American constitutional order (Milbank 2007). This is fundamentally inaccurate. On the contrary, for Judaism we make God present by doing the work that God cannot do, mending the torn fabric of creation. And while ethical conduct and political struggle are clearly central here, ritual and indeed sacramentality in the broader sense of celebrating the divine presence play a central role in Judaism. And Judaism has a rich mystical tradition which, just because it does not promise mystical union in the same sense as the Catholic mystical tradition, does indeed provide a pathway of growth towards God.

An equivocal metaphysics is a metaphysics of participation because to the extent that we exist we authentically share in God's Being, for the simple reason that that is the only Being there is. This is not affected by the fact that contingent being, or what we call *existence*, and the power of Being as such are so radically different that we cannot speak of Being itself even analogically. We see an example of what this looks like in Spinoza. It has become commonplace since Deleuze to view Spinoza as link in the chain of philosophers advocating the univocity of Being leading from Scotus to Heidegger and Deleuze himself. But as Stephen Houlgate (Deonotologistics 2009) and others point out, Spinoza recognizes a radical distinction between Being and beings. God/Nature/Substance are self-caused; the modes are not. This is precisely the difference invoked by ibn Sina and Thomas to justify an analogical metaphysics and by Moshe ben Maimon to justify an equivocal metaphysics. The ontological distinction between Being and beings, or between Substance and Modes itself at once excludes univocity and defines beings or modes as participations in the power of Being as such (Deonotologistics 2009).

Being and Dependent Origination

What does this argument imply for *ways* other than and not syncretized with the dialectical tradition? At least within a postaxial context we are looking at two principal complexes: the debate within the Dharmic traditions regarding the reality of Brahman and Atman and the debate within the Taoic traditions regarding the status, knowability, and name-ability of the Tao and other formulations of the architectonic principle such as *Tian* or *Tai Chi*.

To begin, we must remember that these traditions are not *different answers to the same question* posed and answered by Judaism, Christianity, and Islam, or by Hellenism. They are *different answers* to *different questions*. For the *ways of justice and liberation* (Judaism, Islam, and, with some significant qualifications, Christianity) the fundamental question is how we overcome injustice, individual and collective. For Hellenism, the fundamental question is whether or the what extent and how we can transcend our finitude and contingency. Judaism, Islam, and Christianity all syncretize to a greater or lesser extent with Hellenism, so that the problem of Being and that of Justice become linked together, as we have shown in our analysis up to this point, which has shown that within these traditions metaphysics drives political theology. The question about Being becomes a restatement, in terms of the Hellenic theological problematic, of the question about how and to what extent Justice can be realized. More specifically, the Good as a metaphysical first principle (as for Plato) and ultimately Being as Such with which it is convertible, serve as a ground for a discourse about justice and for ethical judgment, and the way in which Being as Such or any possible Supreme Being is understood frames an understanding of the nature and possibility of sovereignty.

The concern which we see in the dialectical tradition with the problem of finitude and contingency is shared by the Dharmic traditions which we have classed with Hellenism as part of the *way of wisdom*, but the core metaphysical debate within these traditions centers around the question of whether or not things have a "self" or inherent existence and if so where it is located: i.e., the question of Brahman and Atman and the relationship between them and, in the Buddhist variants of the tradition, the question of whether or not things have *svabhava*—inherent existence or an essential nature. Let us see how this develops.

Axial Age and postaxial India presents a broad range of metaphysical doctrines, both within the *astika* traditions which affirm the authority of the Vedas and the *nastika* traditions such as Buddhism and Jaina which do not. In general, all of the *astika* traditions affirm that *something* has substance or self-existence, whether it is atoms, as in the case of the *Vaisheshika* and (to the extent that it is addressed) the *Nyaya* traditions, *prakriti* or matter and *purusa* or spirit in the case of the *Samkya/Yoga* tradition, the creative words of the priests in the case of the *Mimamsa* tradition, or *Brahman* and *Atman* in the case of the *Vedanta* tradition. The *nastika* traditions, on the other hand, tended to be skeptical about claims on behalf of any sort of immaterial principle, though the *Caravaka and Ajivika* both tended towards a materialist doctrine of substance and the *Jaina* towards a *jiva/ajiva* dualism similar to the *Samkya* doctrine. It is really only in the case of Buddhism—and in later *astika* responses to Buddhism—that we find the idea of *svabhava* or self-existence consistently thematized, much less called into question.

While the concept of *pattica samupada* or interdependent origination goes back to the earliest texts of the Pali Canon, the term *svabhava* is not used there. The *Abidharma* allows *svabhava* to *dhammas*, the atomic or momentary point-instants into which more complex phenomena, which lack *svabhava*, can be analysed, though it is not entirely clear whether the term should be understood in this context to refer to self-existence or essential nature. This early view, which was characteristic of the *Sarvastivadins*, also affirmed that past, present, and future all exist in some sense. The *Sarvastivadins* later split into the *Vaibishikas*, who continued to uphold this position, and the *Sautrantikas*, who insisted that only the present is real. This in turn led to the *Theravada* use of the term, which regards *dhammas* as having *svabhava* in the sense of a characteristic nature, but which regards this as radically conditioned and subject to constant change (Harvey 1990).

Strictly speaking the claim that all *dharmas* lack *svabhava* is specific to the *Prajnaparamita* literature and the *Madhyamika* school, where it should be understood in its historical and polemical context as a safeguard against the absorption of Buddhism into emerging Puranic Hinduism, and the *advaita* school in particular, with which the emerging Mahayana otherwise shared many concerns and practices (Walser 2021). The argument runs something like this:

> Svabhāva is by definition the subject of contradictory ascriptions. If it exists, it must belong to an existent entity, which means that it must be conditioned, dependent on other entities, and possessed of causes. But a *svabhāva* is by definition unconditioned, not dependent on other entities, and not caused. Thus the existence of a *svabhāva* is impossible. (Robinson 1957)

The more mature Mahayana Schools, such as the *Tiantai* and the *Huayen*, as well as the various Vajrayana schools, frequently allow that the *tathagatagarbha* or Buddha-nature has *svabhava*, or, as the *Mahayana Mahaparanirvana Sutra* puts it, the *tathagatagarbha* is the *svabhava* of all things. This is view is balanced, however, with a complementary radicalization of the doctrine of interdependent origination, especially in the *Avatamska Sutra*, which argues that everything is implicit in everything else.

This, in turn created an argument, which became particularly developed in India and in the Tibetan *Vajrayana* schools over the meaning of the doctrine, inherited from the *Prajnaparamita* and the still very prestigious *Madhyamika* that all *dharmas* are empty. The *Prasangika* interpretation held that one should argue for the emptiness of all *dharmas* only by showing the logical incoherence of the claim that they have *svabhava*, while the *Svatantrika* attempts to advance positive claims regarding *sunyata* or emptiness itself. This, in turn led to the emergence of the *Rangtong* and *Shentong* schools. The *Rangtong* hold that all *dharmas* are empty of *svabhava* or inherent existence and that this emptiness is not itself an ultimate reality of some kind. Susan Kahn summarizes the *Rangtong* position.

> Ultimate truth does not point to a transcendent reality, but to the transcendence of deception. It is critical to emphasize that the ultimate truth of emptiness is a negational truth. In looking for inherently existent phenomena it is revealed that it cannot be found. This absence is not findable because it is not an entity, just as a room without an elephant in it does not contain an elephantless substance. Even conventionally, elephantlessness does not exist. Ultimate truth or emptiness does not point to an essence or nature, however subtle, that everything is made of. (Kahn 2014)

The *Shentong*, on other hand, argue that while conventional reality is empty of *svabhava* or inherent existence, the *buddhajnana* or *tagthagatagarbha* is in fact the *paramarthasatya* or ultimate reality, putting the stress on nonduality rather than emptiness (Stearns 1999).

There is, in fact, a very simple resolution of the contradiction between these two views—and one that is coherent with an equivocal metaphysics of *Esse*. Specifically, if we say with the *Shentong* that the ultimate reality is the *tathagatagarbha*, then we need to ask what the *tathagatagarbha* might be. But isn't the Buddha-nature simply, on the one hand, an understanding of the authentic nature of reality, understood as interdependent origination and, on the other, an *effective* compassion flowing from this understanding which aims at the liberation and ripening of being? It is, in other words, neither substance nor subject, but rather a relational, transformative generativity which mends the torn fabric of the contingent and conditioned) universe. To put the matter differently, God or Being may not *exist*, but we desire them nonetheless and that desire draws us into Being and as we grow intellectually and morally we recognize that God is not self-existence but rather relationship and generativity. Seeking Being we discover that Being is not existence after all, but something far greater: the capacity to bring things into Being. Liberating ourselves from the illusion that things exist in themselves and that the phenomenal world is ultimately real (and ultimately important), and passing through the recognition that there may not be an ultimate *existing* reality after all (what we might even call two "dark nights"), at least in the sense we naively hoped and believed, we attain a higher understanding of what God *is*.

It is not surprising, from this point of view, that many Jews have found themselves drawn to Buddhism. Both, albeit by different metaphysical pathways, share a spirituality which is focused not on God as a self-existing subject, but rather on the relational generativity which is the presence of the divine in the phenomenal world.

The Way of Harmony

We find a similar attempt in the Chinese tradition to integrate a creative and ordering first principle with a rejection of the idea that this principle is substance or self-existence. While the Chinese tradition is often regarded as less concerned with metaphysical than with ethical questions, the Axial Age in China did lead to significant religious rationalization and produced a number of concepts which attempt to identify and/or characterize the first principle. The most important of these is *Tian*, or Heaven which, while sometimes anthropomorphized at least implicitly (as in the idea that the Emperor is the "Son of Heaven") is generally theorized as an impersonal principle which, interacting with *Kun* or Earth, generates and orders the universe. There is also the concept of the *Tao* or Way, which the Taoist tradition resists defining or even naming, while the Confucian tradition sees it as the source of particular natural and moral principles. Finally, in the course of the interaction between these two traditions we see the emergence of the concepts of *taiji* and *wuji*, the Great Ultimate (literally the Great Tent Pole) and the Non-Ultimate, or Non-Being. These different theorizations of the first principle are brought together in the *daoxue* synthesis, most fully in Zhoudunyi's cryptic *Explanation of the Diagram of the Great Ultimate*.

If the Dharmic variant of the *way of wisdom* approaches the problem of finitude and contingency from an utterly different angle than the Hellenic variant, then what we have called the *way of harmony* focuses on a different problem entirely. In China the Axial Age, while still very much a process of religious problematization, rationalization, and democratization, was focused above all on resolving the problem of how to restore the harmony—both within human society and between human beings and the natural world—which had been lost in the emergence of sacral monarchy. The axial age in China also built on what can only be called the Zhou *Revolution*, which introduced the concept of *tian ming* or the mandate of heaven, which qualified sacral monarchy in such a way that the king ruled to the extent and only to the extent that he maintained and restored social harmony.

From here the *way* divides over a number of questions. Is there a principle which grounds harmony as the architectonic value and tells us what it means? Is this principle personal or impersonal? Is it knowable by means of discursive reason or not? Factoring out these possibilities we find:

- *Legalism,* properly *fajia,* which rejects the idea of a first principle and sees harmony as the product of force and law—the sovereign who decides the exception, for which Xi and Jiang seem to have opted,
- *Mohism,* properly *mojia,* which sees harmony as the result of following the law decreed by a personal god,
- *Confucianism,* properly *ruxue,* which sees harmony as grounded in a impersonal principle, associated with *tian* (heaven), the *tao* (the way), and/or *taiji* (the Great Ultimate), which can be known discursively and embodied in laws and rituals, and
- *Taoism,* properly *daojiao,* which also sees harmony as grounded in a impersonal principle, but cautions against any attempt to grasp that principle discursively.

In addition to these various "high traditions," there is the *xiantiandao* or the Way of the Former Heaven, or more broadly the "salvationist tradition" of popular religious movements which put much less emphasis on religious rationalization and instead focus on restoration of pre-imperial and even pre-tributary/pre-patriarchal/pre-sacral monarchic Golden Age before the advent of the state and of exploitation. These traditions focus on a "former" high god, generally represented as feminine, usually as the primordial grandmother out of whom who the universe emerged. These movements were frequent catalysts of peasant revolts.

Each of these traditions had a well-defined social base. The Legalists articulated the position of warlords aspiring to Empire and their advisors. Mohism was actually quite close to this position, but also made a direct appeal to the peasantry, by promising them a larger share of the value added as less was devoted to ritual and other "luxuries." Confucianism appealed to scholars focused on promoting harmony by advising rulers and Taoism to scholars who had withdrawn from the court and even from urban society. There were syncretisms between these schools and with Buddhism, with some Confucians, such as Xunzi, leaning towards Legalism and others towards Taoism (the later Song *daoxue*, which also drew on elements of Cha'an Buddhism). The *xiantaindao* was an organic movement of the peasantry but interacted and syncretized with the high traditions in ways which still need deeper investigation.

In this context the principal divide between the schools is between those that acknowledge an impersonal first principle and those that do not. Why impersonal? Because a personal god is always the reflex of a monarch, and the Mohist tendency to personalize *Tian* marks their school as an attempt to build an alliance between rulers or would be rulers and the people *against* the aristocracy. In this sense they are not too far from the Legalists, who allow no first principle whatsoever—in the interest of making the Emperor actually supreme. In either case the result is a decisionist political theology not unlike that of Christianity. The Confucians, on the other hand, insist on an impersonal *Tian* to which the Emperor is accountable. Taoism carries this further by denying the possibility of *naming* the *Tao* or capturing it in discursive conceptual formulations, laws, or rituals. While this does not mean that there should be no political authority, it makes legitimation problematic at best. After an extended struggle between the Confucians and the Taoists around these questions—a reflection of resistance in the South and among non-court intellectuals to the Han appropriation of the Confucian tradition—the two traditions flowed together and joined with *Cha'an* Buddhism to form the normative *daoxue*, which was summarized in Zhou Dunyi's cryptic *Explanation of the Diagram of the Great Ultimate*, with its first line:

> *Wuji er Taiji*
> Non-Being therefore Being.

While this metaphysics prefers to hold open the paradox rather than to attempt a discursive formulation which captures it (and the limitations of discursive formulations), it is nonetheless very close to the equivocal metaphysics of *Esse* which we are advocating, especially in two key respects. First, it affirms a first principle, but not necessarily its substantial existence. Second, this first principle is manifest primarily in innerworldly activity ordered to the restoration of harmony and the cultivation of human capacities and the ripening of being generally.

We can see traces of this dynamic in the contemporary debate around "socialism with Chinese characteristics." It is only an impersonal first principle, interpreted by a broad stratum of scholars committed to self-cultivation and to serving the people that can serve as a check on Empire. This stratum is the "deep state" on which Emperors depend but which they also fear and resent. Now the Communist Party—any communist party actually—is, foundationally, a party of intellectuals, whether of what Gramsci called traditional humanistic or clerical intellectuals who come to the side of the working classes or organic intellectuals drawn from the working classes themselves and formed in the struggle against Capital. And the "wisdom" of these intellectuals is fundamentally that there is a *way* or law of history, which even the party must obey and a mandate of history from which it derives its authority.

When, after creating a broad popular front which successfully prosecuted a prolonged popular war against the Japanese, Mao began to try to consolidate his power, his first target was Liu Shaoqi, who advocated "self-cultivation" in the Confucian tradition as a model for party cadres. And the Cultural Revolution was fundamentally an attack on the party as an *institution* which could not help but limit the power of a supreme leader.

Xi and Jiang say that the Communist Party is the "deep constitution" of China. But they are walking a very fine line, since what they mean by the party is not the broader, transhistorical institution, but rather its central leadership and specifically its General Secretary: the "sovereign who decides the exception." They want a party which legitimates but does not hold accountable. And this is a contradiction. A healthy party legitimates precisely because it holds accountable, and ensures that the people can find redress for wrongs and correction of errors in policy and strategy without questioning the socialist order itself. A party which reduces Communism to a vague *xinxue* and "socialist spiritual civilization" to anti-spitting campaigns (and far worse, to campaigns against liberal and democratic rights) will inevitably fail in its task of legitimation.

Against Sovereignty

The analysis we have advanced has profound implications at the political theological level. In order to see this, we need merely extend Durkheim's insight that religious symbols are collective representations of the social order to include conceptual formations. A univocal metaphysics in which God exists in the same way as creatures but is infinitely powerful implies a purely decisionist political theology in which the ethics and law are simply matters of power, and sovereign brings the ethical and legal order into being by means of a foundational act of "divine" violence, deciding its boundaries and decreeing exceptions. It does not really matter if this sovereign is an emperor or dictator of some kind, the People, hypostatized in the General Will, or a revolutionary party. An analogical metaphysics in which God *is* pre-eminently but creatures participate in this Being implies a divided sovereignty in which the divine nature is represented by spiritual lords who serve as guarantors of a pre-existing moral and legal order—the eternal and natural laws—but without absolute efficacy, and the human nature of Christ is presented by the temporal lord who, however imperfectly, tries makes this law effective. An equivocal metaphysics, finally, in which God *is*, but does not strictly *exist* as a thing alongside others, and in which contingent beings, while drawn into existence by the attractive power of God, remain trapped in their contingency, *implies that sovereignty is impossible and an illusion.* This is because without involvement with contingent being that would imply change (and thus be contradiction with the divine nature), God can act only as final cause. And because of this, while in the final instance God is the only real cause of everything, much of what God causes—indeed *all* of what God causes—are incomplete, inadequate, and often profoundly problematic attempts at the divine. The ethical and legal order are inherent in the divine nature and inspire us to mend the torn fabric of the universe—something which God cannot do, as it would imply a knowledge of particulars and an involvement with contingency which contradicts the divine nature—but it can never be fully effective.

This framework can be extended, albeit imperfectly, to the Dharmic and Taoic traditions. While many of the Dharmic traditions, both *astika* and *nastika,* acknowledge something like gods, it is only within the context of Vedanta that this concept is well developed. And it is only within the context of *dvaita* Vedanta (which teaches that God is a separate, transcendent, personal being) that we find a personal God of the sort that appears in Augustinian Christianity and Asharite Islam—perhaps as a result of influence from these traditions. Indeed, the division between *dvaita* and *vishishtadvaita* Vedanta (which argues that Brahman is both present in and distinct from Atman) is quite similar to that between univocal and analogical metaphysics in Christianity.

Advaita Vedanta, on the other hand, argues that Atman *is* Brahman. This amounts to an argument that contingent being is an illusion. The difference with Buddhism is primarily in regard to whether or not the first principle is or has self-existence. Since *everything* is Brahman was based. Instead, we regard the state as one of many institutions which seek to penetrate and transform, without the implication that it either can or should be the agent of a global, revolutionary, structural transformation of the social order. Our vision, in this sense draws very significantly on that of the Right Opposition and especially of Gramsci, but differs in that Gramsci and his interpreters have often understood hegemony as a form of sovereignty rather than as a different way of understanding power. It also draws on insights from libertarian socialists who have stressed that we need to actually cultivate the social order we want to build, whether in the "belly of the beast" or in marginal, liminal, or liberated spaces. But we reject the utopianism of this tradition which seems to assume that we can forgo the work of building and exercising power, engaging institutions, and resisting fascism, with armed struggle if necessary.

Social Ontology

This recognition that sovereignty is an illusion and an impossible ideal is, furthermore, simply one dimension of a broader social ontology. Specifically, because the phenomenal world is not *fully* real, but only a participation in or even a trace of the power of Being as Such, a distinction is created between various levels or degrees of reality, both in the sense of degrees of participation in Being as Such (formal, physical, chemical, biological, rational, etc.) and in the sense of the way in which we *know* these systems. There is thus a fundamental distinction between the level of ordinary experience and common sense—the outer or *zahir* level of knowledge—and the underlying structures behind what we experience, along with the *end* to which they are ordered, which constitutes the hidden or *batin* level of reality. It is not that the phenomenal world is *just* an illusion or has no reality. On the contrary, it (quite literally) *matters* because they things we experience are subject to cause and effect and have an impact on the degree to which things participate in Being and the extent to which we are able to mend the torn fabric of the universe. Nor is it proper to say that the *batin* level of reality which becomes increasingly accessible through formal and transcendental abstraction and spiritual practice, especially under the regulation of an equivocal metaphysics, is *fully real*. Rather, from the moment we understand that there is something which *is* in a radically different sense than the phenomenal world, and that behind what we experience lie structures ordered to this end, we can begin to dig closer to that reality. But claiming that *batin* knowledge is full or absolute is profoundly mistaken and the source of sectarian delusions.

Things like *sovereignty* belong to the manifest or *zahir* level of reality, or are, at least, very close to that surface. We all know "who is in charge." We can all check the org chart. Distinctions between *reign* and *rule* and the Leninist understanding of state power represent attempts to dig a bit deeper. Just winning an election doesn't really mean that you are in charge. There is the *deep state* and there is an entire social structure and ideological apparatus in which the hegemony of the ruling class is inscribed. Thus, the Leninist attempt to "smash the state" and replace it with the party and the soviets, something that was never fully carried out, but which allowed a much more profound break with the past than any change of government ever could. But the party is still a formal organization and power is not something which one *has* and is even less something one simply *gets* by being in a certain formal role. The legal-rational, bureaucratic *mana* associated with office is real, to be sure, and is enough to make most ordinary people go along. But most ordinary people are politically passive and are not fully engaged trying to accomplish something. Power is, rather, built and exercised in relationship and so behind the formal structure of an organization we find informal networks which, while themselves not absolutely real, get us much closer to the heart of things. These networks are structured and constrained by formal organizations, but it is through the networks and not the formal organization that power is built and exercised and purposes actually realized. And so as we approach the question of what communism looks like once we have understood that sovereignty is an illusion and realized that socialism, with its focus on state power, was never really a form of transition to communism, we are not just turning away from that obsession with state power (and formal organization); we are turning towards the actual power of Being as Such, or at least is trace in the complex networks of relationships through which people actually come together to accomplish their aims.

Let us now see what this looks like at the strategic level.

Politics

The Underlying Social Theory

In order to do this we need first to address the question of whether or not our metaphysical and political-theological analysis has any implications for the underlying social theory and theory of change on which the communist project has historically been based. We have already established in our earlier works that the historical materialist claim that history is driven purely and simply by the contradiction between the forces and relations of production or by class struggle (actually two different claims themselves) is in itself inadequate, as it does not account adequately for more purely material factors (ecosystems, the physical, chemical, and biological levels of organization on the basis of which they emerge, and indeed the underlying structure of spacetime), as opposed to technological and economic factors, which is what historical materialists generally mean by the "material base." Nor does it account for the teleological ordering of matter to Being as Such, which becomes conscious in humanity. With this in mind we have proposed a tripartite model of causation which includes:

- Material Factors, i.e., the physical, chemical, and biological organization on the basis of which human societies emerge,

- Structural Factors, i.e., the technological, economic, political, cultural, and psychological structures which emerge in order to facilitate humanity's struggle to *Be*, and

- Teleological Factors, both the Power of Being as Such, which draws all things into Being, and the diverse ways in which it is perceived and theorized under diverse social conditions: what we call spiritual and civilizational ideals.

Social change takes place for a variety of reasons.

- As an adaptation to changing material conditions,

- Through the development of new structures which change the way in which we seek Being,

- Through the emergence of new spiritual and civilizational ideals.

All of these factors are conditioned by each other. Fundamental change, however, is a result of profound contradictions between the material conditions, social structures, and the civilizational ideal. Structural change occurs when structures are no longer adequate to the civilizational ideal or the material conditions. Civilizational change occurs when civilizational ideals lose credibility.

The actual process of social change is also multidimensional and varies considerably. The leading factor is always the development of new spiritual and civilizational ideals (or variants thereof) and the creation of new structures by which to realize them. So long as the hegemonic spiritual and civilizational ideal retains credibility and there are no fundamental contradictions between material conditions, structures, and ideals, change may be gradual and incremental. But where contradictions become serious more radical change is inevitable. Marx was mistaken, however, to assume that this change inevitably takes the form of revolution—much less the sort of consciously planned and organized revolution which he and his interpreters envisioned. On the contrary, transitions by decadence, in which old structures gradually decay and new ones emerge in the ruins, are probably most common (think the crisis of the Roman Empire and the emergence of Christendom). Transitions by civilizational collapse are also a permanent possibility, especially where existing forms cease to be effective adaptations to material conditions.

As our analysis in the preceding chapters suggests, we are currently entering such a period of profound and multidimensional civilizational crisis. On the one hand, industrial technology has led to potentially catastrophic climate change, created conditions in which the emergence of new pandemics is likely, led to resource depletion, and large-scale poisoning of the planet. On the other hand, the commodification of labor power has alienated human beings from their essential nature, which consists in seeking meaning and engaging in creative activity and nurturing relationships which support continued human development. As a result, they take refuge in authoritarian patriarchal and racist ideologies, leading to the continuous emergence and re-emergence of fascism. The hegemonic civilizational ideals, meanwhile, have increasingly lost credibility. With the exception of a small core of investors in the technology sector, along with their acolytes in the scientific-technical and financial intelligentsia, people no longer believe that scientific, technological, and economic progress will liberate them from finitude, and the alienation generated by the commodification of labor power, by alienating human beings from their essential nature, undercuts support for the humanistic ideal in its liberal, democratic, and communist forms. Older ideals (axial or postaxial) retain some salience, but they are, frequently as not, embraced in reactive and reconstructed forms as part of a broader authoritarian complex rather than as authentic *ways* of being human and of growing spiritually.

Within this context, two things stand out. First, because of the gravity of the climate crisis and the enduring and essentially permanent danger of fascism, a popular front politics of broad unity among those willing to resist fascism and address developments which could threaten civilizational collapse is necessary. This popular front should, in principle, be very broad, including not just the peasantry, working classes, and much of the petty bourgeoisie, but also the liberal bourgeoisie, which is itself increasingly threatened by the emergence of Capital as an autonomous intelligence as well as the new stratum of capitalist magnates. The challenge is that all of these classes are themselves vulnerable to authoritarian psychology and thus to fascist hegemony, so that even building the popular front becomes a kind of institutional and cultural trench warfare.

Second, because of the devastating impact of alienation, there is no spontaneous social basis for the communist project. We need to actually rebuild communities and institutions in order to create the context for advancing this project. While elements of popular front policy—increasing the social wage and reducing market pressure—can help in this process, ultimately it requires engaging every single individual, community, and institution on the planet.

Let us see what this looks like in practice.

The Popular Front

General Considerations

Historically, the international workers movement understood the transition between capitalism and communism as involving an intermediate form of social organization, *socialism*, in which the conditions for communism are gradually created and capitalist forms of oppression gradually effaced. From the very beginning this was understood as involving two principal features. First, the proletariat or an alliance between the proletariat and other revolutionary classes (the peasantry, the petty bourgeoisie, the national bourgeoisie, etc.) had to seize state power, generally through the medium of a workers' party of some kind, whether by means of an electoral struggle, insurrection, or a prolonged popular war.

Second, the new revolutionary government would gradually eliminate private property in the means of production, generally through nationalization. The idea was that because the workers control the party, the party the state, and the state the means of production then by some "transitive property of control" the workers would control the means of production and the wage relation would be negated at least formally. No one ever pretended that this was sufficient for communism which, as Marx put it, required the "positive" or substantive abolition of private property and of the wage relation. But the idea that either electoral struggle or revolution had or was creating workers' states was central to the legitimation of both social democracies and socialist states such as the USSR, China, and the states which emerged from the national liberation movements.

This idea was intimately bound up with the idea of the "dictatorship of the proletariat." Marx did not invent this term. This was the work of Joseph Weydemeyr (Weydemeyer 1852) who published an article called "The Dictatorship of the Proletariat" which drew on the example of Cromwell's dictatorship and of the Committee of Public Safety in the English and French Revolutions to theorize what a first step towards communism, based on the seizure of power by the proletariat, might look like. But Marx did embrace the concept, while remaining open to both peaceful and violent paths to revolutionary power.

We have already seen that this approach did not create a viable pathway towards the decommodification of labor power. On the contrary, where the road to power was electoral, the result was a social liberalism which, on the one hand, certainly reduced market pressure and increased the possibilities of rational autonomy for members of the working classes, but which, *under the conditions of the post-WWII "Fordist" regime of accumulation*, stabilized capitalism rather than overcoming it. Where the road to power was by means of insurrection or prolonged popular war the result was a more radical restructuring of social relations, but also a concentration of power in the ruling party which was ultimately incompatible with the ideal of rational autonomy. Imperial restoration replaced communism as the actual aim.

Those who remained committed to the communist project but who found fault with actually existing socialism historically moved in one of three directions. Libertarian socialists, drawing on both earlier anarchist tendencies and "left" tendencies during the uprisings in Germany and elsewhere which accompanied the Russian Revolution and the end of WWI, insisted that the idea of a worker's rule be embodied in radically democratic and decentralized mechanisms such as workers councils or Soviets, and not in the vanguard party. Another group, following Trotsky, continued to uphold the necessity of a vanguard party but argued that the Soviet Union and later China and the states which emerged from the national liberation struggles were "bureaucratically deformed workers' states" which remained socialist but which needed an internal revival of democracy or even an internal democratic revolution—though it was never really explained what this would look like. While always popular among a section of the humanistic intelligentsia, this tendency never found significant popular support within the so-called workers' states or among the working classes elsewhere. Those who followed Mao argued that the persistence of petty commodity production under socialism (both the wage relation and small peasant and crafts production and mercantile activity) created a basis for the constant re-emergence of capitalist tendencies, including within the revolutionary party itself. The Soviet Union, in this view, was no longer socialist, but rather state capitalist and imperialist. Resisting such tendencies required intense ideological struggle to purge the party of "capitalist roaders," a process which not surprisingly became a lever for sectarian warfare between many different power blocs and which very nearly destroyed Chinese civilization.

Over time, the importance attached to the nationalization of the means of production has declined, especially for social democrats, as against income transfers and an increased social wage and even socialist states have privatized parts of their economies and reintroduced market mechanisms alongside state planning. Many social democratic and social liberal parties, furthermore, participated in the neoliberal assault on the welfare state. This, in turn, has led to the emergence of new "democratic socialist" tendencies which aim at carrying out a full-blown revolutionary transformation by largely electoral means, without a vanguard party (though many "democratic socialist" formations such as Democratic Socialists of America appear, in fact, to have been largely hegemonized by *de facto* Leninists). At the same time libertarian socialists, rejecting the strategic priority of state power, have carried out quite radical transformations of small liberated zones (parts of Chiapas and Kurdistan) but who have been limited in the scope of their activity and vulnerable to repression by the states which still claim their territory. Those charged with defending the legitimacy of socialist states, on the other hand, such as Jiang Shiqong, argue, as we have seen, that the goal of communism should be taken figuratively as a spiritual ideal, and not as a concrete strategic goal.

Throughout this process humanistic tendencies which have focused on the destructive power of the alienation engendered by the commodification of labor power—including the effective elimination of the mass base for socialism and its transformation into a mass base for fascism—have been marginalized, partly because of the pessimism of their analysis and partly because of their failure to imagine a strategic road forward. And while Gramsci's argument that communists should aim not merely at state power, but rather at cultural hegemony has been broadly influential across a broad spectrum of communist tendencies, it has generally been operationalized in a way that focuses on penetration of and positioning in key institutions and in exercising broad cultural influence through the media of social communication rather than on deep organizing, engagement, and transformation.

What we are proposing does not represent a complete break with historic socialism and the communist movement, but it is a fundamentally new approach. Like libertarian socialists we reject the idea that capturing state power is paramount. But unlike them we attach great importance to who is exercising state power and how it is being exercised, and do not negate the importance of state institutions among those that we seek to engage and transform. Like social democrats we believe that incremental reforms are meaningful and sometimes transformative, greatly enhancing the lives of the vast majority. Unlike social democrats, we do not think that focusing on reforms is an end in itself, but see a focus on the right reforms, carried out in the right way, under the right circumstances, as having the potential to invisibly lead to fundamental structural transformations. Like Leninists, and especially like Leninists after the emergence of the popular front strategy in 1935, we see the struggle against fascism, where it is a danger, as our first priority, and we believe that this requires a broad popular front which includes the liberal bourgeoisie. And like them we believe that communists must lead the popular front, even if from behind the scenes, because the bourgeoisie is always vacillating and unreliable. But unlike them we believe that fascism is a permanent danger and that the popular front is therefore permanent and not just a temporary strategic alliance or a characteristic of a certain stage of the revolution. And because we believe that Capital is emerging as an autonomous force independent of the historic bourgeoisie, we believe that the bourgeoisie itself, even as it remains an exploiting class, is increasingly excluded from meaningful power and stripped of its historic freedoms. Like Gramsci and Mao, we believe in the revolutionary potential of the peasantry and the need to create the spiritual conditions for communism. Like Gramsci and unlike Mao we believe that this comes about through the gradual penetration and transformation of institutions and not through dogmatic "study and struggle" sessions and rituals of public humiliation. Unlike Gramsci, perhaps because capitalism has done so much damage over the years, we don't believe that meaningful, functional institutions are always there to be penetrated and transformed, and that in any case the superficial "ideological" level at which the humanistic intelligentsia is used to operating is adequate, and instead argue that we must build and rebuild institutions and engage individuals at a much deeper level around what it means to be human, challenging authoritarian patriarchal and racist formations and cultivating *ways* of being human which promote growth and development, drawing out the practical implications of these emerging commitments, and creating communities which provide nurture and accountability. Finally, with the Leninist tradition, we affirm the necessity of a conscious leadership, but reject the idea that this leadership must take the form of a single, compact organization practicing military discipline and that it is necessary or even desirable for one organization, no matter how advanced, to have a monopoly on power (which, given our critique of the whole concept of sovereignty, we believe to be impossible anyway). And we do not believe that this conscious leadership is immune to the alienation generated by the commodification of labor power, or from patriarchy and racism. It must be composed of people living lives consecrated to spiritual discipline and self-cultivation as well as to the struggle for social justice.

Antifascism

When fascism first emerged in the 1920s it was widely regarded as an aberration—something which needed to be explained, to be sure, especially since so many workers ended up supporting fascist parties, but which was a specific feature of a specific historic period during which some bourgeoisies, having gotten a late start on building the colonial empires which turned out to be necessary in order to compensate for the declining rate of profit in capital intensive sectors of the economy, leveraged popular religious, nationalistic, and even democratic ideologies in order to legitimate militarizing the population in order to carry out wars of conquest against more advanced adversaries. And there *is* a certain historic specificity about what the Axis was trying to accomplish in the 1930s and 1940s. But this analysis misses the fact that fascism as a mass psychology and a mass movement is generated spontaneously by capitalism itself, through the alienation generated by the commodification of labor power. Fascism was not invented by the would-be imperialist sectors of the bourgeoisie in Germany, Italy, Japan, Spain, and Portugal. It was leveraged by them. And as we have seen, there is good reason to believe that both Stalin and the national liberation movements leveraged similar political structures and ideological dynamics (if for morally more defensible causes), which in turn resulted in the radical deformation of the socialist and national liberation projects in a fascistoid direction.

What is essential in fascism is the *radical, visceral, reactive* rejection of the liberal ideal of rational autonomy. It is not sufficient for an ideology to be fascist that it believes that rational autonomy must be balanced by other values or that its cultivation requires what some might regard as "conservative" practices and institutions, such as intellectual and moral discipline, stable and supportive family structures, etc. Indeed, even the incorrect belief that rational autonomy requires private property and free markets is not in itself fascistic. Fascism, on the contrary, represents a hatred of rational autonomy itself and a conscious embrace of submission.

This is why fascism is always constitutively anti-Semitic. In the popular imagination it is the Jew, and above all the Jewish intellectual, who is the carrier and agent of the humanistic ideal, of the conviction that everything is open to question and that debate and deliberation are themselves valuable spiritual disciplines. And it is precisely the organic anti-Semitism of the Christian tradition which allowed Europe to legitimate not only the conquest of Asia, Africa, and the Americas, but also their total assimilation to Christianity or its secular offshoots. And so where the Jew represents for the fascist the internal enemy who doesn't merely rally the intelligentsia around the ideal of freedom, but organizes it and forms it for battle, it is the (newly de-)colonized peoples migrating in to "his" cities and pouring across the borders of "his" country as immigrants who the fascist sees as a threat to both his privilege and to his Christian identity as someone who has submitted unconditionally to Christ (or Capital) and who is thus defined by submission. The same is true of women, whose rejection of patriarchy threatens the social order because it threatens to withdraw the unpaid labor which women perform creating and sustaining and reproducing the real social fabric which capitalism and fascism destroy. *Jews, women, and historically colonized peoples are experienced as such a threat that fascists are willing to sacrifice their own freedom in order to prevent others from realizing theirs.*

Within actually existing capitalism there are two principal mechanisms by which someone can be judged unfit for freedom. The first is by becoming a criminal. Thus the criminalization of African Americans, of immigrants, of Muslims, and now of women. The other is by way of the Protestant Ethic, which in its secularized form equates full humanity with productivity and regards the unproductive as effectively damned. The first mechanism dehumanizes targeted groups without regard to their social class. Highly privileged and even wealthy African Americans are stopped and abused and even summarily executed by police for no reason; bourgeois women are now very much in danger of incarceration or worse should they have an abortion in certain states. The second mechanism focuses on class, though it still has racial overtones. Those unable to produce a surplus for Capital—and thus unproductive—are effectively stripped of all other rights, which open up only once one has demonstrated the ability to get and keep a job. And of course, the disabled are special targets, as they often cannot be made "productive" in the capitalist sense. This latter mechanism is more appealing to liberals who are susceptible to arguments that people are unproductive due to personal choices, or that if they are not, enjoy such a low quality of life anyway that they may as well die.

It is this latter mechanism which defines the way in which fascism penetrates even social liberal governments such as that of Joe Biden. The pandemic created a labor shortage which gave the less skilled elements in the working class their first real increase in income in decades and the new petty bourgeoisie/professional middle class increased flexibility and work/life balance. Clawing back these gains has become the first priority of the bourgeoisie generally, as they threaten to undo in short order decades of neoliberal austerity. Thus the decision that we must live with COVID, suspend all of the temporary enhancements in the social safety net, and force people back into offices—even though such policies threaten even more serious long term labor shortages due to the disability which results from Long COVID.

These dynamics make an effective popular front strategy an extremely delicate operation. There are good reasons why those authentically dedicated to the interests of the working classes and historically oppressed communities—whether they theorize this commitment in communist terms or not—would be hesitant to work with social liberals, especially when they are compromised by fascistic influences. But we are so far from being able to contest elections under our own banners with any hope of meaningful victories that attempting to do so amounts to willingly bringing open fascists to power. And so we support the liberal bourgeoisie while we struggle with it . . .

That said, it is important to be clear what we struggle around. The "democratic socialist" left has staked out an essentially maximalist position, demanding massive policy concessions focused on the interests of their core constituency—mostly lower new petty bourgeois millennials—which have very little support in other sectors of the population, while underestimating the importance of combatting racism, and of defending reproductive rights and the rights of the LGBTQ community, the attack on which is the principal tactic of fascism in the present period. And to the extent that there is room to strengthen the safety net and thus reduce market pressures on the working classes, it is through a defense of the pandemic emergency measures and resistance to the renewed attacks on the disabled on which the democratic socialist Left, with its *faux* workerism, has been soft at best.

Struggle within the popular front is first and foremost about defending the liberal ideal (freedom of conscience, expression, and political participation) and especially its extension to women and historically exploited communities while thematizing and criticizing the ideological mechanisms—anti-Semitism, racism, patriarchy, and ableism—and the authoritarian psychology by means of which conservatives and liberals and socialists alike are transformed into fascists. Second, we need to actively resist the mechanism by which the humanistic intelligentsia has historically been rendered impotent: the ideal of the value free "professional" who offers expert technical advice rather than exercising intellectual and moral leadership. We must, in other words, defend the space we need to lead and organize effectively. The aim is to push fascism back far enough for us to move from a primarily defensive posture and begin to press for enduring changes which make the freedoms we are defending meaningful for the vast majority.

The Question of Reforms

The communist movement has, historically, taken a wide range of positions with respect to reform, a question which has often, though not always, been bound up with that of participation in electoral struggle in "bourgeois" democracies. Engels, for example, argued in *Socialism: Utopian and Scientific*, that communists should participate in electoral struggle because capitalist development would lead to proletarianization and, as the proletariat grew, so too would the electoral power of the Social Democratic Party, until it was winning solid majorities, bringing the working class to power. For Engels this was an illustration of one of the three laws of the dialectic: that quantitative change, at a certain point, became qualitative in nature. This reflected, we now know, a simplistic and naïve understanding of the state and of the power of Capital and has more than once led naïve communists and socialists to assume that it was enough to win elections, only to find themselves toppled by a coup when they dared act as if they had a mandate for revolutionary social transformation. For my own generation the case of Allende remains decisive, even if it also led to an equally one-sided emphasis on the "necessity" of armed struggle.

From here thinking on reform evolved in two different directions. Social democrats moved from imagining that electoral majorities mean the political power of the working class to imagining that incremental reforms would *by themselves* eventually add up to a socialist transformation—until, in the latter part of the last century, with no such transformation in sight in spite of some very strong welfare states, social democrats themselves took "responsibility" for reversing many of these reforms, and in particular in tightening labor markets and thus exacerbating the effects of commodification.

The truth is, however, that the idea of revolutionary transformation by means of incremental reform has never really been tested comprehensively. The unambiguous verdict of the communist movement against this approach—at least until the emergence of Eurocommunism in the 1970s—was based not on the extent to which it contributed to the principal economic aim of communism—the decommodification of labor power—but rather the fact that it obviously did not lead the Communist Party to "state power." Since then, communist thinking on reform has taken one of four avenues. The Communist Right, represented by Eurocommunism, adopted electoralism wholesale, in a way which left little real distinction between their position and that of the social democrats, something which lead very quickly to the liquidation or marginalization of the communist parties of Europe. The Communist center—what remains of both the old pro-Soviet parties and the antirevisionist trend, including its more moderate Maoist elements, followed Lenin's strategy of advancing "transitional demands"—demands which are not socialist in character but which are popular and on which the bourgeoisie cannot deliver. The model here is Lenin's own strategy in the October Revolution of demanding "land, bread, and peace." The idea is that the people will shift their support to the Communist Party, as they did in Russia in 1917, and bring the party to power without even a significant plurality of the population even understanding what communism is, much less supporting it. Later variants of this strategy generally derive from the popular front strategy which emerged in the struggle against fascism, and popular fronts for national liberation, in which communists proved themselves the most effective leaders, either bringing themselves to power or at least building up a broad popular base. In general, this strategy worked well as a path to state power in national liberation struggles where communists were in a position to build a powerful peasant army. But in the electoral struggle in advanced capitalist societies, it simply made communists a divisive force in an already fractured Center-Left bloc, aiming as they were first and foremost to discredit their electoral partners and swing "the masses" behind themselves. Indeed, it is not too much to say that the use of "transitional demands" by the Left since the 1980s has been based on a fundamental misreading of Lenin. In *Left Wing Communism, an Infantile Disorder* Lenin (Lenin 1920/2012) identifies transitional demands as appropriate in and only in a *revolutionary situation*. This is a situation in which not only can't the working classes live in the old way; the ruling classes can no longer govern in the old way, and there is already a very significant level of mass resistance. It is not clear that such a situation has *ever* existed in the United States, and it has existed in Europe only at moments when a nation state is suffering a total military defeat, but not foreign occupation—e.g., in various ways Russia and then Germany towards the end of and immediately after the First World War. Apart from this a "revolution" in the Leninist sense—i.e., the capture of state power by a revolutionary party which is otherwise very far from having the informed support of the vast majority—is simply impossible. Left Wing Communists have generally rejected electoral participation and reform altogether, while Democratic Socialists have attempted to accomplish by means of electoral struggle a total revolutionary transformation of society.

From this point of view, there really is very little difference between the Communist Center, the Communist Left, and so called "democratic socialists" who advance more radical demands primarily with the aim of undercutting their partners in the popular front. Whatever else they may claim all, in effect, "aim the main blow" at reformists and somehow imagining that they can win over a majority, or at least enough people to seize and hold state power.

Where does this leave us? Our own approach to reforms is very different. First, as we have indicated above, the alienation generated by the commodification of labor power makes fascism a permanent danger, so that a broad popular front against fascism remains a constitutive part of communist strategy. This means engaging not just elements which might eventually be won over to communism, but also the liberal bourgeoisie and upper petty bourgeoisie, represented by liberal conservative, centrist, and social liberal parties. While the principal purpose of the popular front is to resist fascism, it also provides a context in which we can catalyze dialogue around which reforms are necessary, when, and why.

Second, we stress that communism requires a habitable planet, a healthy population, a complex economy, and a complex of political, social, and cultural institutions which allow human beings to pursue a broad range of different *ways of being*. This in turn requires enlightened and capable governance, and many reforms are worth pursuing on this basis alone: they conserve and advance the human civilizational project generally, which is a condition for creating a communist civilization and which is worthwhile in its own right. While many reform struggles—around climate change, for example—offer us opportunities to constrain Capital and point out the limits of market mechanisms, this is not always the case and it shouldn't have to be for us to support them.

Third, however, very modest reforms which have been around for a very long time *do* address a specifically communist aim—the decommodification of labor power, an aim to which historical socialism did not contribute any more than social democracy and which we do not yet know how to realize completely. *In short, anything which de-links work and income and reduces pressure on people to sell their labor power advances the cause of communism.* What this means is that land reform, social security, unemployment insurance, universal basic incomes, and income transfers of any kind from the bourgeoisie to the proletariat reduce the economic pressure on the proletariat and increase both its potential collective bargaining power and the personal autonomy of individual workers. The same is true of increases to the "social wage," i.e., collective services such as health, subsidized housing, transportation, education, etc. that are provided without any out of pocket expense to individuals. Similarly, financing these transfers by means of taxes on wealth or, where that is not possible, steeply graduated taxes on income, constrain the power of the bourgeoisie and improve our political position.

In this sense, the most communist thing ever done by communists was something most communists thought was "bourgeois" in character: land reform. Land reform and investments in the social wage and in infrastructure, education, research, and development represent the positive civilizational legacy of the socialist era.

It is often assumed, as we noted in an earlier chapter, that the neoliberal reaction against the welfare state was motivated, as its advocates claimed it was, by economic factors leading to a decline in the rate of profit. Versions of this explanation are as widespread on the Left as they are on the Right, though the Left generally stresses the effects of the export of capital to low wage, low technology, low skill activities in the Third World on the productivity of basic industry in the First, or of the advance of the national liberation movements on the "superprofits" which could be extracted from the Third World in order to fund income transfers. The first of these phenomena is almost certainly real. The second claim is more questionable and very difficult to assess. But what we do know is that the welfare state makes workers less pliable and more difficult to exploit. And this is, in fact, what the bourgeoisie itself claimed, just prior to their assault, in their attack on "entitlements." And much as a large section of the bourgeoisie may have supported the welfare state as a way of supporting effective demand and thus stabilizing capitalism, we know that there were sections of core capital which resisted it from the beginning. And it is not just about profit levels. It is also about power. Workers who don't have to work all the time are in a better position to organize and bid for power.

Fourth, we should note that while the social liberal regime of the post-WWII period *did* contribute to capitalist stabilization, this was in large measure a result of the consumer demand led character of the "Fordist" regime of accumulation, which required an expanding mass market in consumer durables such as automobiles in order to ensure continued growth. Today, some sectors of Capital have abandoned the idea that they require a mass consumer base entirely, aiming to live off surplus redistributed by means of exotic financial instruments or monopoly rents on technological platforms, while the proletariat (and much of the new petty bourgeoisie) is increasingly replaced by robot servants and large language models. Under these conditions social liberal reforms and especial income transfers do not stabilize the hegemonic regime of accumulation, but rather sustain an opposition across social classes which might otherwise succumb to annihilation, while giving them to space to think and grow and organize.

Finally, while the disabling effects of the pandemic have given the proletariat, at least in the US, a sort of tragic reprieve from its secular loss of leverage, the long-term tendency is clear. The formation of a unified market in labor and capital leads to the formation of a single world wage, and technological progress drives the value of labor power down towards zero: a point at which even capitalism become quite impossible, and creating the conditions for the sort of transhumanist dystopia envisioned by the Dark Enlightenment. The proletariat and the liberal bourgeoisie may pursue social liberal measures for very different reasons: to stabilize the system or to gradually chip away at the commodification of labor power, but communists can embrace *both* aims. A civilizational collapse serves no one, and the remedy against it advances our cause. It restores the commons and frees humanity from the inevitability of wage slavery. We may not yet know how to get all the way to this goal, but we can get a lot closer than we are, and in the process build a civilization which is both more stable and sustainable and more humane.

This said, we should be clear that a strong popular front and a commitment to incremental reform does not mean that we stand down and simply support whatever the liberal bourgeoisie brings forward. On the contrary, this would be catastrophic. First, the liberal bourgeoisie is constitutively incapable of understanding that Capital produces and reproduces fascism and instead assumes that fascism is simply a mark of "backwardness," whether in the sense of a rootedness in technologically obsolete forms of production or in the sense of lack of education and isolation from the cosmopolitan currents which make the liberal bourgeoise (in its own imagination) so "enlightened." In this sense, while the bourgeoisie was, in fact, the protagonist of the liberal revolution, there is a profound contradiction between the liberalism of the class and its bourgeois character, even if the two also depend on each other. The freedom of the bourgeoisie depends on its capacity to extract a surplus from the proletariat through the formally consensual mechanism of the marketplace and the commodification of labor power. But as we have seen the commodification of labor power not only renders the freedom of the proletariat meaningless; it also generates the alienation which forms the ideological and psychological basis for a fascism which eventually undoes the freedom even of the bourgeoisie.

More broadly, the bourgeoisie is constitutively incapable of taking decisive action to secure its own long-term interests where those conflict with its short-term enjoyment. This is apparent in the peculiar position of the class with respect to climate change: it accepts the science and the need for radical action but then simply refuses to take it, generally blaming the limits of the liberal order and democratic practice and the backwardness of the masses.

It is, furthermore, not at all difficult for this sort of weakness in the face of political challenges to degenerate very quickly into opportunism and covert fascism. There is no better illustration of this than the behavior of the liberal bourgeoisie during the current pandemic. While initially far more supportive of lockdowns, curfews, mask mandates, and other mitigation measures than the more reactionary sectors of the bourgeoisie, the liberal bourgeoisie globally has been unable to resist the demands of both a general population, too ill informed and immature to accept the possible necessity of what might be decades long restrictions on its "fun," and of elements within its own ranks to limit the economic impact of the pandemic, which weakened the bourgeoisie as a whole in relation to the proletariat for the first time in decades. The result has been an implicitly and, in some cases, explicitly eugenic policy which silently "takes advantage" of the (potential) opportunity presented by a mass die off of unexploitable surplus population to reduce the burden of the growing percentage of the population which is no longer productive in the capitalistic sense. And it does this without recognizing that the result may well be quite the opposite: more mass disability than mass death and a rising dependency ratio which requires funding that can come only out of its profits.

Finally, it is vitally important that we resist the principal means by which the liberal bourgeoisie attempts to hegemonize the humanistic intelligentsia and undercut the formation of the communist leadership: professionalism and technocracy. The liberal bourgeoisie is very careful to keep opportunities for upward mobility and real privilege to those members of this class who agree to provide "value neutral" technical advice and not to exercise their historic vocation as teachers and as "radical critics of everything existing." And of course, while there are elements of the humanistic intelligentsia which are already fully proletarianized, most members of this social category occupy an ambiguous new petty bourgeois position in which they continue to enjoy not just wages in excess of the reproduction rate but also modest control over their work—provided they never use that autonomy to challenge the bourgeoisie. And yet that is precisely what we need to do—not to be sure, by undercutting the popular front and dismantling the barriers to fascism, but by doing the hard work of deep organizing, building a network of conscious leaders and organization by organization, institution by institution, rebuilding the social fabric and de-alienating themselves and the working classes.

Popular Front and Empire

Before we turn to a more detailed account of the nature of this deep organizing, however, there is one remaining question regarding the popular front that we must answer. That is the question of our relationship with Empire and with its spiritual reflex, the Church—and its analogs in other civilizational traditions and the *Sangha,* the ulema, *etc.* On the one hand, we have shown that it is precisely the syncretism between the socialist project and projects of imperial restoration which doomed historic socialism as a form of transition to communism. And one of the most delicate questions for the popular front occurs when the liberal bourgeoisie (or in the case of an analogous formation in, say China, the party leadership) "shows its true imperial colors" and engages in vicious oppression of colonized peoples. How does one maintain a popular front with a liberal bourgeoisie which is in the process of bombing into oblivion peasant villages in Vietnam because they aspire to full national liberation and radical land reform, or subsidizing death squads torturing to death peasants in El Salvador for the same reason? Or, similarly, how does one unite with the Communist Party of China in supporting its many policies on behalf of humanity and the human civilizational project when it is engaged in genocide against the Uyghurs?

At the same time, we have also seen that Empires can be authentic carriers of spiritual and civilizational ideals. Thus, the United States and the Liberal International Order which it leads is, clearly, a sort of imperial formation and one which makes the hegemony of Capital possible. But it is also the defender of liberal rights protected by rule of law and of authentic if imperfect structures of democratic accountability. China is both an authentically socialist society which has lifted millions from desperate poverty and which authentically carries spiritual traditions reaching back to the Axial Age which focus on the cultivation of virtue as the foundation of social justice, *and* an Empire involved in the brutal repression of the Uyghur people. India is both an attempt at a liberal, democratic, and pluralistic society which leverages the distinctive religious diversity and syncretism of Indian society and, increasingly, a subcontinental empire controlled by a party with roots in historic fascism. *Dar-al-Islam* is both an attempt to actually create a just social order on a global scale and an (admittedly fractured) Arabizing world empire.

Two points follow. First, there is not just one popular front but many: one with the liberal bourgeoisies of North America, Europe and Oceana, another with the Chinese Communist Party, and yet others with what remains of a liberal, democratic, and pluralist India and with those elements in *Dar-al-Islam* which emphasize doing justice above Empire. Second, a popular front politics cannot wash its hands of Empire. It is only by constructive engagement with civilizational empires that we will save humanity from Capital. But this engagement must always be critical. We defend the liberal ideal but show that capitalism is actually incompatible with it. We affirm the enormous contributions of Chinese civilization and the ideal of harmony and self cultivation, as well as the staggering achievements of the Chinese Communist Party, but stand against the decisionist political theology promoted by Xi and Jiang and the authoritarian politics it seeks to legitimate, especially as expressed in the current political line and leadership of the Communist Party. We affirm the contributions of the Dharmic traditions to humanity's quest for wisdom and enlightenment and the achievement of the Indian state in creating and maintaining liberal and democratic institutions for more than 70 years, but also stand against the idea of Hindutva and the deep seated anti-Islamism which is present in many variants of Buddhism. We affirm that *Dar-al-Islam* really is an authentic attempt to establish a just social order, but reject the idea that this comes about by means of submission. We affirm the legitimacy and indeed the value of a Jewish state but reject the idea that it must sell its soul to a fascist party in order to survive. Authentic revolution is always a complex and contradictory process.

Finally, as we try to point towards a *way* of being human which transcends both Capital and Empire, we must ensure that we are actually building power—including the actually capacity to live and govern in a new way. It is to that task that we now turn.

Beyond Cultural Hegemony

Gramsci's Theory

Our starting point in this regard is Gramsci's theory of hegemony, which has been central to our strategic perspective for the past 40 years. In order to be understood properly, Gramsci's concept of hegemony must be understood in its original theoretical context, in contrast with *dictatorship* and *transformism*. Dictatorship, for Gramsci, is fundamentally rule by force and is inevitably weak because of the limits to what people can be compelled to do. Transformism refers to the strategy of the more moderate *Destra Storica* and *Sinistra Storica* which governed Italy after the *Risorgimento*, and which stitched together ruling coalitions among various factions and parties mostly by trading concrete concessions, marginalizing the far Right and the far Left alike. This is a more stable approach to rule, in that it builds consent, though only at a cost, as it makes it difficult to carry out any sort of systematic social transformation.

Hegemony is a strategy by which a class presents its own organic interests and vision in ways that make the vast majority of people adopt those interests and that vision as their own and by which the class structures the political "rules of the game" so that, even in a context of open dialogue, debate, and deliberation, it always wins. This has generally been interpreted to mean a focus on culture, in part because many of Gramsci's most salient examples are from this arena. Gramsci's theory, for example, played a critical role in the communist engagement with ethnic and national identity and with religion in the struggle against imperialism (Mansueto 1988). Hegemony, however, also includes things like electoral structure and legal tradition which can significantly affect the balance of power. Thus, Christendom used the Christian ideal of love as expressed in care and service to legitimate feudal structures in which people gained access to land and thus to sustenance by performing agricultural, military, or religious services—an arrangement which, stripped of this "halo," was ultimately just a protection racket. Capitalist societies mobilize the liberal ideal of rationally autonomous human beings freely pursuing their own understanding of what it means to be human, and entering only in to consensual relationships which are mutually advantageous in order to legitimate the instrumentalization of the vast majority, who have no real alternative but to consent to the commodification of labor power and the wage relation.

Communist hegemony is a situation in which *the people as a whole find in the communist ideal the deepest and fullest realization of their own beliefs and values and in which the state and legal system and indeed all institutions are structured in such a way as to favor communist power and progress towards the decommodification of labor power, without requiring repression of any kind.*

Contradictions

Clearly Gramsci's concept of hegemony represents a fundamental advance in communist strategy—and especially over earlier theories of the "dictatorship of the proletariat." But there are a number of problems which it presents, which we have, in the past, not adequately addressed. First, Gramsci's strategy is based in significant measure on his analysis of fascism and is, at the most basic level, an attempt to turn the fascists' own methods against them. Thus, fascism draws on religious, nationalistic, racial, or even democratic symbols and ideology to legitimate the militarization of the society in defense of or in support of the conquest of a colonial empire. Gramsci argues that the Communist Party should counter by showing how communism is the real fulfillment of the Christian ideal and of the liberal, democratic, and national revolutions (Portelli 1972). In fact, however, this was already happening the in the Soviet Union, as Stalin turned away from directly communist towards nationalist strategies of legitimation. And the approach is, in fact, definitive of the strategy of the communist led national liberation movements, beginning with China, even if the explicit connections between "socialism" and its "Chinese characteristics" are just now being drawn out clearly. One need only examine the case studies contained in Eric Wolf's *Peasant Wars of the Twentieth Century* to see this (Wolf 1969). *And this did not make the resulting socialism a form of transition to communism in the sense of the decommodification of labor power. On the contrary, all of these revolutions ultimately took on fascistoid characteristics.*

Second, even if we find a way to evade this problem, Gramsci's strategy does not so much depart from the primacy of state power as it simply understands state power in a more complex way, as emerging from consent built on principles, values, and identity and guaranteed by legal and political structures.

Third, finally, Gramsci's strategy has been operationalized largely as a mandate to penetrate key institutions and then use them to exercise a broad cultural influence through the arts, religion, education, mass media, etc. Again, this is a significant advance, but it does not go far enough. The question is what sort of influence we need to exercise, either from within existing institutional structures or in the broader cultural arena. *More specifically, cultural hegemony needs to be exercised at the deep level of* batin (hidden) *networks and not just at the* zahir *level of formal organizations.*

Deep Organizing

What we are suggesting is that it is not enough to redirect existing social institutions either by means of penetration and control or by means of broad cultural influence. Rather, we must:

- Rebuild them and the networks of relationships and living communities on which they depend, and
- In the process and as the principal long-term impact of this work, radically transform the human beings who shape and are shaped by them.

The need to rebuild institutions is implicit in our forgoing analysis. While throughout much of its history Capital has exercised a sort of formal domination over nonmarket institutions, limiting and instrumentalizing them, its long-term tendency is to fracture, erode and destroy them. This is because the alienation generated by the commodification of labor power undercuts humanity's connatural knowledge of its authentic ends and orients everyone toward selling themselves in order to survive and consume—what Fromm (Fromm 1943) called the "marketing orientation." People spend more and more time working and less and less time engaged in relationship building and self-cultivation.

This means, fundamentally, living and acting not just at the surface or *zahir* level at which institutions consist of formal organizations oriented towards shared aims and governed by shared norms, but also at the hidden or *batin* level, at which we will still find at least the *trace* of authentic human beings seeking Being in the multiform ways we have developed over the course of our history. This is the level at which economic institutions exist not for the accumulation of Capital but in order to produce the means of subsistence which makes it possible for humanity to pursue higher ends. It is the level at which political institutions exist not in order to engage in conquest and extract surplus from dependent populations or in order to create the conditions for the accumulation of Capital, but rather as *fora* for deliberation around both the ends of human life and the means to achieve those ends, and for building and exercising the power necessary to realize them. It is the level at which the media of social communication exist not to confuse and misdirect but rather to inform and as an arena for dialogue, debate, and deliberation. Schools exist not to render people exploitable but rather to cultivate free human beings and engaged citizens with a mature spirituality capable of effectively resisting instrumentalization. And religious institutions exist not in order to lull people to sleep but rather to awaken and enlighten.

We must work in all of these arenas, and across all of humanity's spiritual and civilizational traditions. But how?

We *do* have a model for this. All of the great social movements of the past century had as their foundation the difficult work of *organizing*. While this work looks somewhat different and the language may differ significantly depending on whether we are discussing the labor movement, the civil rights movement, the women's movement, electoral movements, community organizing of various kins, or the political organizing carried out by the Communist Party and the organizations which split from it in order to create a leadership which could guide all of these movements, they all had at their foundation certain basic organizing universals:

- engaging people *individually* around their self-interest and, to various degrees, challenging them to see that self-interest in a broader way,
- bringing people together around shared self-interest in order to build power, and
- applying pressure, whether through public demonstrations, direct action (nonviolent or otherwise), lobbying, or electoral action, on carefully chosen targets in order to make it in *their* interest to meet well defined demands, which are crafted not only to solve problems or achieve policy goals, but to build the power of the movement.

This is true whether or not the movements themselves centered the task of organizing (such as the labor movement and community organizing, *some* electoral organizing, whether on the old "machine" model or by organizations attempting to adapt that model for new purposes and *some* party-building work) or lived off organizing done by others, such as the civil rights movement, which depended on the capacity of African American pastors to deliver congregations for nonviolent direct action campaigns which would have been impossible if those pastors had not already been adept organizers themselves. It is even true of the women's movement which in many ways comes closest, among the movements of the past century, to the kind of deep, *longue durée* organizing we will advocate. I will draw primarily here on the language of congregation based or institutionally based community organizing, which I learned from the Industrial Areas Foundation and which is also practiced by Faith in Action, the Gamaliel Foundation, and the Direct Action Research and Training Center. I was drawn into this particular form of organizing both because, leveraging congregations as a base, it inevitably engaged people around questions of meaning and value and because, at its best, it also worked to transform those organizations in ways which helped them serve their mission more adequately.

This was a particular concern of the Industrial Areas Foundation during the 1980s when I worked with them in Texas and built the sponsoring committee for Dallas Area Interfaith. To be clear, I never regarded the model as fully adequate, and aimed to join it with training in social analysis and theological reflection designed to help members of the congregation see the struggle for justice generally and the communist project in particular as a logical extension of their existing convictions.

These efforts were quickly marginalized by the rightward turn on the part of the Catholic hierarchy and the decision of the IAF to prioritize efforts to build state and national networks in order to bring pressure to bear on Congress and on state legislatures (an effort which had limited success, and only at the state level) and on school reform and housing projects (which had, at least, more staying power). I also overestimated the possibility of theological transformation within a Christian context and we all underestimated the devastating impact of the pedophilia scandal, which effectively liquidated the moral authority of the Catholic hierarchy, undercutting the IAF's main strategic asset.

This said, the IAF model provides a good starting point for understanding the deep, *longue durée* approach to organizing I am proposing, both because I have conserved much of the model and because this provides an opportunity for me to explain how and why I have modified it. Let us begin with that model as I learned it. The organizing process begins when a group of religious leaders approaches the IAF and asks for assistance in building the power necessary to act effectively on its values in the public arena. Or, more often, the IAF works through its established networks to get one or two religious leaders to put together a group which makes such an invitation. Organizers then begin doing individual relational meetings in these congregations, testing out their potential and identifying a core of leaders. At this stage there is more emphasis on teaching organizing universals, building leadership capacity, and raising funds than on action of any kind. After a year or two a sponsoring committee is formed, organizers are hired, and the organizing process begins in earnest. Organizers will conduct literally hundreds and sometimes thousands of individual relational meetings in order to identify leaders, engage them around their self-interest, and challenge them to see that self-interest in a broader light. Small groups will come together to identify problems, frame them as issues which can be leveraged to build power, and identify and research targets on whom the organization might act to advance its agenda and expand its power. Eventually an assembly comes together and, with guidance from the organizers, decides which initiatives to pursue. While in its early days the IAF had a reputation for highly confrontational if also rather creative tactics (e.g., having hundreds of people deposit and withdraw pennies from a bank which was engaged in redlining) in reality the principal tactic is the accountability session with an elected official at which demands are presented and the official pressed to make a public, often written commitment to act in a certain way. There is also ample use of backchannel tactics leveraging the individuals to whom the target is likely to listen and with which the organization or its leaders have some influence. Historically this approach was used primarily to address very local issues such as redlining by individual banks or specific problems in particular schools.

By the time I was working with them in the late 1980s, the IAF was building metropolitan and statewide organizations and pressing legislatures to raise the state minimum wage, to invest more in infrastructure, and to engage in various education reform strategies. The plan was to move on to a national network which would act similarly on Congress, but this never materialized, and both the IAF and the other networks have mostly focused on housing, workforce, and education initiatives at the metropolitan level.

What do we take from this approach and where do we differ? First, we share much of the IAF's understanding of how human beings operate and how power is built, but we set it in a much broader theoretical context, rooted in our broader social theory and social ontology. Human beings are, like everything else in the universe, constituted by relationships. Lacking inherent existence, we are fundamentally nodes in complex networks of relations, physical, biological and social. The underlying matter from which we arise was formed in distant stars billions of years ago. We are brought into being by the union of two individuals whose genetic and later social contribution to our development passes on elements drawn from billions of years of evolution and millennia of history. We are sustained by an exchange of energy with our environment which allows the emergence of the complex structures and capacities which nature and nurture both shape and we grow and develop through interaction with others at the intellectual and affective levels.

As finite and contingent beings which lack the power of Being as such and are thus driven by self-interest. This is not the same thing as being selfish or egoistic. On the contrary, our interests (from *inter* and *esse*) are what we connected to, what we know and seek and value. Ultimately what we seek is the power of Being as such, but we seek it under diverse and changing material conditions and in spiritual forms. The more developed we are the more nearly we come to understanding what we seek—and also that it is not something which can *have* but rather something we exercise and (partially) become.

In order to realize our interests, we need power, which (as *potere*) is the verb *to be able to,* the capacity to accomplish things. Power (at the social level) requires two people, a purpose, and a plan. The more people (and the more developed the people) involved, the higher the purpose and the better the plan, the more power we have and the more nearly we realize the ends of human life.

It is important here to distinguish *power* from *control* and *coercion*. Control is fundamentally about preventing things from happening. It is sometimes necessary. We clearly want to control the spread of fascism, for example. But it does not by itself allow us to realize the ends of human life. Coercion is about removing obstacles. When exercising coercion, we ask "What do I want?," "What is in my way?," and "How do I remove these obstacles?" Again, coercion is sometimes necessary. But realizing the ends of human life is not just about removing obstacles, but rather about developing capacities. When we are exercising power, we ask "What are my interests?," "Who else is involved?," "What are their interests?," and "How do I realize my interests and build my power?"

At the macrosociological level, power is stored, as it were, in institutions, as the potential for effective action. It consists in organized money, which allows us to pay people to do things they would not otherwise be free or willing to do, organized people, networks of people sharing common aims and a common understanding of how to achieve them, and organized *mana*, the respect enjoyed by people who embody widely held values which can sometimes inspire people to act in ways they otherwise wouldn't.

Now here is where begin not so much to differ with the IAF but to push certain of their insights much further than they have. Institutions are not the same as formal organizations, which are a *zahir* phenomenon, and they are not simply the set of all formal organizations of a certain type. *The University* is not simply the set of all universities; the Church is not simply the set of all churches. Rather institutions are *batin* networks operating in, through, and under formal organizations in pursuit of the ends which define them. In the case of the University, this end is, fundamentally, seeking wisdom and forming people to lead this search and to act on what they find in the public arena. These ends are, furthermore, at once given in natural law, as ways of seeking the Power of Being as Such and the product of social and historical evolution, as we understand Being in new and more profound ways.

Deep organizing acts on institutions, not (just) formal organizations. It leverages the potential latent in institutions, the organized money, organized people, and organized mana, in order to support both the conservation and transformation of the institution, and in order to pursue its aims under natural law.

This allows us to clarify one of the key areas where we *do* differ rather markedly from the Industrial Areas Foundation and the other institutionally based organizing networks. The IAF organizes formal organizations and leverages their power in order to affect public policy. We organize institutions and leverage the power we build in order to inflect their aims and to help them realize those aims.

This said, we share a common method: the *individual relational meeting*. As taught by the Industrial Areas Foundation, the individual relational meeting involves the following steps:

- Begin the conversation with something you know or suspect is of interest to the person.
- Pose an agitational question. By this is meant a question which provokes real thought and reflection. It can be as simple as "Why?" or "What do you mean by?"
- Get the person's story. What people have done tells us more about who they are and what they value than what they say.
- Probe for more meaning. Use each story as the starting point for deepening the conversation and drawing out new insights and interests.
- Reinterpret experience in a way that leads to action. It is at this point that the individual relational meeting differs most clearly from the in-depth interview.
- Respect the iron rule. Never do something for someone which they can do for themselves.

The aim of an individual relational meeting is to develop a *self-interest map* of the potential leader and, if there is sufficient potential, to build a public relationship. A self-interest map is essentially an analysis of the person's principal interests and relationships and allows the organizer to assess the person's leadership potential. It should include, at a minimum:

- What is the person trying to accomplish in life, with as much specificity as possible across different time frames? Why? How?
- What are the person's key relationships? Who do they listen do? Who listens to them?
- What have they actually done? What does that tell us about their abilities?

Potential leaders are generally classified as follows:

- Passives: Passive individuals are survival oriented and have very few interests or are too fearful to act on them.
- Followers: Followers have limited interests and will support others acting on their interests but are not likely to take initiative and lack a following.
- Tertiary Leaders: Tertiary leaders are interested in concrete *problems*. These may be very simple (getting a stop sign at the end of the block) or very complex (e.g., racism or climate change), but their

focus is on the problem and its solution rather than on building power over the long run. They are thus often interested in technical questions and on what are currently called "best practices" (and are vulnerable to arguments made on these bases). They tend not think politically. They have followers, sometimes many, who share an interest in a common problem, and they have the social skills to move those followers to action. Their timeframe is relative brief: weeks to years. They want to see results and will grow impatient with efforts that don't yield at least *some* immediate progress.

- Secondary Leaders: Secondary leaders are interested in *issues*. They understand—or can be taught—how to analyze a problem, break it down into actionable elements, and leverage that action to build power. They have networks of tertiary leaders. Their timeframe is intermediate. They understand that things take time, but act within the framework of their lifetimes.

- Primary Leaders: Primary leaders, who I prefer to call *institutional* leaders, are interested in principles and values and in building, conserving, and transforming institutions which serve those principles and values over the *longue duree*. They have networks of secondary leaders and, at the higher levels, other primary leaders. Their time frame is at least multi-generational.

The IAF makes a sharp distinction between private and public relationships. Where private relationships are made with people we like, in order to feel known and loved, and tend to be spontaneous, public relationships are developed with people we respect, in order to accomplish something, and are more formal and involve real accountability. This is a valuable distinction and one that we press those we organize to master early on, given that many people have no public relationships and given that meaningful leadership is possible only for those who can transcend, at least in part of their life, the need to be liked.

At the same time, for those who are prepared, we teach a higher form of relationship which is focused on the all-sided growth and development of those we engage. This brings what has historically been the private work of care into the public arena, albeit at a much higher level, and public standards of intentionality and accountability into the private realm. When successful, this sort of relationship becomes an enduring friendship in the Aristotelian sense.

With this in mind our practice of the individual relational meeting differs from that of the IAF and other organizing networks in that we:

- engage people more directly around questions of meaning and value, and on what they want to accomplish in life, rather than just around problems, issues, etc. allowing us to
- hone in more closely on the level of *batin* networks, and
- focus more on conserving and transforming institutions than on leveraging organizations in order to affect public policy.

Because the IAF is focused primarily on leveraging the organized money, people, and mana of formal organizations in order to affect public policy, the official leadership of these organizations *has* to be supportive, even if the organizers privately acknowledge that this or that pastor or bishop, for example, is a tertiary leader at best. To the extent that we are trying to do the same, similar concessions are necessary, though this puts the effort more nearly in the popular front rather than the deep organizing arena. But since we are primarily focused on transforming the institution itself, while we will inevitably engage the official leadership, it will rarely be our focus. Instead, we are looking at transforming culture and practice on the ground as it were, working with and through the most developed leaders we can identify and cultivate, regardless of their formal roles in the organization.

Beyond conducting individual relational meetings to identify potential leaders, our approach diverges more significantly. While we may well come away from a period of getting to know a new organization with a sense of its problems, and may decide to transform these problems into issues which we can leverage to build power, applying pressure to the official leadership to move or move on, this can never be our principal focus. Our emphasis, on the contrary, is on

- identifying potential leaders,
- cultivating the leaders we have identified and
- *doing the ordinary work of the institution differently.*

What are we looking for? Fundamentally, we are looking for big-picture thinkers with an insatiable thirst for wisdom and justice and for helping their people grow and develop across all dimensions of life. We need people with a very long-term perspective. The ability to think in terms of power (among other things) is critical, as well as the desire to have a profound impact (for the good) on the historical process. We obviously need people with a range of skills, so being a big picture thinker does not mean that everyone needs to be a social theorist or a philosopher. We need people who can lead in every conceivable field and discipline. And of course, the ability to identify, recruit and train other leaders is also essential—or at least the ability to learn how to do so, using the method of individual relational meeting outlined above.

The process of cultivating the leaders we have identified is a delicate one. It is essential that people cultivate the ability to decide for themselves what it means to be human, in the context of a profound grasp of the ongoing historical and contemporary debate around this question. This is, of course, the aim of a traditional liberal education, but we find that very few people actually develop this capacity on the basis of formal education alone. And the development of this capacity is, furthermore, not identical with the other capacities cultivated by the liberal arts—logical and persuasive written and oral communication in whatever passes for the standard or elite sociolect of the individual's native language—and hopefully several others, a facility for mathematical formalization and argument, reading, analyzing and interpreting texts and other cultural artifacts (including a broad mastery of humanity's artistic, musical, literary, and dramatic traditions), scientific observation and experiment, social research and analysis, and a mastery of the fundamental theories across the physical, biological and social sciences and the natural and social history on which those theories are largely based. There are people who are capable of deciding where they stand and why whose natural talents lie elsewhere than in the liberal arts and sciences who may choose not to invest very heavily in their development but who can nonetheless make significant contributions to our work. And we need to be very cautious about a sort of neuropsychological and cultural homogenization which results from forcing people through an education process which, for example, massively favors certain ways of engaging the world over others or which effectively destroys the dialects, sociolects, and cryptolects of the oppressed. It must be remembered that while for the vast majority of us today, in the fractured terrain we inhabit, the path to virtue leads through discursive or acquired wisdom, this is not the highest path. That, rather, is the path of connatural knowledge and we need always to be open to the possibility that the hidden leader with no formal education may actually turn out to be far more advanced than we are—in effect, one of the *tzadikim nishtarim*.

The first practical task of a leader is to identify and cultivate other leaders, and it is in this activity that we must first begin to involve the leaders we identify. But depending on the context, we may also want to encourage them to undertake increasingly complex actions, projects, or campaigns within the organization. *The aim here is, as we noted above, to do the ordinary work of the organization differently*. What we are looking for is a graded series of very slight inflections of the organization's work, which edges it ever closer to its authentic purpose. These initiatives will need to be accompanied by multi-tiered deliberation, gradually initiating the most advanced into a deeper understanding of what we are actually trying to accomplish, while providing intermediate leaders with a rationale which speaks to their interests and values. The more backward can be neutralized by horse trading or, if need be, by the judicious application of political pressure.

Finally, spiritual practice is an organic and constitutive dimension of our strategy. Everything depends on the quality of leadership and the quality of leadership depends in significant measure on its level of spiritual development. How we direct the leaders we identify, and whether we direct them ourselves or point them towards others depends on the tradition in which they were formed, our own tradition and capacities, and what the leader in question will and will not do. But it is vital that they have access to the resources they need in order to find meaning in a struggle which is incredibly protracted and in which victory is always partial and relative.

In this process, in the absence of legitimate *formal* leadership, we act as organizers or operatives "errant." We are "errant" because there is no fully legitimate formal leadership. There is no fully legitimate formal leadership precisely because the development of capitalism has eroded the institutions which would ordinarily fulfill this role. Historically this would have been communities of advanced spiritual practitioners with a calling to or charism for civilizational leadership and transformation. Efforts to build new institutions—such as the historic revolutionary vanguard parties—have failed. And we stand back, at least for the moment, from the focus on trying to create one such a new organization, since there seems to be no well-developed constituency for such an effort or a consensus on how to proceed. And so like the medieval knights errant or the Chinese *youxia* we act on our own, going where we are most needed and can contribute the most to the struggle. This does not mean that we do not recognize and respect authentic leadership when we find it or exercise leadership by ourself—or that we act by preference on our own. On the contrary, the idea of network is that we engage, collaborate, and learn from each other and accomplish things together which we could not if acting alone. We are always searching for teachers and students and friends.

Finding Our Way

This bring us to our final point. *Communism, even when it is disentangled from Christian political theology and renounces both messianism and godbuilding, remains a spiritual project.* We need now to specify what that project involves.

We have already seen the roots of the communist project in the humanistic secularism which emerged from the Radical Aristotelianism and ultimately from the interaction of Hellenism, and dialectics in particular, with Judaism. We have seen how the project was deformed in a messianic and utopian direction by the hegemonic Christian political theology and also how attempts to free it from that theology and to define a path to communism rooted in other spiritual and civilizational traditions have both born real fruit and been limited and deformed themselves to the extent that they have become ideologies of imperial restoration. And we have articulated a syncretic theology, a *way of ways* intended not as the "One Way," but rather as a network of pathways which grounds both our political activity and our spiritual practice. It remains, having highlighted the critical role of spiritual practice in our work, to say something about what that practice looks like.

What Is a Mature Spirituality?

Humanity has left its childhood. During our childhood we navigated the world through images and stories. The images we gained from our sensory experience and the stories we crafted from memory and conversation. We always knew that there was more to the world than these images and stories could capture. That is why there were always competing stories and competing versions of stories. The truth, it was understood, transcended anything that our images and stories could capture. Indeed, their aim was not so much to capture reality as to point us towards new experiences which deepened and ripened us.

Now we are also leaving our long and turbulent adolescence, during which we learned the power of concept and argument—the power of theory. This adolescence, which began in the Axial Age and which culminated in the Enlightenment, did indeed bring us closer to understanding reality, allowing us to look behind the images which we garner through the senses and to uncover the underlying structures of the universe—and, more important, the deeper meanings of the stories that we tell. And again, the wisest humans always knew that the Truth was at once far simpler and far more profound than any theory could comprehend. Like images and stories concepts and arguments point us towards the truth and set us on quests which deepen and ripen us. But Truth itself they cannot capture or contain.

Skepticism was, from the very beginning, a constitutive dimension of the Axial Age and Enlightenment awakenings, and it played an important critical role in reminding us that *nothing* is literally true. But it also served to legitimate those who argued that there is no Truth, no Good, no Beauty and that claims about justice are just ways of legitimating acts of power: that the Sovereign is he (and it is always *he*) who decides the exception. This was the function of Sophism and the Caravaka School and the *faxjia* in the Axial Age and it is the function of poststructuralism and deconstruction in our own time. The result is that the people slip into despair and act as though there is nothing more than what we experience with the senses, and the only purpose of what we experience is to help us survive and to give us a bit of pleasure along the way. Capital, that mindless intelligence, meanwhile, rapes the planet and its people, and then renders us all redundant.

As we enter the early years of our maturity as a species we need to find a way to use these various ways of knowing and of being properly. Image and story, concept and argument alike serve to ground and articulate our underlying conviction that the universe is, in the end, ultimately meaningful, pointing towards—and pointing us towards—the One which is the power of Being as such. But they also serve to strip us of the illusions that this ultimate meaning revolves around us and to understand that we will never realize what we naturally seek—to be God. And they help us understand that the aim of our desire is actually something quite different than we first imagine: that it is not impassible substance which can endure forever, nor infinite subjectivity, capable of realizing its will, but rather a relational, transformative, generativity which brings all things into Being and through which we all live in each other's embrace.

Each of the *ways* on which we draw in our synthesis highlights distinctive elements of this realization, and different ways of getting there. The *ways of the former heaven* remind us that humanity was once confident of the ultimate meaningfulness of the universe, not because we were naive or because nothing bad ever happened, but because we lived within the creative cycles of life in communities which nurtured us, even if they also sometimes constrained our seeking. The Dharmic variants of the *way of wisdom* teach us that our quest for *svabhava* or self-existence is an illusion, either because, as for the Buddhists, *nothing* has the power of Being as Such, and we all live in each others' embrace, or because, as for *Advaita Vedanta* we already *are* that Being. The Buddhist tradition puts forward the Noble Eightfold Path: right view, right resolve, right speech, right action, right livelihood, right effort, right mindfulness, right concentration (*Dhammacakkappavattana Sutta*). While each of the eight elements of the path has a specific significance in various Buddhist schools, we can divide the path into three dimensions:

- Cultivating a correct understanding of the nature of reality, or *Seeking Wisdom*,
- Acting consistently on this understanding and therefore *Doing Justice*, and
- Learning from this practice of doing justice so that we are transformed by it through spiritual practice of various kinds and thereby *Ripening Being*.

The various Hindu schools qualify this by pointing out that not everyone is ready to pursue Enlightenment, and that pleasure, power, and ethical conduct and social justice are all, when properly pursued, legitimate aims of life. Hinduism also points out that there are many different ways to *Seek Wisdom*, including devotion and psychophysical discipline as well as theory and contemplative practice—insights that later Buddhism accepted.

The Hellenic variant of the *way of wisdom* is actually just a bit less narrowly intellectualist, suggesting that the cultivation of the intellectual virtues, by focusing us on progressively higher goods, will also lead to the flourishing of the moral virtues which involve forming our will and our passions so that they seek these higher goods. The Jewish *way of justice and liberation* focuses us simply on *da'ath 'elohim*, the knowledge of God that we have in the just act, while at the same time providing a complex discipline of legal scholarship centered on determining what justice means in any particular case, a discipline which is intended, once again, to form us intellectually and morally in a way that orders us to the good. And the *Da Xue* brings all of these various elements together:

> The ancients who wished to illustrate illustrious virtue throughout the kingdom, first ordered well their own states. Wishing to order well their states, they first regulated their families. Wishing to regulate their families, they first cultivated their persons. Wishing to cultivate their persons, they first rectified their hearts. Wishing to rectify their hearts, they first sought to be sincere in their thoughts. Wishing to be sincere in their thoughts, they first extended to the utmost their knowledge. Such extension of knowledge lay in the investigation of things.

Later developments of the *dao xue*, drawing on Taoist and Buddhist sources, would add an emphasis on the *xin xue* or "learning of the heart" as well as the investigation of things, and identify it with contemplative practice, generally in the Cha'an tradition.

We can now systematize the various elements of our synthesis as follows.

First, we need to cultivate a correct understanding of reality. This means not the inculcation of a particular doctrine or worldview, but the cultivation of the capacities necessary to see things clearly as they are. Since all knowledge begins with the senses, the "investigation of things" is indeed the first step and this must include the study of the physical, biological, and above all the social world, including most especially the study of history, without which it is quite impossible to overcome the alienation generated by the commodification of labor power and to understand the historical specificity of capitalist relations of production. But knowledge moves from sensation to abstraction, and so theory is also an essential component of the intellectual transformation required. Specifically, people need to master the skills of totalization (the elaboration of rational taxonomies), formalization (e.g., through logic, mathematics, and formal semiotics), and transcendental abstraction (through teleological explanation in the sciences and in metaphysics). Concretely this means a solid foundation in the formal sciences, physics, chemistry, biology, and the social sciences and their application, as well as in epistemology, cosmology, metaphysics, and value theory (ethics and aesthetics). The aim must be to get people to the point where they can take and defend a position regarding disputed questions, and draw on their historical and theoretical formation to navigate practical situations.

This said, while we do not need everyone to share the same metaphysical doctrine, there are certain constraints on what sort of worldview can promote action on behalf of justice and the full development of human capacities. Specifically, people need to mature beyond the belief that they are in some sense the center or purpose of the universe, whether in the sense of being under the care of an omnipotent and transcendent God who, for some inexplicable reason, is concerned with what they do and with rewarding or punishing them for it or in the sense of being the "leading edge" of the evolutionary process. A spiritually mature humanity must accept the reality of contingent being and the fact that it cannot be transcended, and that any God worth the name *is* in a radically different way that we exist: outside space and time, acting only as a teleological attractor or final cause, absolutely and purely generative (and in that sense certainly "loving"), but not in any sense a cosmic parent or caretaker—or for that matter a cosmic judge and disciplinarian. To use more technical language, *a mature spirituality is impossible on the basis of a univocal metaphysics which teaches that everything exists in the same way we do and that if God exists, it is as a being alongside others, albeit infinitely powerful, and that if there is not, then because everything exists in the same way, we can actually build God.*

At the same time, we must also mature beyond the adolescent temptation of nihilism, which is always present as we discover that the universe is not about us and that God is so vastly different from us as to be no source of easy comfort as we confront the inevitability of death and the impermanence of all we care for. We must be able to find meaning—authentic, compelling meaning that gives us greater joy than any salvation religion or technological optimism ever could—in the work we *can* do. If we understand the universe as drawn into Being by the power of Being as such, then the reality and eternal and unlimited generativity of that power must become the source of an eternal and unlimited joy, because whatever it is we could seek and whatever it is we could imagine creating already *is* and our lives can become, if we will let them, an unshackled enjoyment of this Beauty. If, on the other hand, we prefer to think of the universe as network of relationships governed by interdependent origination, then we must find joy in the fact that we live in each other's embrace, always and forever a part of each other and everyone else a part of us. Our bodies and minds may perish utterly, and if we are clear minded, we realize that this happens over and over again even in this lifetime as we change and grow, but we persist in all that we touch.

Fleeting as we are, we authentically live in our *otherselves*. And because our existence now is impermanent and insubstantial anyway—it is not *inherent existence* of the sort which could continue without change—the persistence we have in others is as real as what we are now and indeed more so, as it is the immanent generativity which is the authentic ground of the universe. And the knowledge we have of this is the knowledge of enlightening beings, one and many, eternal but acting in space and time, once again, as a teleological attractor.

Second, as we have noted, we must act consistently on the basis of a correct understanding the nature of reality. This leads us to *Do Justice*—i.e., both to act in such a way as to seek each good in proportion to its intrinsic value, and thus work towards promoting the growth and development of all things, i.e., *Ripening Being*, and to creating institutions which promote this growth and development or *Doing Justice* in the narrower sense. This is work which only we can do. We human beings occupy a unique place in the great chain of Being, able to theorize the infinite and necessary power of Being as Such, but trapped in what amounts to a contingency hell, bound by ontological barriers which even God cannot break. The phenomenal world, as beautiful as it is and as much as it is a participation in the power of Being as such, is also inevitably broken. And seeking Being under conditions of finitude and contingency, on the basis of a limited understanding of reality, we inevitably deepen these fractures and create structures which exploit and oppress each other. But we can also work to mend the torn fabric of the universe by transforming these structures and building new ones—what the kabbalists call the great work of *Tikkun Olam*.

Doing Justice has, furthermore, two profound effects on the cultivation of wisdom. First, struggling for justice, we are drawn outside of and beyond ourselves and realize in ways not otherwise possible that we are not at the center of the universe and that no degree of intellectual and moral excellence can free us from the contingency in which we are trapped or allow us to master contingent reality and somehow fix it definitively. We mend physically, biologically, and socially the fabric of a reality which is torn at the metaphysical level. Second, in the just act we become the presence of the power of Being which we seek, knowing connaturally what we only knew *of* on the basis of discursive reason. For this reason, where Buddhism teaches that the we make the transition from an analytic understanding of the nature of reality to an experiential understanding primarily through meditation, we teach that this transition happens through ethical conduct, with meditation and other spiritual practice being a means of harvesting and processing the results of that experience.

This, in turn, means that *Doing Justice* leads inevitably to *Ripening Being*. The task of *Ripening Being* is precisely to guide people as they develop intellectually towards an increasingly mature understanding of the world, to help them discern their particular calling, their particular way of *Doing Justice*, to mentor, nurture, and hold them accountable as they act, and to help them process the results of this experience through liturgy, community, and ultimately contemplative practice.

What Does the Transition Look Like?

Many readers are, at this point, no doubt wondering what the next steps in the human civilizational project might look like. What is the "end game?" My answer is twofold. First, there is no "end game." Having broken with the Christian political theology which historically deformed the communist movement, we reject on principle the political apocalyptic in which the Revolution "comes" and human suffering ends. While we believe that communism is a real social state in which the commodification of labor power has been transcended (and not replaced by new restored coercive ways of organizing labor power), finitude and contingency will not only remain, but will likely give rise to continuing challenges, including structures which are oppressive or otherwise inadequate to the task of ripening Being. Second, the comparative historical study of fundamental structural and civilizational transformations suggests that "revolution" in the sense of a seizure of state power leveraged to carry out fundamental changes in the end to which a particular society was ordered and the means by which it pursued those ends, is actually very rare. The English, French, and Russian Revolutions and their clones are very much the exception. We have already seen that significant progress towards our strategic aim—the decommodification of labor power—can be made by "reformist" means, even if there is no history of complete structural or civilizational transitions by means of reform alone. Far more common than either reform or revolution are transitions by decadence in which old institutions gradually decay and new institutions are built, often out of the "raw materials" of those left behind. This is a possibility which Samir Amin (Amin 1978/1980) suggested more than 40 years ago. And it remains possible, of course, that the climate crisis and possibly the development of AI are so far advanced what we will experience a civilizational collapse or something very close to it.

In either case the work we are doing makes a profound difference Over the *longue durée,* it builds power which is as deep as it is broad. This, and this alone, will put us in the position to engage major global actors, to sustain and redirect the popular front, and to lead governments and other major formal organizations if that becomes a priority at a particular time. Second, it means that even without "state power" or effective control of institutions, we are beginning to set the agenda and lead humanity in a very different direction. It also means that we are prepared to lead in the event of a civilizational collapse or profound decadence, when the new structures required may well be something we cannot even now envision.

This power will be deployed in two very different but equally important ways. First, we hope and work for a transition by reform, in which popular front governments begin to take both climate change and the pandemic seriously and make the investments in solar and other clean energy sources necessary to wean us off of fossil fuels, and in the infrastructure necessary to effectively contain this and future pandemics while securing liberal rights for all (including the rights of historically colonized and oppressed peoples, women, and those who challenge historic gender norms), respecting democratic accountability, and encouraging authentic pluralism in which people can live and work together while pursuing fundamentally different ways of being human. Within this popular front our role will likely vary considerably from place to place. Our "distinctive" as communists will always be to struggle to reduce the pressure on people to sell their labor power in order to survive, taking into account what is economically prudent and politically possible at any given time and place. But we also bring a broader and more profound understanding of what is required to resolve the ecological crisis (transcending industrial technology), of what liberal and democratic rights look like when they are fully developed, and of the profound ideological and psychosocial transformations which are necessary in order to overcome racism, patriarchy, and gender oppression. Thus, our historic advocacy for hortic/ neoalchemical technologies which cultivate the latent potential of matter in for complex organization rather than breaking down existing organization to release energy and do work (Mansueto 2010b, 2012). Thus our vision of democracy as a deliberation around the *ends* of human life as well as the *means,* and our conviction that life as a free human being presupposes the capacity to decide for oneself, in the context of historic debates, what it means to be human (Mansueto 2014, 2016). These are all likely areas in which we will bring to bear our developing power and relationships to deepen the work of the popular front in advanced industrial/information societies with (until recently) fairly secure liberal and democratic orders and growing pluralism.

There remains, however, significant work to be done determining what a popular front strategy looks like societies which do *not* respect liberal rights and which severely limit democratic deliberation. In those—the vast majority—which are not the product of socialist revolutions, the struggle for liberal and democratic rights will likely be the principal priority for some time to come. This will also be true in liberal and democratic countries in which established rights are under threat by rising fascism. Socialist countries, on the other hand, represent a more complex challenge. The experience of *glasnost* and *perestroika* in the Soviet Union, which led not to a more democratic socialism, but to capitalist restoration and the establishment of Russia as the planet's premier promoter of fascism, raises questions about prioritizing "opening" without also reaffirming the historic long term aim of socialism, which is the decommodification of labor power. While it is thus up to our Chinese comrades to decide exactly how to navigate this complex situation, we are inclined to suggest struggling both around the foundational role of liberal and democratic rights in the communist project and around the long-term aim of decommodifying labor power.

Second, however, we prepare for a descent into fascism and/or a civilizational collapse. The kind of *batin* networks we are building provide both the most secure foundation for resistance and the reservoir of the knowledge—and hope—which will be necessary to rebuild. We are the hidden guardians of humanity's unique contributions to the universe—*seeking wisdom, doing justice, and ripening being*—and we will not allow distinctively human ways of being to be crushed by those who misunderstand what it means to be human. Exhausted though we may be, we carry on. We cannot control what will happen to us or what we will become. But understanding that the universe has never been about us and that the *theosis* we desire is quite impossible, we live and breathe the knowledge that we can nevertheless do work which even God cannot, mending the torn fabric of the universe, finding meaning, connecting, challenging, and nurturing each other, and thus knowing the only possible human joy.

Bibliography

Acemoglu, Daron, and Restrepo, Pascual. (2020). Robots and Jobs: Evidence from US Labor Markets. *Journal of Political Economy*, 128(6), 2188–244.

Adam, David. (2022). Covid's True Death Toll: Much Higher than Official Records. *Nature*, 603(7902), 562.

Agamben, Giorgio. (1995/1998). *Homo Sacer: Sovereign Power and Bare Life*. Stanford, CA: Stanford University Press.

———. (2000/2005). *The Time that Remains: A Commentary on the Letter to the Romans*. Stanford, CA: Stanford University Press.

———. (2003/2005). *State of Exception*. Stanford, CA: Stanford University Press.

———. (2007/2011). *The Kingdom and the Glory: For a Theological Genealogy of Economy and Government*. Stanford, CA: Stanford University Press.

———. (2010/2012). *The Church and the Kingdom*. Stanford, CA: Stanford University Press.

———. (2011/2013). *The Highest Poverty*. Stanford, CA: Stanford University Press.

———. (2012/2012). *Opus Dei: An Archaeology of Duty*. Stanford, CA: Stanford University Press.

———. (2013/2015). *Pilate and Jesus*. Stanford, CA: Stanford University Press.

———. (2013/2017). *The Mystery of Evil: Benedict XVI and the End of Days*. Stanford, CA: Stanford University Press.

Aglietta, Michel. (2001). *A Theory of Capitalist Regulation*. London: Verso.

Amadeo, Kimberley. (2022, July 27). The Economic Outlook in the United States in 2022 and Beyond. *Balance*. https://www.thebalancemoney.com/us-economic-outlook-3305669.

Amin, Samir. (1978). *The Law of Value and Historical Materialism*. New York: Monthly Review.

———. (1979/1980). *Class and Nation, Historically and in the Current Crisis*. New York: Monthly Review.

———. (1980/1982). *The Future of Maoism*. New York: Monthly Review.

———. (1988/1989). *Eurocentrism*. New York: Monthly Review.

Anderson, Benedict. (1991). *Imagined Communities: Reflections on the Origin and Spread of Nationalism*. Rev. ed. London: Verso.
Anderson, Perry. (1974a). *Passages from Antiquity to Feudalism*. London: New Left Review.
———. (1974b). *Lineages of the Absolutist State*. London: New Left Review.
Aquinas, Thomas. (1272/1952). *Summa Theologiae*. Chicago: Encyclopaedia Britannica.
Aristotle. (c. 350 BCE/1946). *Politics* (E. Barker, Trans.). Oxford: Clarendon.
———. (c. 350 BCE/1952). *Metaphysics* (R. Hope, Trans.). New York: Columbia University Press.
———. (c. 350 BCE/1973a). *De Anima* (R. McKeon, Trans.). In R. McKeon (Ed.), *Introduction to Aristotle*, pp. 153–251. Chicago: University of Chicago Press.
———. (c. 350 BCE/1973b). *Physics* (R. McKeon, Trans.). In R. McKeon (Ed.), *Introduction to Aristotle*, pp. 142–247. Chicago: University of Chicago Press.
Arvidsson, Stefan. (1999). Aryan Mythology as Science and Ideology. *Journal of the American Academy of Religion*, 67(2), 327–54.
Augustine. (386/1969). "*Contra Academicos*: A Critique of Skepticism." In J. Wippel and A. Wolter (Eds.), *Medieval Philosophy*, pp. 33–42. New York: Free Press.
———. (426/1972). *The City of God*. (H. Bettenson, Trans.). New York: Penguin.
Avineri, Shlomo. (2017). *The Making of Modern Zionism: The Intellectual Origins of the Jewish State*. Boston: Basic.
Bachofen, Johann Jacob. (1861/2003–2008). *An English Translation of Bachofen's Mutterrecht (Mother Right) (1861): A Study of the Religious and Juridical Aspects of Gynecocracy in the Ancient World*. Vols. 1–5. Lewiston, NY: Edwin Mellen.
Badiou, Alain. (1998/2005). *Being and Event* (O. Feltham, Trans.). New York: Continuum.
———. (2002/2003). *Saint Paul: The Foundation of Universalism*. Stanford, CA: Stanford University Press.
———. (2006/2009). *Logics of Worlds: Being and Event*. Vol. 2. New York: Continuum.
Balthasar, Hans Urs von. (1968). *Love Alone*. San Francisco: Ignatius.
Barbour, Ian. (2000). *When Science Meets Religion*. San Francisco: Harper.
Bat-Zvi, Chaya. (2017, May 15). The Jewish Antinomian Origins of Cultural Marxism. *YouTube*. https://www.youtube.com/watch?v=X_yoLxcANic.
Bataille, Georges. (1973/1989). *Theory of Religion*. New York: Zone.
Baumol, W. J., and Bowen, W. G. (1965). On the Performing Arts: The Anatomy of Their Economic Problems. *American Economic Review*, 55(1/2), 495–502.
Belo, Fernando. (1974). *A Materialist Reading of the Gospel of Mark*. Maryknoll: Orbis.
Benjamin, Walter. (1921/1978). Critique of Violence (E. Jephcott, Trans.). In P. Demetz (Ed.), *Reflections: Essays, Aphorisms, Autobiographical Writings*, pp. 277–300. New York: Schocken.
Benoist, Alain de. (1977). *Vu de droite. Anthologie critique des idées contemporaines*. Paris: Copernic.
Bernstein, Eduard. (1899/1909). *Evolutionary Socialism: A Criticism and Affirmation* (E. C. Harvey, Trans.). New York: B. W. Huebsch.
Bessire, Lucas, and Bond, David. (2014). Ontological Anthropology and the Deferral of Critique. *American Ethnologist*, 41(3), 440–56.
Bettelheim, Charles. (1976). *Class Struggles in the USSR*. Vol. 1. New York: Monthly Review.
———. (1978). *Class Struggles in the USSR*. Vol. 2. New York: Monthly Review.

Betz, Hans Dieter. (2005). Saint Paul: The Foundation of Universalism. *Journal of Religion*, 85(2), 304–5.

Bonald, Louis de. (1796/1859). Théorie du Pouvoir Politique et Religieux. In J.-P. Migne (Ed.), *Œuvres Complètes de M. de Bonald*, pp. 122–953. Paris: Migne.

———. (1796/1859). Essai Analytique sur les Lois Naturelles de l'Ordre Social. In J.-P. Migne (Ed.), *Œuvres Complètes de M. de Bonald*, pp. 954–1049. Paris: Migne.

———. (1858). *Œuvres Complètes de M. de Bonald*. 3 vols. Paris: Jacques-Paul Migne.

Bonaventura (1274/1970). Quaestiones disputate de Scientia Christi. In E. Fairweather (Ed.), *A Scholastic Miscellany*. New York: Macmillan.

Bourdieu, Pierre. (1983/1986). The Forms of Capital. In J. G. Richardson (Ed.), *Handbook of Theory and Research for the Sociology of Education*, pp. 241–58. Westport, CT: Greenwood.

———. (1988/1996). *The Political Ontology of Martin Heidegger*. Stanford, CA: Stanford University Press.

Boyer, Paul, and Nissenbaum, Stephen. (1978). *Salem Possessed*. Cambridge: Harvard University Press.

Brand, Paul, and Yancey, Philip. (1980). *Fearfully and Wonderfully Made: A Surgeon Looks at the Human and Spiritual Body*. Grand Rapids: Zondervan.

Brenner, Robert. (1998). The Economics of Global Turbulence. *New Left Review*, 229, 1–264.

Buchholz, Peter. (1968). Perspectives for Historical Research in Germanic Religion. *History of Religions*, 8(2), 111–38.

Budiansky, Stephen. (1999). *The Covenant of the Wild*. New Haven: Yale.

Bultmann, Rudolf. (1941/1971). *The Gospel of John: A Commentary*. Philadelphia: Westminster John Knox.

Bureau of Economic Analysis, US (BEA). (2021). Shares of Gross Domestic Income: Compensation Of Employees, Paid: Wage and Salary Accruals: Disbursements: To Persons. *FRED, Federal Reserve Bank of St. Louis*. https://fred.stlouisfed.org/series/W270RE1A156NBEA.

Burkhart, Brian. (2019). *Indigenizing Philosophy Through the Land*. Lansing: Michigan State University.

Burgin, Angus. (2012). *The Great Persuasion: Reinventing Free Markets Since the Depression*. Cambridge, MA: Harvard University Press.

Calcagno, Antonio. (2016). Badiou's Suturing of the Law to the Event and the State of Exception. *Journal of French and Francophone Philosophy*, 24(1), 192–204.

Caputo, John. (1982). *Heidegger and Aquinas: An Essay on Overcoming Metaphysics*. New York: Fordham.

———. (2006). *The Weakness of God*. Bloomington: Indiana University Press.

Caputo, John D., and Alcoff, Linda Martín. (2009). *St. Paul Among the Philosophers*. Bloomington: Indiana University Press.

Castro, E. Viveiros de. (1998). Cosmological Deixis and Amerindian Perspectivism. *Journal of the Royal Anthropological Institute*, 4, 469–88.

Centers for Disease Control and Prevention (CDC). (2024, May 17). Wastewater Surveillance. *COVID Data Tracker*. https://covid.cdc.gov/covid-data-tracker/#wastewater-surveillance.

Cicero. (51 BCE/1928). *De Republica* (C. W. Keyes, Trans.). http://attalus.org/info/republic.html.

Coker, Christopher. (2019). *The Rise of the Civilizational State*. Medford, MA: Polity.

Collins, Randall. (1998). *The Sociology of Philosophies*. Cambridge, MA: Belknap.
Commager, Henry Steele. (1950). *The American Mind: An Interpretation of American Thought and Character Since the 1880s*. New Haven: Yale University Press.
Conomos, Dimitri E. (1984). *Byzantine Hymnography and Byzantine Chant*. Brookline, MA: Hellenic College.
Cook, Francis. (1977). *Hua-Yen Buddhism: The Jewel Net of Indra*. University Park: Pennsylvania State University Press.
Cook, Michael, and Crone, Patricia. (1977). *Hagarism: The Making of the Islamic World*. Cambridge: Cambridge University Press.
Coomaraswamy, Ananda Kentish. (1987). *Metaphysics*. Princeton, NJ: Princeton University Press.
Crenshaw, Kimberlé. (1989). Demarginalizing the Intersection of Race and Sex: A Black Feminist Critique of Antidiscrimination Doctrine, Feminist Theory, and Antiracist Politics. *University of Chicago Legal Forum*, 1, 139–67.
Crone, Patricia. (2004). *God's Rule: Government and Islam*. New York: Columbia University Press.
Crossan, John Dominic. (1991). *The Historical Jesus: The Life of a Mediterranean Jewish Peasant*. San Francisco: Harper.
———. (2007). *God and Empire: Jesus Against Rome, Then and Now*. San Francisco, CA: HarperSanFrancisco.
Dahm, Helmut. (1988). *Philosophical Sovietology: The Pursuit of a Science*. Dordrecht: Reidel.
Daly, Mary. (1984). *Pure Lust*. Boston: Beacon.
———. (1998). *Quintessence*. Boston: Beacon.
Dante Alighieri. (1300–1318/1969a). *Commedia* (J. D. Sinclair, Trans.). New York: Oxford.
———. (1300–1318/1969b). *De Monarchia*. Indianapolis: Bobbs-Merrill.
Darwin, John. (2007). *After Tamerlane: The Global History of Empire Since 1405*. London: Allen Lane.
de Ste. Croix, C. E. M. (1982). *The Class Struggle in the Ancient Greek World: From the Archaic Age to the Arab Conquests*. London: Duckworth.
Deleuze, Gilles. (1968/1994). *Difference and Repetition*. New York: Columbia University Press.
Deleuze, Gilles, and Guttari, Felix. (1980/1987). *A Thousand Plateaus*. Minneapolis: University of Minnesota Press.
Den Uyl, Douglas J. (1983). *Power, State and Freedom: An Interpretation of Spinoza's Political Philosophy*. Assen, Netherlands: Van Gorcum.
Denton, Sally. (2012). *The Plots Against the President*. New York: Bloomsbury.
Diamond, Jared. (1987, May). The Worst Mistake in the History of the Human Race. *Discovery*, 64–66.
———. (1997). *Guns, Germs, and Steel*. New York: Norton.
Dobbs-Weinstein, Idit. (2000a). Gersonides the Supercommenator on Aristotle: The Decisive Forgotten Link Between Averroes and Spinoza. In M. Miklos (Ed.), *Problems in Arabic Philosophy*. Berlin: Klaus Schwarz Verlag.
———. (forthcoming). *Necessity Revisted: Spinoza as a Radical Aristotelian*. Leiden: Brill.
Dugin, Alexander. (2021, January 18). Theoretical Principles of Great Awakening Based on the Fourth Political Theory. *Katehon* (blog). https://katehon.com/en/article/theoretical-principles-great-awakening-based-fourth-political-theory.

Duhem, Pierre. (1909). *Etudes sure Léonard de Vinci*. Paris: n.p.
Dunn, J. (1995). *A Contemporary Crisis of the Nation State*. Washington, DC: Council on Foreign Relations.
Duns Scotus, John. (1301/1965). *A Treatise on God as First Principle* (*De Primo Principio*) (A. Wolter, Trans.). Chicago: Franciscan Herald.
Durkheim, Emile. (1893/1964). *The Division of Labor in Society*. New York: Free Press.
———. (1897/1951). *Suicide*. New York: Free Press.
———. (1911/1965). *Elementary Forms of Religious Life*. New York: Free Press.
Dussel, Enrique. (1992). *1492: L'occultation de l'autre*. Paris: Éditions Ouvrières. https://enriquedussel.com/txt/Textos_Libros/45.1492_l.occultation_de_l.autre.pdf.
———. (2008). *Twenty Theses on Politics*. Durham: Silliman University Press.
Eckstein, Walter. (1944). Rousseau and Spinoza: Their Political Theories and Their Conception of Ethical Freedom. *Journal of the History of Ideas*, 5(3), 259–91.
Economist. (2022, October 25). The Pandemic's True Death Toll. *Economist*. https://www.economist.com/graphic-detail/coronavirus-excess-deaths-estimates.
Edelman, Marc. (2013). What are Peasants? What Are Peasantries? A Briefing Paper on Issues of Definition. Paper prepared for the first session of the Intergovernmental Working Group on a United Nations Declaration on the Rights of Peasants and Other People Working in Rural Areas, Geneva, July 15–19, 2013. https://www.ohchr.org/sites/default/files/Documents/HRBodies/HRCouncil/WGPleasants/MarcEdelman.pdf.
Engels, Frederick. (1880/1940). *The Dialectics of Nature*. New York: International.
———. (1880/1978). Socialism: Utopian and Scientific. In R. C. Tucker (Ed.), *Marx-Engels Reader*, pp. 683–717. New York: Norton.
———. (1884/1948). *The Origins of the Family, Private Property, and the State*. Moscow: Progress.
———. (1895/1978). Introduction to Marx's *Class Struggles in France, 1848–1858*. In R. C. Tucker (Ed.), *Marx-Engels Reader*, pp. 556–76. New York: Norton.
Etzioni, Amitai. (1993). *The Spirit of Community: Rights, Responsibilities, and the Communitarian Agenda*. New York: Crown.
Eusebius of Caesarea. (336/1893). Oration in Praise of the Emperor Constantine. In vol. 1 of P. Schaff (Ed.), *Nice and Post Nicene Fathers*, Series II (A. C. McGiffert, Trans.), pp. 1478–540. Grand Rapids: Christian Classics Ethereal Library.
Evola, Julius. (1934/1995). *Revolt Against the Modern World*. Rochester, VT: Inner Traditions.
Ewing, Thor. (2008). *Gods and Worshippers in the Viking and Germanic World*. Stroud, UK: Tempus.
Faye, Guillaume. (1998/2000). *L'Archéofuturisme*. Paris: L'Aencre, 1998.
———. (2000/2016). *La Colonisation de l'Europe: discours vrai sur l'immigration et l'Islam*. Paris: L'Æncre.
Federici, Silvia. (2004). *Caliban and the Witch: Women, the Body, and Primitive Accumulation*. New York: Autonomedia.
Feuer, Lewis. (1987). *Spinoza and the Rise of Liberalism*. New Brunswick, NJ: Transaction.
Fèvre, Raphaël. (2021). *A Political Economy of Power: Ordoliberalism in Context, 1932–1950*. New York: Oxford University Press.

Fiorenza, Francis Schüssler. (1977/2012). Political Theology as Foundational Theology. *Proceedings of the Catholic Theological Society of America*, 32, 142–77. https://ejournals.bc.edu/index.php/ctsa/article/view/2881.

Food and Argiculture Organization (FAO). (2020). Global Forest Resources Assessment. https://www.fao.org/3/ca9825en/ca9825en.pdf.

Foucault, Michel. (1971/1980). *Language, Counter-Memory, Practice: Selected Essays and Interviews*. Ithaca, NY: Cornell University Press.

Frank, Andre Gunder. (1998). *ReOrient: Global Economy in the Asian Age*. Berkeley: University of California Press.

Fromm, Erich. (1941). *Escape from Freedom*. New York: Holt Reinhart Winston.

———. (1947). *Man For Himself*. New York: Holt Reinhart Winston.

———. (1966). *Ye Shall Be As Gods*. New York: Holt Reinhart Winston.

Frost, Peter. (2015, January 3). The Emerging Synthesis in Human Biodiversity. *Evo & Proud* (blog). https://evoandproud.blogspot.com/2015/01/sometimes-consensus-is-phony.html.

Fuerst, John. (2015, June 20). The Nature of Race. *Open Behavioral Genetics*, 169.

Gabriele, Matthew, and Perry, David. (2021). *The Bright Ages*. New York: Harper.

Garrett, Aaron. (2003). "Was Spinoza a Natural Lawyer?" *Cardozo Law Review*, 25(2), 627–41.

Garton, Vincent. (2020, February 5). "Jiang Shigong's Chinese World Order." *Palladium*. https://www.palladiummag.com/2020/02/05/jiang-shigongs-vision-of-a-new-chinese-world-order.

Gernet, Jean. (1985). *History of Chinese Civilization*. Cambridge: Cambridge University Press.

Gilson, Etienne. (1936). *The Spirit of Medieval Philosophy*. New York: Scribner's.

———. (1952). *Being and Some Philosophers*. Toronto: Pontifical Institute of Medieval Studies.

———. (1968). *Dante and Philosophy*. Glouster, MA: Peter Smith.

Gimbutas, Marija. (1991). *Civilization of the Goddess*. San Francisco: Harper.

Gleason, Sarell Everett. (1936). *An Ecclesiastical Barony of the Middle Ages: The Bishopric of Bayeux, 1066–1204*. Cambridge, MA: Harvard University Press.

Goerner, E. A. (1965). *Peter and Caesar*. New York: Herder and Herder.

Gogol, Nikolai. (1836/2011). *The Nose*. New York: Frederick A. Stokes. http://www.gutenberg.org/files/36238/36238-h/36238-h.htm#Page_67.

Gottwald, Norman. (1979). *The Tribes of Yahweh*. Maryknoll, NY: Orbis.

Gould, Warwick, and Reeves, Marjorie. (2001). *Joachim of Fiore and the Myth of the Eternal Evangel in the Nineteenth and Twentieth Centuries*. Oxford: Clarendon.

Graeber, David, and Wengrow, David. (2021). *The Dawn of Everything: A New History of Humanity*. New York: Farrar, Straus, and Giroux.

Gramsci, Antonio. (1948). *Il materialismo storico e la filosofia di Benedetto Croce*. Torino: Einaudi.

———. (1949a). *Il Risorgimento*. Torino: Einaudi.

———. (1949b). *Note sul Macchiavelli, sulla politica, e sullo Stato Moderno*. Torino: Einaudi.

———. (1949c). *Gli intelletualli e l'organizzazione di cultura*. Torino: Einaudi.

———. (1950). *Letteratura e vita nazionale*. Torino: Einaudi.

———. (1951). *Passato e presente*. Torino: Einaudi.

———. (1954). *L'Ordine Nuovo*. Torino: Einaudi.

———. (1966). *La questione meridionale.* Roma: Riuniti.
Grant, Edward. (1978). Cosmology. In D. Lindberg (Ed.), *Science in the Middle Ages*, pp. 265–302. Chicago: University of Chicago Press.
———. (1996). *Planets, Stars, and Orbs: The Medieval Cosmos.* Chicago: University of Chicago Press.
Green, Thomas Hill. (2006). *Lectures on the Principles of Political Obligation.* New Jersey: Lawbook Exchange.
Gregory, Peter N. (1981). The P'an-Chiao System of the Hua-Yen School. *T'oung Pao*, 67(1–2), 10–41.
Grosfuguel, Ramon. (2013). The Structure of Knowledge in Westernized Universities: Epistemic Racism/Sexism and the Four Genocides/Epistemicides of the Long Sixteenth Century. *Human Architecture: Journal of the Sociology of Self-Knowledge*, 11(1), 73–90.
Grosghal, Dov, and Kruse, Kevin. (2019, August 6). How the Republican Majority Emerged. *Atlantic.* https://www.theatlantic.com/ideas/archive/2019/08/emerging-republican-majority/595504.
Gryson, R. (1982). The Authority of the Teacher in the Ancient and Medieval Church. *Journal of Ecumenical Studies*, 19, 176–87.
Guenon, René. (1929/2007). *The Crisis of the Modern World.* Varansi: Indica.
Guttierez, Gustavo. (1973). *The Theology of Liberation.* Maryknoll, NY: Orbis.
Hamilton, Elizabeth. (2003). The Celts and Urbanization: The Enduring Puzzle of the Oppida. *Expedition Magazine*, 45(1). https://www.penn.museum/sites/expedition/the-celts-and-urbanization.
Harvey, Peter. (1990). *Introduction to Buddhism: History, Teachings, and Practices.* Cambridge: Cambridge University Press.
Hatch, Nathan. (1977). *The Sacred Cause of Liberty: Republican Thought and the Millennium in Revolutionary New England.* New Haven: Yale University Press.
Hayden, Brian. (1986). Old Europe: Sacred Matriarchy or Complementary Opposition? in A. Bonanno (Ed.), *Archaeology and Fertility Cult in the Ancient Mediterranean*, pp. 17–30. Amsterdam: Gruner.
———. (1998). An Archaeological Evaluation of the Gimbutas Paradigm. *Pomegranate*, 6, 35–46.
Hayek, F. A. (1973). *Rules and Order.* Vol. 1 of *Law, Liberty, and Legislation.* Chicago: University of Chicago Press.
———. (1988). *The Fatal Conceit.* Chicago: University of Chicago Press.
Hegel, G. W. F. (1807/1967). *Phenomenology of Mind* (J. B. Baillie, Trans.). New York: Harper.
———. (1817/1990). *Encyclopaedia of the Philosophical Sciences (Outline)* (S. Taubeneck, Trans.). New York: Continuum.
———. (1830/1971). *Encyclopaedia of the Philosophical Sciences* (W. Wallace, Trans.). Oxford: Oxford University Press.
Heidegger, Martin. (1928/1968). *Being and Time.* New York: Harper and Row.
———. (1936/2012). *Contributions to Philosophy (Of the Event)* (R. Rojcewicz and D. Vallega-Neu, Trans.). Bloomington: Indiana University Press.
———. (1941/1979–1987). *Nietzsche.* San Francisco: Harper and Row.
———. (1977). *The Question Concerning Technology.* New York: Harper and Row.
Heimart, Alan. (1966). *Religion and the American Mind: From the Great Awakening to the Revolution.* Cambridge, MA: Harvard University Press.

Heywood, Paolo. (2017). *The Ontological Turn. Open Encyclopedia of Anthropology.* https://www.anthroencyclopedia.com/entry/ontological-turn.

Hobhouse, L. T. (1994). *Liberalism and Other Writings.* Cambridge: Cambridge University Press.

Hobsbawm, Eric. (1959). *Primitive Rebels.* New York: Norton.

———. (1991). *Nations and Nationalism Since 1780: Programme, Myth, Reality.* Cambridge: Cambridge University.

Hobson, John Atkinson. (2000). *The Crisis of Liberalism: New Issues of Democracy.* Boston: Adamant.

Holzer, Harry J. (2022, January 19). Understanding the Impact of Automation on Workers, Jobs, and Wages. *Brookings* (blog). https://www.brookings.edu/blog/up-front/2022/01/19/understanding-the-impact-of-automation-on-workers-jobs-and-wages.

Hoppe, Hans-Herman. (2001). *Democracy—The God That Failed: The Economics and Politics of Monarchy, Democracy, and Natural Order.* New Brunswick, NJ: Transaction.

Ibn Rushd. (1979). *Tahafut al-Tahafut* (S. van den Bergh, Trans.). Harrow, UK: Gibb Memorial Trust.

———. (2002). *The Decisive Treatise* (C. Butterworth, Trans.). Salt Lake City: Bringham Young University.

———. (2005). *Averroes on Plato's Republic* (R. Lerner, Trans.). Ithaca: Cornell University Press.

Ibn Sina. (1037/1973). *The Metaphysica of Avicenna (ibn Sīnā)* (P. Morewedge, Trans.). Persian Heritage Series 13. London: Routledge and Kegan Paul.

———. (1037/2005). *The Metaphysics of the Healing.* Edited by M. Maramura. Salt Lake City: Bringham Young University.

Inati, Shams. (2014). *Ibn Sina's Remarks and Admonitions: Physics and Metaphysics: An Analysis and Annotated Translation.* New York: Columbia.

Ismaili Gnosis. (2019, January 25). "The Imamate of James: Brother of Jesus, Successor of Christ, and the Leader of Early Christianity." *Ismaili Gnosis* (blog). https://ismailignosis.com/2019/01/25/the-imamat-of-james-brother-of-jesus-successor-of-christ-leader-of-early-christianity.

Jaspers, Karl. (1953). *The Origin and Goal of History.* New Haven: Yale University Press.

Jensen, Derrick. (2000). *A Language Older than Words.* New York: Context.

———. (2002). *The Culture of Make Believe.* New York: Context.

Jones, A. H. M. (1974). *The Roman Economy.* Oxford: Blackwell.

Jones, Daniel Steadman. (2012). *Masters of the Universe: Hayek, Friedman, and the Birth of Neoliberal Politics.* Princeton, NJ: Princeton University Press.

Kahn, Susan. (2014, September 11). The Two Truths of Buddhism and The Emptiness of Emptiness. *Emptiness Teachings* (blog). https://emptinessteachings.com/2014/09/11/the-two-truths-of-buddhism-and-the-emptiness-of-emptiness.

Kane, Sally. (2019, November 20). The Benefits of Working in a Small Law Firm. *Liveabout* (blog). https://www.liveabout.com/small-law-firm-benefits-2164678

Kavadas, Ted. (2022, May 26). Corporate Profits as a Percentage of GDP. *EconomicGreenfield* (blog). https://www.economicgreenfield.com/2022/05/26/corporate-profits-as-a-percentage-of-gdp-38.

Keynes, John Maynard. (1936). *The General Theory of Employment, Interest, and Money.* London: Palgrave.

Koltaj, Bojan. (2019). *Žižek Reading Bonhoeffer: Towards a Radical Critical Theology*. New York: Springer.
Krebs, Pierre. (2012). *Fighting for the Essence*. London: Arktos.
Kyrtatas, Dimitris. (1987). *The Social Structure of Early Christian Communities*. London: Verso.
Laclau, Ernesto. (1977). *Politics and Ideology in Marxist Theory*. London: Verso.
———. (2005). *On Populist Reason*. London: Verso.
Laclau, Ernesto, and Mouffe, Chantal. (1985). *Hegemony and Socialist Strategy*. London: Verso.
Land, Nick. (2013). *Dark Enlightenment*. n.p. https://www.thedarkenlightenment.com/the-dark-enlightenment-by-nick-land.
———. (2017, May 25). A Quick and Dirty Introduction to Accelerationism. *Jacobite*. https://jacobitemag.com/2017/05/25/a-quick-and-dirty-introduction-to-accelerationism.
Lederman, Doug. (2019, November 26). The Faculty Shrinks, but Tilts to Full-Time. *InsideHigherEd*. https://www.insidehighered.com/news/2019/11/27/federal-data-show-proportion-instructors-who-work-full-time-rising.
Lenin, Vladimir Ilyich. (1894/1959). *The Development of Capitalism in Russia*. Moscow: Progress.
———. (1902/1929). *What is to Be Done?* New York: International.
———. (1905/1962). Two Tactics of Social Democracy. In vol. 9 of *Collected Works*, pp. 15–140. Moscow: Progress.
———. (1908/1970). *Materialism and Empiriocriticism*. Moscow: Progress.
———. (1916/1963). Imperialism. In vol. 1 of *Selected Works*, pp. 667–766. Moscow: Progress.
———. (1916/1976). *Philosophical Notebooks*. Vol. 38 of *Collected Works*. Moscow: Progress.
———. (1920/1964). Left Wing Communism: An Infantile Disorder. In vol. 31 of *Collected Works*, pp. 17–118. Moscow: Progress.
Lenski, Gerhard, and Lenski, Jean. (1982). *Human Societies*. New York: McGraw Hill.
Lerner, Eric. (1991). *The Big Bang Never Happened*. New York: Random.
Levin, Nora. (1977). *While Messiah Tarried: Jewish Socialist Movements, 1871–1917*. New York: Schocken.
Lim, Jie-Hyun. (2019). Nationalizing the Bolshevik Revolution Transnationally: Non-Western Modernization Among Proletarian Nations. In C. Chatterjee et al. (Eds.), *The Global Impacts of Russia's Great War and Revolution: Book 2. The Wider Arc of Revolution (Part 2)*, pp. 177–200. Bloomington: Slavica.
Lindberg, David, ed. (1978). *Science in the Middle Ages*. Chicago: University of Chicago Press.
———. (1992). *The Beginnings of Western Science*. Chicago: University of Chicago Press.
Locke, John. (1690/1967). *Two Treatises on Government*. London: Cambridge University Press.
Lubac, Henri de. (1979). *La Postérité spirituelle de Joachim de Flore*. Paris: Lethielleux.
Lukacs, Gyory. (1923/1971). *History and Class Consciousness*. Cambridge: MIT Press.
———. (1953/1980). *The Destruction of Reason*. London: Verso.
Ma, Xisha, and Meng, Huiying. (2011). *Popular Religion and Shamanism*. Leiden: Brill.
MacAleer, Graham. (1996). Saint Anselm: An Ethics of *Caritas* for a Relativist Agent. *American Catholic Philosophical Quarterly*, 70, 163–78.

Maccoby, Hyam. (1987). *Mythmaker: Paul and the Invention of Christianity*. London: SCM
———. (1991). *Paul and Hellenism*. London: SCM
———. (2003). *Jesus the Pharisee*. London: SCM.
MacIntyre, Alisdair. (1981). *After Virtue*. Notre Dame: University of Notre Dame Press.
———. (1988). *Whose Justice? Which Rationality?* Notre Dame: University of Notre Dame Press.
Mahabharata. (1955). (P. C. Roy, Trans.). Calcutta: Oriental. https://www.holybooks.com/mahabharata-all-volumes-in-12-pdf-files/Upanishads.
Maistre, Joseph de. (1775–1821/1965). *The Works of Joseph de Maistre*. Edited by Jack Lively. New York: Macmillan.
Makdisi, George. (1989). Scholasticism and Humanism in Classical Islam and the Christian West. *Journal of the American Oriental Society*, 109(2), 175–82.
Mannermaa, Tuomo. (2005). *The Christ Present in Faith*. Philadelphia: Fortress.
Mansueto, Anthony. (2002). *Religion and Dialectics*. Lanham, MD: University Press of America.
———. (2012). *Knowing God: The Journey of the Dialectic*. Eugene, OR: Pickwick.
———. (2016). *The Ways of Wisdom*. Eugene, OR: Pickwick.
Mansueto, Anthony, with Mansueto, Mary. (2005). *Spirituality and Dialectics*. Lanham, MD: Lexington.
Maritain, Jacques. (1936). *Humanisme intégral. Problèmes temporels et spirituels d'une nouvelle chrétienté*. Paris: Fernand Aubier.
Marsden, George. (1980). *Fundamentalism in American Culture*. New York: Oxford.
Martin, Keith D. (2010). *A Liberal Mandate: Reflections on Our Founding Vision and Rants on How We Have Failed to Achieve It*. Silver Spring, MD: Weit.
Marx, Karl. (1843/1970). *Contribution to the Critique of Hegel's Philosophy of Right* (A. Jolin and J. O'Malley, Trans.). Edited by Joseph O'Malley. Cambridge: Cambridge University Press.
———. (1843/1978). For a Ruthless Criticism of Everything Existing. In R. C. Tucker (Ed.), *Marx-Engels Reader*, pp. 12–15. New York: Norton.
———. (1844/1978). *Economic and Philosophical Manuscripts*. New York: Norton.
———. (1846/1978). The German Ideology. In R. C. Tucker (Ed.), *Marx-Engels Reader*, pp. 46–202. New York: Norton.
———. (1848/1978). The Communist Manifesto. In R. C. Tucker (Ed.), *Marx-Engels Reader*, pp. 469–501. New York: Norton.
———. (1849/1978). Wage Labor and Capital. In R. C. Tucker (Ed.), *Marx-Engels Reader*, pp. 203–17. New York: Norton.
———. (1859/1993). *Contribution to the Critique of Political Economy: Introduction* (N. I. Stone, Trans.). Moscow: Progress.
———. (1863/1963). *Theories of Surplus Value: Part One*. Moscow: Progress.
———. (1863/1971). *Theories of Surplus Value: Part Two*. Moscow: Progress.
———. (1867/1977). *Capital*. Vol. 1. New York: Vintage.
———. (1881/1978). Letter to Vera Zasulich. In R. C. Tucker (Ed.), *Marx-Engels Reader*, pp. 665–75. New York: Norton.
Mayr, Ernst. (1988). *Toward a New Philosophy of Biology*. Cambridge: Harvard University Press.
Meikle, Scott. (1985). *Essentialism in the Thought of Karl Marx*. London: Duckworth.
Merquior, J. G. (1991). *Liberalism Old and New*. Cambridge: Twayne.
Milbank, John. (1990). *Theology and Social Theory*. London: Blackwell.

———. (1991). *Theology and Social Theory*. London: Blackwell.
———. (1997). *The Word Made Strange*. Oxford: Blackwell.
———. (1999). The Theological Critique of Philosophy in Hamman and Jacobi. In John Milbank et al. (Eds.), *Radical Orthodoxy*, pp. 21–37. London: Routledge.
———. (2007). Only Theology Saves Metaphysics: On the Modalities of Terror, In C. Cunningham and P. Chandler (Eds.), *Belief and Metaphysics*, pp. 452–500. London: SCM.
———. (2009). Geopolitical Theology: Economy, Religion, and Empire after 9/11. In M. J. Morgan (Ed.), *The Impact of 9/11 on Religion and Philosophy: The Day That Changed Everything?*, pp. 85–112. New York: Palgrave Macmillan.
———. (2014). *Beyond Secular Order: The Representation of Being and the Representation of the People*. London: Wiley-Blackwell.
Mill, John Stuart. (1989). *"On Liberty" and Other Writings*. Cambridge: Cambridge University Press.
Miller, Jon. (2012). Spinoza and Natural Law. In J. A. Jacobs (Ed.), *Reason, Religion, and Natural Law: From Plato to Spinoza*, pp. 201–21. Oxford: Oxford University Press.
Millerman, Michael. (2014). Heidegger, Left and Right: Differential Political Ontology and Fundamental Political Ontology Compared: Marchart vs. Dugin. *Journal of Eurasian Affairs*, 2(1), 94–104.
Mirowski, Philip, and Plehwe, Dieter, eds. (2009). *The Road from Mont Pèlerin: The Making of the Neoliberal Thought Collective*. Cambridge, MA: Harvard University Press.
Moldbug, Mencius. (2008). *Unqualified Reservations*. https://www.unqualified-reservations.org.
Montesquieu, Charles de Secondat, baron de. (2018). *The Spirit of Law* (P. Stewart, Trans.). n.p. http://montesquieu.ens-lyon.fr/spip.php?rubrique186.
Moore, Barrington. (1966). *Social Origins of Dictatorship and Democracy*. Boston: Beacon.
Mordechai, Lee, et al. (2019). The Justinianic Plague: An Inconsequential Pandemic? *Proceedings of the National Academy of Sciences*, 116(51), 25546–54.
Morgan, Lewis Henry. (1877). *Ancient Society*. New York: Henry Holt.
Mosely, Fred. (2016, September 19). The Decline of the Rate of Profit in the Postwar US Economy. *Marxismo Critico* (blog). https://marxismocritico.com/2016/09/19/the-decline-of-the-rate-of-profit-in-the-postwar-us-economy-a-comment-on-brenner.
Murdoch, John, and Sylla, Edith. (1978). The Science of Motion. In D. Lindberg (Ed.), *Science in the Middle Ages*, pp. 206–64. Chicago: University of Chicago Press.
Mutz, Diana. (2018). Status Threat, Not Economic Hardship, Explains the 2016 Presidential Vote. *Proceedings of the National Academy of Sciences*, 115(19), 4330–39. www.pnas.org/cgi/doi/10.1073/pnas.1718155115.
Næss, Arne. (1989). *Ecology, Community, and Lifestyle*. Cambridge: Cambridge University Press.
Næss, Arne, and Haukeland, Per Ingvar. (1998/1999). *Life's Philosophy: Reason & Feeling in a Deeper World* (R. Huntford, Trans.). Athens, GA: University of Georgia Press.
Nasr, Seyyed Hussein. (1964). *Three Muslim Sages: Avicenna–Suhrawardi–Ibn 'Arabi*. Cambridge, MA: Harvard University Press.
———. (1989). *Knowledge and the Sacred*. Albany: State University of New York Press.

National Center for Education Statistics (NCES). (2021a). Percentage of Degree-Granting Postsecondary Institutions with a Tenure System and Percentage of Full-Time Faculty with Tenure at These Institutions, by Control and Level of Institution and Selected Characteristics of Faculty: Selected Years, 1993–94 through 2018–19. *Digest of Education Statistics.* https://nces.ed.gov/programs/digest/d19/tables/dt19_316.80.asp.

———. (2021b). Percentage of Full-Time Instructional Faculty with Tenure for Degree-Granting Institutions with a Tenure System, by Academic Rank, Sex, and Control and Level of Institution: Selected Years, 1993–94 through 2009–10. *Digest of Education Statistics.* https://nces.ed.gov/programs/digest/d11/tables/dt11_278.asp.

Negri, Antonio. (1991). *The Savage Anomaly* (M. Hardt, Trans.). Minneapolis: Minnesota University Press.

Neusner, Jacob. (1975/1998). *Invitation to the Talmud.* Atlanta, GA: Scholars.

Newton, Isaac. (1687/1999). *The Philosophical Principles of Natural Philosophy* (I. B. Cohen, Trans.). Berkeley: University of California Press.

———. (1700). *The Reasonableness and Certainty of the Christian Religion.* London: n.p.

Niebuhr, H. Richard. (1951). *Christ and Culture.* New York: Harper.

Njoku, Raphael Chijioke. (2020). *West African Masking Traditions and Diaspora Masquerade Carnivals: History, Memory, and Transnationalism.* Rochester, NY: University of Rochester Press.

Origen. (256 CE/1965). *Contra Celsum* (H. Chadwick, Trans.). Cambridge: Cambridge University Press.

Paley, William. (1802/1986). *Natural Theology.* Charlottesville, VA: Ibis.

Palmer, David A. (2008). Les mutations du discours sur les sectes en Chine moderne. *Archives de sciences sociales des religions,* 144. https://journals.openedition.org/assr/17743.

———. (2011). Redemptive Societies in Cultural and Historical Context. *Journal of Chinese Theatre, Ritual and Folklore/Minsu Quyi,* 173, 1–12.

Pandemic Accountability Index (PAI). (2024, April 1). What COVID-19 Does to the Body (Fourth Edition, April 2024). *Pandemic Accountability Index.* https://www.panaccindex.info/p/what-covid-19-does-to-the-body-fourth.

Paul VI. (1965, December 7). *Gaudium et Spes.* https://www.vatican.va/archive/hist_councils/ii_vatican_council/documents/vat-ii_const_19651207_gaudium-et-spes_en.html.

Pawlikowski, John. (1982). *Christ in the Light of Jewish-Christian Dialogue.* New York: Paulist.

Pedersen, Olaf. (1978). Astronomy. In D. Lindberg (Ed.), *Science in the Middle Ages,* pp. 303–37. Chicago: University of Chicago Press.

Phillips, Kevin. (1969/2014). *The Emerging Republican Majority.* Princeton, NJ: Princeton University Press.

Pirenne, Henri. (1937/1939). *Mohammed and Charlemagne.* London: Allen and Unwin

Pius IX. (1870, June 29). "Dei Filius: Dogmatic Constitution on the Catholic Faith." https://www.papalencyclicals.net/councils/ecum20.htm.

Portelli, Hughes. (1972). *Gramsci et le bloc historique.* Paris: Presse Universitaires.

Poulantzas, Nicos. (1968/1974). *Fascism and Dictatorship: The Third International and the Problem of Fascism.* London: Verso.

———. (1974/1978). *Classes in Contemporary Capitalism*. London: Verso.
Puiu, Tibi. (2021, March 11). Ancient Woman May Have Ruled Bronze Age Society in Modern Day Spain. *ZME Science* (blog). https://www.zmescience.com/science/ancient-woman-bronze-age-ruler-04234.
Quijano, Anibal. (2000a). Colonialidad y Clasificación Social. *Journal of World Systems Research*, 6(2), 342–88.
———. (2000b). Coloniality of Power, Eurocentrism, and Latin America. *Nepantla: Views from South*, 1(3), 533–80.
Radhakrishnan, Sarvepalli. (1953). *The Principal Upanishads*. London: Allen & Unwin.
Raschke, Carl. (2012). *Postmodernism and the Revolution in Religious Theory*. Charlottesville: University of Virginia Press.
Ratzinger, Joseph Cardinal. (1984). Instruction Regarding Certain Aspects of the Theology of Liberation. United States Catholic Conference (USCC).
Rawls, John. (2005). *A Theory of Justice*. Cambridge: Harvard University Press.
Reeves, Marjorie. (1999). *Joachim of Fiore & The Prophetic Future: A Medieval Study in Historical Thinking*. Stroud: Sutton.
Reimann, Matt. (2017, August 11). These Wall Street Millionaires Literally Plotted to Overthrow the President. *Timeline*. https://timeline.com/business-plot-overthrow-fdr-9a59a012c32a.
Ritschl, Albrect. (1882/1900). *The Christian Doctrine of Justification and Reconciliation*. Edinburgh: T&T Clark.
Robinson, Richard H. (1957). Some Logical Aspects of Nagarjuna's System. *Philosophy East & West*, 6(4), 291–308.
Rodenberg, Erik. (1991). Defense of Maria Gimbutas' Thesis About Old Europe (Maria Kvilhaug, Trans.). *Modern Matriarchal Scholars* (blog). http://mmstudies.com/scholars/gimbutas-defense.
Roepke, Wilhelm. (1948). *Civitas Humana: A Humane Order of Society*. London: William Hodge.
Roper, Willem. (2020, November 10). Productivity Versus Wages: How Wages Have Stagnated in America. *World Economic Forum*. https://www.weforum.org/stories/2020/11/productivity-workforce-america-united-states-wages-stagnate.
Rosenthal, Michael. (1998). Two Collective Action Problems in Spinoza's Social Contract Theory. *History of Philosophy Quarterly*, 15(4), 389–409.
———. (2001). Tolerance as a Virtue in Spinoza's *Ethics*. *Journal of the History of Philosophy*, 39(4), 535–57.
———. (2003). Spinoza's Republican Argument for Toleration. *Journal of Political Philosophy*, 11(3), 320–37.
———. (2013). The Siren Song of Revolution: Spinoza on the Art of Political Change. *Graduate Faculty Philosophy Journal*, 34(1), 111–32.
Roser, Max. (2016, December 23). Proof That Life Is Getting Better for Humanity, in 5 Charts. *Vox*. https://www.vox.com/the-big-idea/2016/12/23/14062168/history-global-conditions-charts-life-span-poverty.
Rousseau, Jean-Jacques. (1762/1962). *Le contrat social*. Paris: Freres.
Ruether, Rosemary. (1974). *Faith and Fratricide*. New York: Harper.
Rukmini S. (2019). The BJP's Electoral Arithmetic. In M. Vaishnav (Ed.), *The BJP in Power: Indian Democracy and Religious Nationalism*, pp. 37–50. Washington, DC: Carnegie Endowment for International Peace. https://carnegieendowment.org/research/2019/04/the-bjp-in-power-indian-democracy-and-religious-nationalism?lang=en#the-bjps-electoral-arithmetic.

Russell, James. (1994). *The Germanization of Early Medieval Christianity: A Sociohistorical Approach to Religious Transformation*. New York: Oxford University Press.
Sartre, Jean Paul. (1943/1993). *Being and Nothingness*. New York: Washington Square.
Schmitt, Carl. (1921/2014). *Dictatorship: From the Origin of the Modern Concept of Sovereignty to Proletarian Class Struggle*. Cambridge: Polity.
———. (1922/2005). *Political Theology: Four Chapters on the Concept of Sovereignty* (G. Schwab, Trans.). Chicago: University of Chicago Press.
Schuon, Frithjof. (1992). *Echoes of Perennial Wisdom*. Bloomington: World Wisdom.
Schweitzer, Albert. (1906/2001). *The Quest of the Historical Jesus: A Critical Study of Its Progress from Reimarus to Wrede* (W. Montgomery, Trans.). Philadelphia: Augsburg Fortress.
Segundo, Juan Luis. (1976). *The Liberation of Theology*. Maryknoll: Orbis.
———. (1985). *Theology and the Church*. New York: Harper.
Sereni, E. (1968). *Capitalismo nelle campagne*. Torino: Einaudi.
Sewell, William. (1980). *Work and Revolution in France*. New York: Cambridge University Press.
Shigong, Jiang. (2018/2020). Philosophy and History: Interpreting the "Xi Jinping Era" through Xi's Report to the Nineteenth National Congress of the CCP (D. Ownby, Trans.). *Reading the China Dream* (blog). https://www.readingthechinadream.com/jiang-shigong-philosophy-and-history.html.
———. (2020/2020). Empire and World Order (D. Ownby, Trans.). *Reading the China Dream* (blog). https://www.readingthechinadream.com/jiang-shigong-empire-and-world-order.html.
Slobodian, Quinn. (2018). *Globalists: The End of Empire and the Birth of Neoliberalism*. Cambridge: Harvard.
Smith, Huston. (1995). *The World's Religions: Our Great Wisdom Traditions*. New York: HarperOne.
Solle, Dorthee. (1974). *Political Theology*. Philadelphia: Fortress.
Spinoza, Benedict. (1674, June 2). Epistle 50, Spinoza to Jarig Jellis. http://www.faculty.umb.edu/gary_zabel/Courses/Spinoza/Texts/Spinoza/let5050.htm.
———. (1677/1955). *Ethics*. New York: Dover.
———. (1677/2007). *Theological-Political Treatise*. Cambridge: Cambridge University Press.
Stearns, Cyrus. (1999). *The Buddha from Dolpo: A Study of the Life and Thought of the Tibetan Master Dolpopa Sherab Gyaltsen*. Albany: State University of New York Press.
Stone, Merlin. (1976). *When God Was a Woman*. London: Dorset.
Thapar, Romila. (2002). *Early India: From the Origins to 1300*. Berkeley: University of California Press.
Theissen, Gerd. (1982). *The Social Setting of Pauline Christianity*. Philadelphia: Fortress.
Thibault, Paul. (1972). *Savoir et pouvoir: philosophie thomiste et politique cléricale au XIXme siècle*. Quebec: Université de Laval.
Thoreau, Henry David. (1857/2011). *Walden*. Boston: Ticker and Fields.
Tipler, Frank. (1994). *The Physics of Immortality*. New York: Doubleday.
Tocqueville, Alexis de. (1835/2003). *Democracy in America*. New York: Penguin.
Tolstoy, Leo. (1909/1975). *The Inevitable Revolution*. London: Housman's. https://www.marxists.org/archive/tolstoy/1909/the-inevitable-revolution.html.

Tsung-Mi. (828–35/1995). *Yuan jen lun [Inquiry in to the Origin of Humanity]* (P. N. Gregory, Trans.). Honolulu: Kuroda Institute.

Unger, Roberto Mangabeira. (2014). *The Religion of the Future.* Cambridge, MA: Harvard University Press.

Vansina, Jan. (1984). Western Bantu Expansion. *Journal of African History,* 25(2), 129–45.

Voskuilen, Thijs, and Sheldon, Rose Mary. (2008). *Operation Messiah: St. Paul, Roman Intelligence, and the Birth of Christianity.* London: Valentine Mitchell.

Wade, Lizzie. (2020, May 14). From Black Death to Fatal Flu, Past Pandemics Show Why People on the Margins Suffer Most. *Science.* https://www.science.org/content/article/black-death-fatal-flu-past-pandemics-show-why-people-margins-suffer-most.

Wallace, Claire. (2023, March 17). Physician Suicide Rate Higher than Any Other Profession. *Becker's ASC Review.* https://www.beckersasc.com/asc-news/physician-suicide-rate-higher-than-any-other-profession.html.

Wallerstein, Immanuel. (1974). *Capitalist Agriculture and the Origins of the European World Economy in the Sixteenth Century.* Vol. 1 of *The Modern World System.* New York: Academic.

———. (1980). *Mercantilism and the Consolidation of the European World Economy, 1600–1750.* Vol. 2 of *The Modern World System.* New York: Academic.

———. (1989) *The Second Era of Great Expansion of the Capitalist World Economy, 1730–1840s.* Vol. 3 of *The Modern World System.* New York: Academic.

Walser, Joseph. (2015, February 27). Reading Nāgārjuna as a Political Philosopher. Unpublished paper presented to *The Columbia Society for Comparative Philosophy,* February 27, 2015.

———. (2020). *Genealogies of Mahayana Buddhism: Emptiness, Power, and the Question of Origin.* New York: Routledge.

Wansbrough, John. (2004). *Quranic Studies.* New York: Prometheus.

Williams, Paul. (1989). *Mahayana Buddhism.* New York: Routledge.

Weber, Max. (1918/2004). Science as a Vocation. In R. Livingstone (Ed.), *The Vocation Lectures,* pp. 32–94. New York: Hackett.

Weisskopf, Thomas E. (1979). Marxian Crisis Theory and the Rate of Profit in the Postwar US Economy. *Cambridge Journal of Economics,* 3, 341–78.

Wolf, Eric. (1969). *Peasant Wars of the Twentieth Century.* New York: Harper.

Wolfendale, Peter. (2009, August 3). "Deleuze, Spinoza and Univocity." *Deontologistics* (blog). https://deontologistics.co/2009/08/03/deleuze-spinoza-and-univocity.

Woodson, Hue. (2021). The One Who Decides on the Exception: The Sovereign and Sovereignty in Slavoj Žižek's Political Theology after Carl Schmitt and Giorgio Agamben. *International Journal of Žižek Studies* 15(1). https://zizekstudies.org/index.php/IJZS/article/view/1166.

Wörsdörfer, Manuel. (2013). Von Hayek and Ordoliberalism on Justice. *Journal of the History of Economic Thought,* 35(3), 291–317. https://ssrn.com/abstract=2354436.

Wright, Colin. (2008). Event or Exception? Disentangling Badiou from Schmitt, or, Towards a Politics of the Void. *Theory and Event* 11(2). https://muse.jhu.edu/article/240327.

Wu, Tong, et al. (2017). Economic Growth, Urbanization, Globalization, and the Risks of Emerging Infectious Diseases in China: A Review. *Ambio,* 46(1), 18–29.

Yao, Xinzhong. (2000). *An Introduction to Confucianism*. Cambridge: Cambridge University Press.

Yovel, Yirmiyahu. (2001). *Spinoza and Other Heretics*. Princeton, NJ: Princeton University Press.

Zerzan, John. (2012). *Future Primitive Revisited*. Port Townsend, WA: Feral.

Zimmer, Heinrich. (1951/1989). *Philosophies of India*. Reprint, Princeton, NJ: Princeton University Press.

Zitara, Nicola. (1971). *L'unita d'Italia, Nascita di una colonia*. Milano: Jaca Boo.

Žižek, Slavoj. (1999). *The Ticklish Subject: The Absent Core of Political Ontology*. New York: Verso.

Zorn, Daniel-Pascual. (2020, August 21). "Kant—A Racist?" *Public History Weekly* 8. https://public-history-weekly.degruyter.com/8-2020-8/kant-a-racist.